CHARLES IVES was born in Danbury, Connecticut, in 1874. His father, a bandmaster, also taught music theory, piano, and violin. He fostered in Charles not only a love of music but also a fierce unconventionality in his approach to it. Charles Ives attended Yale University, where he studied composition with Horatio Parker and organ with Dudley Buck. After his graduation in 1898, he divided his time between working in the insurance field, composing, and playing the organ in various churches. Since the career of a composer was even less lucrative in those days than it is today, Ives devoted his regular working hours to the insurance firm he founded in 1907, and composed in his spare time. Ives & Myrick became one of the largest and most successful insurance agencies in the country.

Ives' major works were written between 1906 and 1916, and after 1919 he wrote mostly songs. His music, largely inspired by American subjects, was distinguished by an extraordinary originality. He experimented with polytonality, polyrhythms, quarter-tones, and other modernistic devices long before they appeared in the works of European composers. He composed five symphonies, many shorter orchestral works, several string quartets, four violin sonatas, choral works, piano sonatas, and 114 songs. Very little of this music was played in public until 1939—when Ives was 65. Since then his works have been performed in Europe as well as in America and he has been recognized and honored as a uniquely American composer and an artist of imposing stature and creativity. He died in 1954.

CHARLES IVES

ESSAYS BEFORE A SONATA

The Majority
and Other Writings

Edited by HOWARD BOATWRIGHT

W. W. Norton & Company
New York • London

ISBN 0-393-31830-3

Printed in the United States of America

W. W. Norton & Company, Inc.
500 Fifth Avenue, New York, N.Y. 10110
http://www.wwnorton.com

W. W. Norton & Company Ltd.
10 Coptic Street, London WC1A 1PU

1 2 3 4 5 6 7 8 9 0

CONTENTS

FOREWORD

AFTER Charles Ives died on May 19, 1954, Mrs. Ives decided to present his manuscripts to the Library of the Yale School of Music. The music manuscripts were transferred from the Ives home in Redding, Connecticut, to New Haven in the fall of 1955, and the Ives Collection was inaugurated with appropriate ceremonies on February 22, 1956.

Even before these manuscripts were moved from Redding, John Kirkpatrick had begun the task of sorting and organizing them, which resulted in his first temporary catalogue in 1960.

Naturally, the music manuscripts were a matter of first concern, and it was not until January, 1959, that other manuscript materials from Ives' study were brought to the Collection. These materials ranged from complete essays and articles to memos, fragments, and scribblings on the margins of letters, newspaper clippings, and wall calendars. A start towards classifying them had been made by Mrs. Ives as she emptied drawers and shelves, but the literary manuscripts had never received the attention devoted to the musical ones (the latter had been photostated between 1927 and 1934), and they were still in a state of disorder when they were brought to the Collection.

The largest and most important manuscript contained in the material was that of Ives' book, *Essays Before A Sonata*. The presence of this manuscript (previously thought to have been lost) opened the possibility for a new edition of the *Essays*, which in its privately printed edition of 1920 had not been deemed suitable for literal reprinting by those who had considered it. The manuscript offered the opportunity to consult with the author, as it were, in correcting various lapses which had occurred in the 1920 book.

Further sorting out of the manuscripts revealed the large unpublished essay, "The Majority," and numerous versions of Ives' other political and economic fantasies. On music, specifically, there were the rough drafts of well-known prefaces and program notes for Ives pieces, including the "Postface" to *114 Songs*. Also, there were the materials relating to Ives' one article in the sphere of speculative music theory: "Some Quarter-tone Impressions."

A tally of the literary manuscripts reveals an interesting fact: most of what Ives wrote in words did not concern music directly. If music itself were his concern, he wrote music. But he used words to provide the general philosophical support for his compositions, and, of course, words were the principal weapon when his idealism led him (around 1918) away from attempting to reform the musical conventions of his youth towards attacking the weaknesses of our national and international life, as he saw them.

2

One wishes to read the writings of any exceptional creative artist in the hope that some insight might be gained or that some clue might be found to the magic which separates such a person from the ordinary run. That geniuses never really tell us their secrets directly, and that they would not be able to even if they tried, does not stop us from looking yearningly at all the material they leave behind them, and from wanting to know more about the personalities that gave forth the miracles which are the works of art themselves.

Charles Ives, while he wrote very little which describes any of the steps on the musical peaks he scaled, left a considerable amount of prose which tells us in a vivid way what manner of person he was. The more we know about him as a person, the less difficult it is for us to understand his unique development as a composer, and to reconcile the apparently contradictory elements in his musical style.

The writings have all the overt characteristics of the music—idealism, fervor, humor, loose organization, deep humanity, spirituality, lack of discrimination or inhibition, occasional brilliance, occasional confusion, and an unmistakable Americanism. But there is one thing that ought not to be expected of them, and that is the element of genius which flows through and transcends all the music's qualities, good and bad, for Ives was a musical genius, not a literary one. We must not read his essays on Emerson, Thoreau, politics or economics as critically as though they were written by a specialist in those subjects. The writings are the underside, so to speak, and they give us a rounded view of Ives the man, not better attainable in any other way.

As far as Ives himself was concerned, it would seem doubtful that he thought any less of his pet political and economic schemes than of his music. The fact is that from the beginning of World War I up to about 1921 he composed virtually no new music, but he turned out pages and pages of prose. What accounted for this shift of activity, hardly to be expected of a dedicated composer, was his passionate embrace of life in the whole, of which music, business, and concern with people, the nation, and the world were all inseparable parts. It is appropriate, then, that the first published collection of Ives' writings includes materials as diverse as *Essays Before a Sonata* and "The Amount to Carry," which is a business document. To the discerning eye, however, even the latter relates basically to Ives the composer. Its final sentence, speaking of the way to business success, gives an Ives formula to artistic success: the way should be "simple enough to be understood by the many, and complex enough to be of some value to all!"

3

The present volume is a selection of the larger, more complete items of prose in the Ives Collection. The qualifying criteria were:

1. Sufficient size. The smallest item included here (with the exception of those utilized in notes) is a page and a half long.
2. Completeness. Even the less well-organized and well-preserved manuscripts are entities as they stand.
3. Present unavailability. The volume includes previously unpublished material, or that which is no longer in print.

4. Self-sufficiency. Preface material or detailed technical commentary on individual works which is not readable without the music at hand is excluded, as is also some purely technical material relating to the insurance business.

Occasionally content, and not size, has suggested that certain items would be more suitably grouped with what John Kirkpatrick calls "commuting memos" (possibly written on train rides between Redding and New York). Perhaps the remaining material may find its place later on in volumes which also include Ives' letters. Up to the present time, correspondence of a personal nature remains the property of Mrs. Ives.

4

On the occasion of the meeting of the International Musicological Society in New York, in September, 1961, the publishers produced a limited presentation edition of *Essays Before A Sonata*. Because this portion of the book was issued first, the "Introductory Note" contains some material which otherwise might have been included at this point. The discussion of editorial problems found there is in some ways applicable to the whole volume, and the acknowledgments in the final section should be repeated here with further thanks to the individuals mentioned. Only one minor symptom of two-stage publication remains which may concern the reader: references made in Part One to writings in Part Two do not give page numbers, while references from Part Two to Part One are specific.

It is hoped that this selection of writings will help to give the reader a clearer picture of the unique personality behind the music of Ives— a music which seems to be moving steadily towards its place not only in that small repertoire which first established the character of the "new music" in the twentieth century, but towards its position as a highly important segment of the American musical heritage.

Howard Boatwright

School of Music, Yale University
New Haven, Connecticut, 1962

PART ONE
ESSAYS
BEFORE A SONATA

INTRODUCTORY NOTE

FOR some composers, one work, more than any other, may become a channel through which the streams of philosophical concept, musical technique, and style flow in singular unity. For Charles Ives, the Concord Sonata* was such a work. It reflects programmatically, and also in deeper, less obvious ways, the influence of the Concord Transcendentalists; it is representative of Ives' highest achievements in richness of harmony and freedom of rhythm; and it is stamped unmistakably both with the highly individual personality of the composer and, in an unaffected way, with cultural symbols of the time and place. As Cowell says, no American can hear it without the shock of recognition.

The essays written by Ives to accompany the Concord Sonata occupy a similar, or perhaps even more predominant, position among his literary efforts. Other than his music, these essays tell us more than anything else does about the man. Through the ideas he chooses to borrow, as well as through his own forcefully expressed ideas, we understand better his approach to the specific musical and stylistic problems of the composer as well as to the more general problems of

---

* The full title is *Second Pianoforte Sonata—"Concord, Mass., 1840–1860."* In the Preface to *Essays Before A Sonata* the date is given as 1845.

the artist in society—the latter being problems to which he found an atypical, and widely misconstrued, solution.

Ives must have come into early contact with the Concord writers whose work was to affect him so deeply. There is an allusion in the *Essays Before A Sonata* to the comfort he derived from Thoreau at the time of his father's death, which occurred in 1894, Ives' first year in college. Cowell says (p. 36) that Ives submitted an undergraduate essay on Emerson to a Yale literary magazine, which, however, was rejected. By 1904, Ives had composed an *Orchard House Overture*, named for the Concord home of the Alcotts. The fascination for Concord persisted, as on their honeymoon in 1908 Mr. and Mrs. Ives visited the town. The main work on the Sonata began in the year after this, and was finished about 1915. The Iveses again visited Concord in 1916; the Essays were in process at that time. It can be seen from all these circumstances how sustained and consistent was Ives' interest in the town and its philosophers. The Sonata and Essays were the culmination of years of thought and work, and Concord and its "divinities" were immersed in the ferment of Ives' creative activity from his student days onward.

Ives was among the earliest to accomplish two musical revolutions— one being against the limits and fetters of conventional techniques, and the other against the weak, European–derived style of American composers at the time. If we concede that his gift was extraordinary in the first place, it is still interesting to examine the circumstances that may have led him to take steps that were inconceivable to the musicians who were his teachers and fellow students.

Ives' unconventionality was already in evidence by the time he entered Horatio Parker's theory classes at Yale. This was not because he was a "primitive" of some sort (a conception still widely entertained). On the contrary, he had been so thoroughly trained by his father, town musician of Danbury, Connecticut, and so thoroughly drenched in the platitudes of Victorian church music through his experiences as a church organist (he was something of a child prodigy in this respect) that his contact with Parker meant very little except repetition, and perhaps some expansion, of techniques he already knew. He compared Parker unfavorably, as a teacher, with his father. Besides teaching Bach to his son, George Ives had been a lively musical experimenter. He had rigged up a device to play in quarter-tones, and young Charles had seen him try to reproduce the exact sounds of church bells on the piano (George Ives had "absolute pitch"). The memory of his father's experimental spirit may have been a strong influence, but this alone would not seem a sufficient foundation for the wide-ranging artistic independence Ives achieved. More likely it was the impact on his receptive, imaginative, and ambitious mind of passages in Emerson such as the following:

> The objection to conforming to usages that have become dead to you is that it scatters your force. It loses your time and blurs the impression of your character. . . . But do your work, and I shall know you. Do your work, and you shall reinforce yourself. ("Self-Reliance," *Essays 1*, II, 55.)
> Let me admonish you, first of all, to go alone; to refuse the good models, even those which are sacred in the imagination of men, . . . Imitation cannot go above its model. The imitator dooms himself to hopeless mediocrity. ("An Address," I, 143.)

In deciding to go his own way rather than to follow the direction of Parker, fellow-student David Stanley Smith, and others who felt that study in Germany was the only proper cap for a musical education, he may have recalled Emerson's famous words to the American scholar, dating from 1837, but still pertinent: "We have listened too long to the courtly muses of Europe" ("The American Scholar," I, 113). And in searching for an honest American style, Emerson's essay "Self-Reliance" must have been a special encouragement, particularly a passage such as the following:

> And why need we copy the Doric or the Gothic model? Beauty, convenience, grandeur of thought and quaint expression are as near to us as to any, and if the American artist will study with hope and love the precise thing to be done by him, considering the climate, the soil, the length of the day, the wants of the people, the habit and form of the government, he will create a house in which all these will find themselves fitted, and taste and sentiment will be satisfied also. (*Essays 1*, II, 81.)

If Emerson provided the philosophical support for Ives' artistic independence, Thoreau did likewise for his approach to the business of living. His attitude about his music was like Thoreau's, who said in *Walden* ("Economy," p. 21), ". . . instead of studying how to make it worth men's while to buy my baskets, I studied rather how to avoid the necessity of selling them." Ives deliberately chose a profession other than music to avoid the necessity of having to sell his compositions (he knew also that unless he compromised, he could not sell them), and never in his life was he able to resign himself to any contract likely to bring him any profit from that source. The impact of *Walden* on his conscience never left him, in spite of his successful career in the business circles of New York.

With Emerson and Thoreau—two of the underlying forces in the shaping of Ives' art and life—as overt subjects of the music, it is not surprising that Ives' creative force reached an exceptional level of intensity in the Concord Sonata. The same intensity extends in this context to those other Concord figures, Hawthorne and the Alcotts, who are also the subjects of movements of the Sonata, and of Essays.

2

Ives, in his Preface, gives details concerning the composition and publication of the Essays and the Sonata in 1920. Many eccentricities of the text of the Essays are better understood, however, in the light of biographical facts not mentioned by Ives in his Preface.

Ives' decision after finishing college to make his livelihood in business did not mean at all that he intended to reduce his efforts at composing. Since the days were occupied, he used the nights and weekends for composition, and, on this sort of schedule, he managed to produce in the period 1898–1918 a quantity of works sufficient for the lifetime of many composers. The disorderly condition of most of the manuscript material resulted, to a large extent, from the fact that Ives had no time to spend over mere orthography when his head was bursting with new ideas that he could barely find the time to jot down.

Yet, during these years of composing, Ives somehow found the time also to read on the philosophy of art, to reread Emerson and Thoreau, and to read a number of essays and books about these men. His reading, if not that of a scholar, was of a more than respectable range for a businessman or a composer; it was remarkable for one who was both. It seems likely, considering the extent to which he covered the material on Emerson and Thoreau available at the time, and from the selection of sources on the philosophy of art, that Ives planned his reading for some time to lead toward the writing of these essays. Cowell says (p. 53) that he began to collect and expand notes for the Essays in 1915, on completion of the Sonata. The entry of the United States into World War I must have stopped his work on the Essays as it stopped his composing (see autobiographical notes in Cowell, pp. 75-76). After a period of extremely hard work in connection with the Red Cross and the Liberty Loan drive, he suffered an attack in October, 1918, which forced his absence from business for six months and left him with a permanently damaged heart. After this, Ives seems to have decided to get some of his major works into presentable form as soon as possible. Although he gained some extra time to work on these projects during his convalescence, a sense of hurry, illness, and emotional disturbance over the war caused the works to see print with more mechanical flaws (this was especially true of the Essays) than they would have contained had no unusual circumstances affected their writer. Later on, when his music was published, Ives became quite the meticulous proofreader, as proofs in the Yale Ives Collection show. In 1947 Ives saw through the press a thoroughly overhauled second edition of the Concord Sonata (Arrow Music Press). In both editions, Ives attempted to approximate his original intention of printing the Essays and Sonata together by placing excerpts from the Essays on pages facing the beginnings of each movement, and in the back. In preparing these excerpts from the 1920 book, Ives made some revisions (these have been noted in the present volume, but no thorough overhaul leading to a second edition of the Essays was ever attempted in Ives' lifetime, although he left at least one excerpt to be included in the second edition "if there happen to be one."

3

The republication of the Essays now, after Ives' death, poses difficult problems. A deceased author cannot be queried, and one must either print his text exactly as he left it in the last approved version, or risk burdening the reader with the explanations and apparatuses of textual scholarship. The latter treatment would probably have annoyed Ives as it did Emerson, who speaks scornfully of the "Third Estate" (with the world and the soul) consisting of "the restorers of readings, the emendators, [and] the bibliomaniacs of all degrees"

("The American Scholar," I, 91). Nevertheless, the condition of the 1920 book and other circumstances have made it both necessary and desirable to produce at this time not a simple reprint, but an edition.

In the Ives Collection at Yale there are manuscripts of the Essays. A first step in making this edition, then, was to compare the manuscripts and the printed book.

An obviously necessary revision of the punctuation in the book could not be undertaken without looking up all the passages in quotation marks, of which there were hundreds. Even if it were decided that bolstering Ives' quotations with reference was unnecessary pedantry, there was no other way to distinguish between real quotations, paraphrases, allusions, or passages placed in quotes to express strong feeling.

Ives casually wove into his prose the names (sometimes only the last name, or even the nickname) of authors, musicians, and public figures no longer well known, and it seemed necessary to try to identify these people for the reader. The same was true of allusions to events which may have been forgotten after the lapse of a quarter of a century.

Ives gave autobiographical notes to the Cowells for use in their book, and it seemed desirable to try to connect autobiographical allusions in the Essays to the descriptions of the same or very similar events in the Cowells' biography.

The final level of editing was a revision of the punctuation, done after collation of the book and manuscript, and the tracing of the quotations.

4

Of the manuscripts of the *Essays Before A Sonata* in the Ives Collection at the Library of the Yale School of Music, one set is an early version (perhaps first draft) of the introductory page (called "Preface" in the present edition), the "Prologue," the Hawthorne chapter, the Thoreau chapter, practically complete, and a few passages for the Emerson chapter. The handwriting is nearly illegible in these manuscript pages. For purposes of this edition, the most helpful clue among the material was a reference to Van Doren's *Thoreau* in connection with certain passages quoted therein from a Thoreau article in *Dial*. This helped to establish the fact that certain of the more obscure quotations in *Essays Before A Sonata* came not from the *Journals* and *Dial* but from Van Doren's study of Thoreau.

The second set of manuscripts is a nearly complete, and much more clearly written copy in which all the chapters are represented. This copy has marginal indications for the typist, and it can be presumed that it is the last handwritten copy made by Ives. The typescript extracted from it may have been the one used by the Knickerbocker Press of New York, who printed the book at Ives' expense in 1920. That typescript is not available, the publisher no longer being in business. Mrs. Ives, in response to my inquiry, said (letter of Feb. 2, 1961) that she did not know of the existence of any copies other than the handwritten ones found in Ives' study and turned over to the Yale Collection. Of these, then, the second set represents the final version available before the printed book itself, and, since it is handwritten, one can be sure that no outside influence has affected it. This is the manuscript which has been collated with the 1920 book.

A comparison of the printed book and the second handwritten copy (hereafter called MS) shows that Ives added some passages to the typescript or proofs. It also shows that someone (typist, editor, or typesetter?) corrected a large number of misspellings, revised the punctuation, and even attempted to improve the sentence structure in many places. Mrs. Ives (in the letter mentioned above) said that she doubted if Mr. Ives had a professional editor prepare the manuscript for the printer. But in any case the work was done, and it would seem unlikely to anyone familiar with Ives' raw prose that he himself did the final polishing, if it can be called that.

Since whatever changes there are were made under Ives' supervision, and with his approval, the printed book must constitute the basic text for any newer edition. A literal printing of the manuscript (if such a thing were possible, considering the number of alternate words and marginal notes) would be no more than a curiosity, and unfair in its emphasis on the eccentricity of Ives' style, which has nothing to do with the seriousness of his thought.

The collation of the book and MS revealed a great many changes in wording—some of no consequence as far as meaning is concerned, and others of distinct interest. The latter have been given in footnotes, always introduced by the symbol MS followed by a colon. No quotation marks are used except those which may have been in the passage itself.

A few misspellings not corrected in the 1920 book have been silently taken care of here. Some misspellings of foreign words have been allowed to stand.

Occasional insertions of "a," "and," "the," and other such words from the manuscript did not seem to justify footnotes, and they have been inserted without comment. Words added by the editor have been placed in square brackets.

The editing of the book (whoever did it) was conservative. On the one hand, it attempts to punctuate normally passages which, in the MS, are like Bradford Torrey's description of Thoreau's punctuation in the manuscript of the *Journals*—"a spattering of dashes and little else." On the other hand, if the intention were to normalize the punctuation, there remains a large number of lapses.

The policy followed in the present edition has been to restore Ives' MS punctuation almost literally in free, rhapsodic passages (which means using a great many dashes), and to normalize still further in the primarily expository passages.

Ives' prose is like Emerson's description of Montaigne's: "It is the language of conversation transferred to a book" (IV, 160). When Ives' sentences look strange, read them aloud, and the necessary timing in articulating the words will explain much of his punctuation. This is more obvious in the MS punctuation than in the revised punctuation of the 1920 book. While most writers use commas for grammatical clarity, to Ives they are "phrasing," in actual time, functioning like the phrasing slurs of musical notation. If more time is required to articulate the sibilants at the end of one word and the beginning of another, he puts a comma to indicate the necessary slight pause. For example, without the slightest grammatical justification the following cases occur in the MS: "Vagueness, is," and "Emerson's, substance."

Ives' syntax being as complex as it is, and the difficulties for the reader already being sufficient, the use of commas in this edition has been reduced to normalcy, for the most part. The various kinds of pauses—commas, semicolons, colons, and dashes—have been interchanged freely, the object being to make the important clauses stand out as clearly as possible in Ives' often very long sentences. No change has been made without keeping in mind one striking instance of a complete alteration in the meaning caused by the absence in the 1920 book of two commas which were present in the MS. The passages were: (Book) "And unity is too generally conceived of"; (MS) "And unity is, too, generally conceived of."

A special feature of Ives' style is his coinage of new hyphenated combinations. Unnecessary ones such as "late-spring," or "city-man" have been eliminated. But highly characteristic combinations such as "manner–over–insistence," and "image–necessity–stimulants" have been allowed to stand. A few hyphenated combinations present in the MS but not in the 1920 book have been noted.

Ives uses quotation marks for direct quotations, indirect quotations, mere echoes of another author's prose, allusion, and to indicate strong feeling, which is quite frequently sarcasm. (See the dedication of the book, in which his ironical quotation marks have been retained; those which were placed around the title of the book on the title page have been removed.)

With the feeling of most typographers strongly against excessive use of quotation marks because they make the page appear to have broken out in a rash, an attempt was made to remove some of the unnecessary ones in the Essays. Naturally, this could not be done until the quotations were traced, and the real ones separated from the dozens of other passages so marked for assorted reasons. But it turned out, after the search was made, that most of the passages were real quotations or strong allusions, though in varying states of disarray. To have removed the quotation marks from all those except the direct quotations accurately given would have prevented the reader from knowing of Ives' awareness in other cases that he was using another writer's words or thoughts. Therefore, the text is still full of quotation marks, good modern practice notwithstanding.

Because of the large number of quotation marks necessarily in the text, the footnotes follow a form which introduces quoted passages after a colon, without quotation marks.

Ives, of course, felt no scholarly obligation to quote other writers with strict accuracy, and there is no intention here to make him look irresponsible by calling attention to the errors in the quoted passages. He was probably following Emerson, who said, "A great man quotes bravely . . ." ("Quotation and Originality," VIII, 174). Apparently

Ives was brave enough, and absorbed deeply enough in his subject to quote frequently from memory. But, whatever the reason, the fact is that scarcely a quotation in the entire book is exactly like its source.

When the differences between Ives' text and the source did not involve changes in meaning, and were only single words or punctuation, the corrections have been made silently in the text, and the source given. If there was an interesting change of meaning (e.g., Thoreau: "They shall live with the license of higher beings"; Ives: "They shall love with the license of higher beings"), or if the whole quotation was drastically altered, the form in the source has been given in a note.

With all the different sorts of annotation required, some of the pages promised to look like those of learned journals in which the appendages outgrow the body. To avoid this extreme, which appeared to be inappropriate with Ives' Essays, the longer notes (except those which are variant text readings) have been placed in the back of the book. In these cases, however, a short note appears on the page to inform the reader of the content of the more extensive one, so that he may decide whether he wishes to pause long enough to turn to the back. All short and simple documentation is on the page, and can be dispensed with quickly.

Ives himself had no fondness for footnotes; the 1920 book has only five. Four of these are acknowledgments of sources (the paraphrase of a passage from *Sartor Resartus,* John C. Grigg's article on Debussy, H. D. Sedgwick's *The New American Type,* and Daniel Gregory Mason's *Contemporary Composers*), and these have been absorbed into the notes of this edition. The remaining one, describing instrumental conceptions of the movements of the sonata, has been left as it is, and is separated by a line from the editor's footnotes on the same page.

The tracing of Ives' quotations has been carried out to a degree not originally contemplated for this edition, for reasons outlined above. Having come so close to completeness, it remains a source of disappointment that a few apparent quotations eluded every search possible within the time limit set for the preparation of this volume. It is possible, Ives' methods being what they were, that some of the unexplained passages still remaining in quotation marks are not quotations at all. It is also possible that some of them will be recognized

by readers, in which case it would be pleasant to add more game to
the spoils of the hunt. No attempt was made to trace the few Biblical
and classical allusions.

5

If there was a wide choice of editions from which Ives might have
drawn his quotations, either the complete works of the author have
been cited, or an edition brought out in New York or Boston in the
period, roughly 1890–1915, has been chosen for the reference.

Most of the titles are sufficiently complete as they occur in the
notes. The following are titles referred to only as "Works" or
"Writings":

The Works of Thomas Carlyle, Centenary Edition (New York, 1899).

The Works of William E. Channing, to which is added *The Perfect Life*
(Boston, 1901).

The Writings of John Burroughs, Riverside Edition (Boston and New
York, 1895).

The Works of Ralph Waldo Emerson, Standard Library Edition (Boston
and New York, 1894).

The Works of Nathaniel Hawthorne, Riverside Edition (Boston and New
York, 1883).

The Works of Oliver Wendell Holmes, Standard Library Edition (Boston
and New York, 1896).

The Works of John Ruskin, ed. E. T. Cook and Alexander Wedderburn
(London, 1903).

The Writings of Henry David Thoreau, Walden Edition (Boston and
New York, 1906). Vol I is *A Week on the Concord and Merrimack
Rivers,* referred to in the notes as "Week." *Walden* is vol. II, referred
to in the notes without the volume number.

The following works are referred to a number of times only by
shortened titles:

Henry and Sidney Cowell, *Charles Ives and His Music* (New York:
Oxford University Press, 1955).

Mark Van Doren, *Henry David Thoreau; a Critical Study* (Boston and
New York, 1916).

Edward Waldo Emerson, *Thoreau, As Remembered by a Young Friend*
(Boston and New York, 1917).

John Kirkpatrick, *A Temporary Mimeographed Catalogue of the Music Manuscripts of Charles Edward Ives (1874–1954) given by Mrs. Ives to the Library of the Yale School of Music, September, 1955.* Compiled by John Kirkpatrick, 1954–60. 114 copies, typed by the compiler, mimeographed at Yale University, bound by Demander Bookbindery, Inc., for the Library of the Yale School of Music. Copyright 1960 by John Kirkpatrick.

The meaning of the symbol MS in the notes has been explained above. The symbol AR refers to the text portions of the 1947 edition of the Concord Sonata, published by the Arrow Music Press (now assigned to Associated Music Publishers, New York).

6

I wish to thank Mrs. Ives for allowing the use of uncatalogued papers in the Ives Collection at the Library of the Yale School of Music. I owe thanks to Professor Brooks Shepard, Librarian, for many courtesies in the use of the Collection.

John Kirkpatrick gave me his encouragement to undertake this project. Without his support and advice, I would not have attempted it.

It is one of the advantages of a university that one can find help when he needs it from experts in fields other than his own. Dr. George Lam, who copes daily with editorial problems more complex than those in Ives, gave me invaluable advice and help, for which I am deeply indebted. I was also able to receive highly appreciated help and counsel from Professor Norman Holmes Pearson.

Finally, Edward McClellan deserves special thanks for his skillful help with the manuscript during inconvenient and unconventional hours, and for much helpful advice.

Howard Boatwright

School of Music, Yale University
New Haven, Connecticut

AUTHOR'S PREFACE

THE following pages were written primarily as a preface or reason for the (writer's) second pianoforte sonata—"Concord, Mass., 1845," —a group of four pieces, called a sonata for want of a more exact name, as the form, perhaps substance, does not justify it.[a] The music and prefaces were intended to be printed together, but as it was found that this would make a cumbersome volume, they are separate. The whole is an attempt to present (one person's) impression of the spirit of transcendentalism that is associated in the minds of many with Concord, Mass., of over a half century ago. This is undertaken in impressionistic pictures of Emerson and Thoreau, a sketch of the Alcotts, and a *scherzo* supposed to reflect a lighter quality which is often found in the fantastic side of Hawthorne. The first and last movements do not aim to give any programs of the life or of any particular work of either Emerson or Thoreau, but, rather, composite pictures or impressions. They are, however, so general in outline that, from some viewpoints, they may be as far from accepted impressions (from true conceptions, for that matter) as the valuation which they purport to be of the influence of the life, thought, and character of Emerson and Thoreau is inadequate.[b]

[a] MS: though the form or substance neither justifies or deserves it.
[b] Inserted in AR:
The first edition together with the book of essays was published in 1920. This sonata was composed mostly in 1909 and 1910, the last movement fully completed in 1915. One of the principal themes and some passages were from an orchestral score—an Overture "Orchard House" (Alcotts), 1904. The first movement is partly from an uncompleted score of an Emerson piano concerto, 1908-09. This movement for piano alone is not exactly an arrangement from the orchestral score. It is rather a kind of free translation, though there are several passages not suggested in the score; but to a great extent, it has much of the form and subject matter from the score sketch. This second edition in some passages contains more of this score than does the first edition, and also has a few revisions made since the first edition was printed.
[One more paragraph explains the use of accidentals in the music.]

ESSAYS
BEFORE A SONATA

O N E

PROLOGUE

HOW far is anyone justified, be he an authority or a layman, in expressing or trying to express in terms of music (in sounds, if you like) the value of anything, material, moral, intellectual, or spiritual, which is usually expressed in terms other than music? How far afield can music go and keep honest as well as reasonable or artistic?[c] Is it a matter limited only by the composer's power of expressing what lies in his subjective or objective consciousness? Or is it limited by any limitations of the composer? Can a tune literally represent a stone wall with vines on it or even with nothing on it, though it (the tune) be made by a genius whose power of objective contemplation is in the highest state of development? Can it be done by anything short of an act of mesmerism on the part of the composer or an act of kindness on the part of the listener? Does the extreme materializing of music[d] appeal strongly to anyone except to those without a sense of humor—or, rather, with a sense of humor?—or, except, possibly, to those who might excuse it, as Herbert Spencer might, by the theory that the sensational element (the sensations we hear so much about in experi-

[c] MS: reasonable, i.e. artistic.
[d] MS: (as evidenced by some modern Germans).

3

mental psychology) is the true pleasurable phenomenon in music
and that the mind should not be allowed to interfere?[e] Does the
success of program music depend more upon the program than upon
the music? If it does, what is the use of the music? If it does not,
what is the use of the program? Does not its appeal depend to a great
extent on the listener's willingness to accept the theory that music
is the language of the emotions and *only* that? Or, inversely, does
not this theory tend to limit music to programs?—a limitation as bad
for music itself, for its wholesome progress, as a diet of program music
is bad for the listener's ability to digest anything beyond the sensuous
or physical-emotional. To a great extent this depends on what is
meant by emotion, or on the assumption that the word as used above
refers more to the "expression of," rather than to a meaning in a
deeper sense—which may be a feeling influenced by some experience, perhaps of a spiritual nature, in the expression of which the
intellect has some part.[f] "The nearer we get to the mere expression
of emotion," says Professor Sturt in his *Philosophy of Art and Personality*, "as in the antics of boys who have been promised a holiday,
the further we get away from art."[g]

On the other hand is not all music program music? Is not pure
music, so called, representative in its essence? Is it not program music
raised to the nth power, or, rather, reduced to the minus nth power?
Where is the line to be drawn between the expression of subjective
and objective emotion? It is easier to know *what* each is than when
each *becomes* what it is. The "Separateness of Art" theory—that art
is not life, but a reflection of it, that art is not vital to life but that

[e] For a passage from Spencer's *Facts and Comments* expressing this theory,
see Note 1.
[f] The passage beginning "Does not its appeal . . ." was rewritten as follows
in AR: If one is willing to go no further than to accept the theory that music
is the language of the emotions and *only* that, the matter is perhaps an insolu-
ble problem; but one becoming more interesting, perhaps more possible of solution, if instead of accepting the term "emotion" only as an "expression of"
itself, it is received in a deeper sense—that is, that it is a feeling influenced by
some experience, perhaps of a spiritual nature, in the expression of which the
intellect has some part.
[g] Henry Sturt, "Art and Personality," in *Personal idealism; philosophical essays
by eight members of the University of Oxford*, ed. Sturt (London and New
York, 1902), p. 307.

life is vital to it—does not help us.[h] Nor does Thoreau, who says not
that "life is art," but that "life is an art,"[i] which, of course is a different thing than the foregoing. Tolstoi is even more helpless to
himself and to us, for he eliminates further. From his definition of
art, we may learn little more than that a kick in the back is a work
of art, and Beethoven's *Ninth Symphony* is not.[j] Experiences are
passed on from one man to another. Abel knew that. And now we
know it. But where is the bridge placed—at the end of the road, or
only at the end of our vision? Is it all a bridge, or is there no bridge
because there is no gulf? Suppose that a composer writes a piece of
music, conscious that he is inspired, say, by witnessing an act of great
self-sacrifice—another piece by the contemplation of a certain trait
of nobility he perceives in a friend's character—and another by the
sight of a mountain lake under moonlight. The first two, from an
inspirational standpoint, would naturally seem to come under the
subjective and the last under the objective, yet, the chances are,
there is something of the quality of both in all. There may have been,
in the first instance, physical action so intense or so dramatic in character that the remembrance of it aroused a great deal more objective
emotion than the composer was conscious of while writing the music.
In the third instance, the music may have been influenced strongly,
though subconsciously, by a vague remembrance of certain thoughts
and feelings, perhaps of a deep religious or spiritual nature, which
suddenly came to him upon realizing the beauty of the scene, and
which overpowered the first sensuous pleasure—perhaps some such
feeling as of the conviction of immortality that Thoreau experienced,
and tells about in *Walden*. "Ah! I have penetrated to those meadows
. . . when the wild river valley and the woods were bathed in so
pure and bright a light as would have waked the dead *if* [italics: Ives]
they had been slumbering in their graves, as some suppose. There
needs no stronger proof of immortality."[k] Enthusiasm must permeate
it, but what it is that inspires an art effort is not easily determined,

[h] "The Separateness of Art" is the third section of Sturt's essay. The idea is
summarized in this sentence on p. 314: Art lies outside the vital needs of our
existence, and therefore must always be an episode.
[i] "The Art of Life—The Scholar's Calling," in *Dial*. Quoted by Ives from
Van Doren, *Thoreau*, p. 91.
[j] For a passage from Tolstoi's *What is art?*, see Note 2.
[k] In the chapter called "Spring," *Writings*, II, 349.

much less classified. The word inspire is used here in the sense of cause rather than effect. A critic may say that a certain movement is not inspired. But that may be a matter of taste; perhaps the most inspired music sounds the least so—to the critic. A true inspiration may lack a true expression, unless it is assumed that if an inspiration is not true enough to produce a true expression—if there be anyone who can definitely determine what a true expression is—it is not an inspiration at all.

Again, suppose the same composer at another time writes a piece of equal merit to the other three, as estimates go, but holds that he is not conscious of wht inspired it—that he had nothing definite in mind—that he was not aware of any mental image or process—that, naturally, the actual work in creating something gave him a satisfying feeling of pleasure—perhaps of elation. What will you substitute for the mountain lake, for his friend's character, etc.? Will you substitute anything? If so, why? If so, what? Or is it enough to let the matter rest on the pleasure, mainly physical, of the tones—their color, succession, and relations—formal or informal? Can an inspiration come from a blank mind? Well, he tries to explain and says that he was conscious of some emotional excitement and of a sense of something beautiful—he doesn't know exactly what—a vague feeling of exaltation, or perhaps of profound sadness. What is the source[1] of these instinctive feelings, these vague intuitions and introspective sensations? The more we try to analyze, the more vague they become. To pull them apart and classify them as subjective or objective, or as this or that, means that they may be well classified and that is about all; it leaves us as far from the origin as ever. What does it all mean? What is behind it all? "The voice of God," says the artist. "The voice of the devil," says the man in the front row. Are we, because we are human beings, born with the power of innate perception of the beautiful in the abstract so that an inspiration can arise through no external stimuli of sensation or experience—no association with the outward? Or was there present, in the above instance, some kind of subconscious, instantaneous, composite image of all the mountain lakes this man had ever seen, blended as kind of overtones with the various traits of nobility of many of his friends embodied in one personality? Do all inspirational images, states, conditions, or whatever

[1] AR: Whence comes the desire for expression? What is the source . . .

they may be truly called, have for a dominant part, if not for a source, some actual experience in life or of the social relation? To think that they do not—always at least—would be a relief. But as we are trying to consider music made and heard by human beings (and not by birds or angels), it seems difficult to suppose that even subconscious images can be separated from some human experience; there must be something behind subconsciousness to produce consciousness, and so on. But whatever the elements and origin of these so-called images are, that they *do* stir deep emotional feelings and encourage their expression is a part of the unknowable we know. They do often arouse something that has not yet passed the border line between subconsciousness and consciousness—an artistic intuition (well named, but —object and cause unknown!) Here is a program!—conscious or subconscious, what does it matter? Why try to trace any stream that flows through the garden of consciousness to its source only to be confronted by another problem of tracing this source to its source? Perhaps Emerson in "The Rhodora" answers by not trying to explain:

> . . . if eyes were made for seeing,
> Then Beauty is its own excuse for being:
> Why thou wert there, O rival of the rose!
> I never thought to ask, I never knew:
> But, in my simple ignorance, suppose
> The self-same Power that brought me there brought you.[m]

Perhaps Sturt answers by substitution: "Now we cannot in the strict sense explain the origin of the artistic intuition any more than the origin of any other primary function of our nature. But if, as I believe, civilisation is mainly founded on those kinds of unselfish human interest which we call knowledge and morality, it is easily intelligible that we should have a parallel interest, which we call art, closely akin and lending powerful support to the other two. It is intelligible too that moral goodness, intellectual power, high vitality, and strength should be approved by the intuition."[n] This reduces, or, rather, brings the problem back to a tangible basis; namely, the translation of an artistic intuition into musical sounds[o] approving and reflecting, or endeavoring to approve and reflect, a "moral good-

---

[m] "The Rhodora: On Being Asked, Whence Is the Flower?," *Works*, IX, 39.
[n] Sturt, p. 328.
[o] MS: into (musical) sounds.

ness," a "high vitality," etc., or any other human attribute—mental, moral, or spiritual.

Can music do *more* than this? Can it *do* this? And if so, who and what is to determine the degree of its failure or success? The composer, the performer (if there be any), or those who have to listen? One hearing, or a century of hearings? And if it isn't successful, or if it doesn't fail, what matters it? The fear of failure need keep no one from the attempt, for if the composer is sensitive, he need but launch forth a countercharge of "being misunderstood," and hide behind it.[p] A theme that the composer sets up as "moral goodness" may sound like "high vitality" to his friend, and but like an outburst of "nervous weakness"[q] or only a "stagnant pool" to those not even his enemies. Expression, to a great extent, is a matter of terms, and terms are anyone's. The meaning of "God" may have a billion interpretations if there be that many souls in the world.

There is a moral in the "Nominalist" and Realist"[r] that will "prove all sums." It runs something like this: No matter how sincere and confidential men are in trying to know or assuming that they do know each other's mood and habits of thought, the net result leaves a feeling that all is left unsaid; for the reason of their incapacity to know each other, though they use the same words. They go on from one explanation to another, but things seem to stand about as they did in the beginning "because of that vicious assumption."[s] But we would rather believe that music is beyond any analogy to word language and that the time is coming, but not in our lifetime, when it will develop possibilities inconceivable now—a language so transcendent that its heights and depths will be common to all mankind.

[p] Omitted in AR: The fear of failure . . . hide behind it.
[q] Omitted in AR: an outburst of "nervous weakness."
[r] Emerson, *Essays 2*, III.
[s] See Note 3 for the passage.

I. "Emerson"

CHARLES E. IVES

T W O

EMERSON

IT has seemed to the writer that Emerson is greater—his identity more complete, perhaps—in the realms or revelation—natural disclosure—than in those of poetry, philosophy, or prophecy. Though a great poet and prophet, he is greater, possibly, as an invader of the unknown—America's deepest explorer of the spiritual immensities—a seer painting his discoveries in masses and with any color that may lie at hand—cosmic, religious, human, even sensuous; a recorder freely describing the inevitable struggle in the soul's uprise, perceiving from this inward source alone that "every ultimate fact is only the first of a new series";[t] a discoverer, whose heart knows, with Voltaire, that "man seriously reflects when left alone."[u] and who would then discover, if he can, that "wondrous chain which links the heavens with earth—the world of beings sub-

[t] "Circles," II, 284.
[u] As the reader becomes acquainted with Ives' freedom of quotation and allusion, he will not be surprised to find in one sentence an exact quotation, as above, and words placed in quotes which may not be quotations at all. The quotation marks in this instance (as often elsewhere in the book) are probably Ives' way of indicating that he was expressing another writer's idea. Of many references to solitude in Emerson, the passage in "Culture," *The Conduct of Life*, IV, 149 ff., seems the most likely source of this allusion.

ject to one law.",^v In *his* reflections Emerson, unlike Plato, is not
afraid to ride Arion's Dolphin, and to go wherever he is carried—to
Parnassus or to Musketaquid.^w

We see him—standing on a summit at the door of the infinite,
where many men do not care to climb, peering into the mysteries of
life, contemplating the eternities, hurling back whatever he discovers
there—now thunderbolts for us to grasp, if we can, and translate—
now placing quietly, even tenderly, in our hands things that we may
see without effort; if we won't see them, so much the worse for us.

We see him—a mountain-guide so intensely on the lookout for the
trail of his star that he has no time to stop and retrace his footprints,
which may often seem indistinct to his followers, who find it easier
and perhaps safer to keep their eyes on the ground. And there is a
chance that this guide could not always retrace his steps if he tried—
and why should he! He is on the road, conscious only that, though
his star may not lie within walking distance, he must reach it before
his wagon can be hitched to it—a Prometheus illuminating a privilege
of the Gods—lighting a fuse that is laid towards men. Emerson reveals
the lesser not by an analysis of itself, but by bringing men towards
the greater. He does not try to reveal, personally, but leads, rather,
to a field where revelation is a harvest-part—where it is known by the
perceptions of the soul towards the absolute law. He leads us towards
this law, which is a realization of what experience has suggested and
philosophy has hoped for. He leads us, conscious that the aspects of
truth as he sees them may change as often as truth remains constant.
Revelation, perhaps, is but prophecy intensified—the intensifying of
its mason-work as well as its steeple. Simple prophecy, while concerned with the past, reveals but the future, while revelation is
concerned with all time. The power in Emerson's prophecy confuses
it with—or at least makes it seem to approach—revelation. It is prophecy with no time element. Emerson tells, as few bards could, of what
will happen in the past, for his future is eternity, and the past is a
part of that. And so, like all true prophets, he is always modern, and
will grow modern with the years—for his substance is not relative but

^v Again, the quotation marks may mean only that Ives is expressing an Emer-
sonian idea. A related imagery is: . . . this one thread [your perceptions], fine
as gossamer, . . . on which heaven and earth are strung (*Natural History of
the Intellect*, XII, 38).
^w "Grass-ground River," Indian name for the Concord River.

a measure of eternal truths, determined rather by a universalist than by a partialist. He measured, as Michelangelo said true artists should, "with the eye and not the hand."[x] But to attribute modernism to his substance, though not to his expression, is an anachronism, and is as futile as calling today's sunset modern.

As revelation and prophecy, in their common acceptance, are resolved by man from the absolute and universal to the relative and personal, and as Emerson's tendency is fundamentally the opposite, it is easier, safer, and, so, apparently clearer to think of him as a poet of natural and revealed philosophy.[y] And, as such, a prophet—but not one to be confused with those singing soothsayers whose pockets are filled, as are the pockets of conservative reaction and radical demagoguery in pulpit, street-corner, [and] bank and columns, with dogmatic fortune-tellings. Emerson as a prophet in these lower heights was a conservative in that he seldom lost his head, and a radical in that he seldom cared whether he lost it or not. He was a born radical, as are all true conservatives. He was too much "absorbed by the absolute," too much of the universal[ist] to be either—though he could be both at once.[z] To Cotton Mather[a] he would have been a demagogue; to a real demagogue he would not be understood, as it was with no self-interest that he laid his hand on reality. The nearer any subject or an attribute of it approaches to the perfect truth at its base, the more does qualification become necessary. Radicalism must always qualify itself. Emerson clarifies as he qualifies, by plunging into rather than emerging from Carlyle's "soul-confusing labyrinths of speculative radicalism." The radicalism that we hear much about today is not Emerson's kind, but of thinner fiber; it qualifies itself by going to "A root" and often cutting other roots in the process. It is usually as impotent as dynamite in its cause, and sometimes as harmful to the wholesome progress of all causes; it is qualified by its failure. But the radicalism of Emerson plunges to all roots; it becomes greater than itself—greater than all its formal or informal doctrines,

[x] In Emerson, *The Conduct of Life*, VI, 171: "An artist," said Michelangelo, "must have his measuring tools not in the hand, but in the eye. . . ."
[y] MS: natural over revealed religion.
[z] "Nominalist and Realist," *Essays* 2, III, 233-234: Very fitly therefore I assert that every man is a partialist; . . . I add that every man is a universalist also. . . .
[a] From 1685 until his death in 1728 Mather was minister of the Second Church, Boston, a pulpit occupied by Emerson, 1829-1832.

too advanced and too conservative for any specific result, too catholic for all the churches—for the nearer it is to truth, the farther it is from a truth, and the more it is qualified by its future possibilities.

Hence comes the difficulty—the futility of attempting to fasten on Emerson any particular doctrine, philosophic, or religious theory. Emerson wrings the neck of any law that would become exclusive and arrogant, whether a definite one of metaphysics or an indefinite one of mechanics. He hacks his way up and down, as near as he can to the absolute, the oneness of all nature, both human and spiritual, and to God's benevolence. To him the ultimate of a conception is its vastness, and it is probably this rather than the "blind-spots" in his expression that makes us incline to go with him but half-way, and then stand and build dogmas. But if we can not follow all the way— if we do not always clearly perceive the whole picture—we are at least free to imagine it; he makes us feel that we are free to do so. Perhaps that is the most he asks. For he is but reaching out through and beyond mankind, trying to see what he can of the infinite and its immensities, throwing back to us whatever he can, but ever conscious that he but occasionally catches a glimpse; conscious that, if he would contemplate the greater, he must wrestle with the lesser, even though it dims an outline; that he must struggle if he would hurl back anything—even a broken fragment for men to examine and perchance in it find a germ of some part of truth; conscious at times of the futility of his effort and its message; conscious of its vagueness but ever hopeful for it, and confident that its foundation, if not its medium, is somewhere near the eventual and absolute good—the divine truth underlying all life. If Emerson must be dubbed an optimist—then an optimist fighting pessimism, but not wallowing in it; an optimist who does not study pessimism by learning to enjoy it; whose imagination is greater than his curiosity; who, seeing the signpost to Erebus is strong enough to go the other way. This strength of optimism—indeed the strength we find always underlying his tolerance, his radicalism, his searches, prophecies, and revelations—is heightened and made efficient by "imagination-penetrative," a thing concerned not with the combining but the apprehending of things.[b]

[b] John Ruskin, "Modern Painters, II," *Works*, IV, 249 (paragraph summary in the margin), reads: Imagination penetrative is concerned not with the combining, but the apprehending of things.

A possession akin to the power Ruskin says all great pictures have, which "depends on the penetration of the imagination into the *true* nature of the thing represented, and on the utter scorn of the imagination for all shackles and fetters of mere external fact that stand in the way of its suggestiveness"[c]—a possession which gives the strength of distance to his eyes and the strength of muscle to his soul. With this he slashes down through the loam—nor would he have us rest there. If we would dig deep enough only to plant a doctrine from one part of him, he would show us the quick-silver in that furrow. If we would creed his "Compensation,"[d] there is hardly a sentence that could not wreck it, or could not show that the idea is no tenet of a philosophy, but a clear (though perhaps not clearly hurled on the canvas) illustration of universal justice—of God's perfect balances; a story of the analogy, or, better, the identity of polarity and duality in Nature with that in morality. The essay is no more a doctrine than the law of gravitation is. If we would stop and attribute too much to genius, he shows us that "what is best written or done by genius in the world, was no one man's work, but came by wide social labor, when a thousand wrought like one, sharing the same impulse."[e] If we would find in his essay on Montaigne[f] a biography, we are shown a biography of scepticism—and in reducing this to a relation between sensation and the morals, we are shown a true Montaigne; we know the man better, perhaps, by this lesser presentation. If we would stop and trust heavily on the harvest of originality, he shows us that this plant—this part of the garden—is but a relative thing. It is dependent also on the richness that ages have put into the soil. "Every thinker is retrospective."[g]

Thus is Emerson always beating down through the crust towards the first fire of life, of death, and of eternity. Read where you will, each sentence seems not to point to the next but to the undercurrent of all. If you should label his a religion of ethics or of morals, he shames you at the outset, "for ethics is but a reflection of a divine personality." All the religions this world has ever known have been

c "Modern Painters, II," *Works*, IV, 278.
d *Essays 1*, II, 89-122.
e Probably not a quotation. For a related passage in Emerson, see Note 4.
f "Montaigne; or The Skeptic," *Representative Men*, IV, 141-177.
g Perhaps not a quotation. For related passages, see Note 5.

but the aftermath of the ethics of one or another holy person; "as soon as character appears be sure love will";[h] "the intuition of the moral sentiment is an insight of the perfection of the laws of the soul";[i] but these laws cannot be catalogued.

If a versatilist—a modern Goethe, for instance—could put all of Emerson's admonitions into practice, a constant permanence would result—an eternal short-circuit—a focus of equal X-rays. Even the value or success of but one precept is dependent, like that of a ball-game, as much on the batting-eye as on the pitching-arm.[j] The inactivity of permanence is what Emerson will not permit. He will not accept repose against the activity of truth. But this almost constant resolution of every insight towards the absolute may get a little on one's nerves, if one is at all partial-wise to the specific. One begins to ask, what is the absolute, anyway, and why try to look clear through the eternities and the unknowable—even out of the other end? Emerson's fondness for flying to definite heights on indefinite wings, and the tendency to over-resolve, becomes unsatisfying to the impatient, who want results to come as they walk. Probably this is a reason that it is occasionally said that Emerson has no vital message for the rank and file. He has no definite message, perhaps, for the literal, but his messages are all vital, as much by reason of his indefiniteness as in spite of it.

There is a suggestion of irony in the thought that the power of his vague but compelling vitality, which ever sweeps us on in spite of ourselves, might not have been his if it had not been for those definite religious doctrines of the old New England theologians. For almost two centuries, Emerson's mental and spiritual muscles had been in training for him in the moral and intellectual contentions, a part of the religious exercises of his forebears.[k] A kind of higher sensitiveness seems to culminate in him. It gives him a power of search-

[h] "The Sovereignty of Ethics," X, 203: Ethics are thought not to satisfy affection. But all the religion we have is the ethics of one or another holy person; as soon as character appears, be sure love will, and veneration, and anecdotes and fables about him, . . .

[i] "An Address," I, 122.

[j] Margin of MS: get better simile?

[k] Oliver Wendell Holmes, in "R. W. Emerson," Holmes' *Works*, XI, 2-8, gives an account of Emerson's genealogy. Emerson's family was remarkable for the long succession of clergymen, and the large number of college graduates counted on its rolls.

ing for a wider freedom of soul than theirs. The religion of Puritanism was based to a great extent on a search for the unknowable, limited only by the dogma of its theology—a search for a path, so that the soul could better be conducted to the next world—while Emerson's transcendentalism was based on the wider search for the unknowable, unlimited in any way or by anything except the vast bounds of innate goodness, as it might be revealed to him in any phenomena of Man, Nature, or God. This distinction, tenuous in spite of the definite *sounding* words, we like to believe has something peculiar to Emerson in it. We like to feel that it superimposes [supersedes] the one that makes all transcendentalism but an intellectual state based on the theory of innate ideas, the reality of thought, and the necessity of its freedom. For the philosophy of the religion[1] (or whatever you will call it) of the Concord Transcendentalists is at least more than an intellectual state. It has even some of the functions of the Puritan church; it is a spiritual state in which both soul *and* mind can better conduct themselves in this world, and also in the next—when the time comes. The search of the Puritan was rather along the path of logic spiritualized, and the Transcendentalist, of reason spiritualized—a difference, in a broad sense, between objective and subjective contemplation.

The dislike of inactivity, repose, and barter drives one to the indefinite subjective. Emerson's lack of interest in permanence may cause him to present a subjectivity harsher on the outside than is essential. His very univeralism occasionally seems a limitation. Somewhere here may lie a weakness, real to some, apparent to others; a weakness insofar as his revelation becomes less vivid—to the many, insofar as he over-disregards the personal unit in the universal. If Genius is the most indebted,[m] how much does it owe to those who would but do not easily ride with it? If there is a weakness here, is it the fault of substance, or only of manner? If of the former, there is organic error somewhere, and Emerson will become less and less valuable to man. But this seems impossible, at least to us. Without considering his manner or expression here (it forms the general subject of the second section of this paper), let us ask if Emerson's sub-

[1] MS: philosophy or religion.
[m] "The Poet," *Essays* 2, III, 11: The young man reveres men of genius, . . . They receive of the soul as he also receives, but they more.

stance needs an affinity, a supplement, or even a complement or a gangplank. And if so, of what will it be composed?

Perhaps Emerson could not have risen to his own if it had not been for his Unitarian training and association with the churchmen emancipators. "Christianity is founded on and supposes the authority of reason, and cannot therefore oppose it without subverting itself. . . . Its office is to discern universal truths, great and eternal principles . . . the highest power of the soul." Thus preached Channing.[n] Who knows but [that] this pulpit aroused the younger Emerson to the possibilities of intuitive reasoning in spiritual realms? The influence of men like Channing—in his fight for the dignity of human nature against the arbitrary revelations that Calvinism had strapped on the church, and for the belief in the divine in human reason—doubtless encouraged Emerson in his unshackled search for the infinite, and gave him premises which he later took for granted instead of carrying them around with him. An overinterest, not an underinterest, in Christian ideal aims may have caused him to feel that the definite paths were well established and doing their share, and that for some to reach the same infinite ends, *more* paths might be opened—paths which would in themselves, and in a more transcendent way, partake of the spiritual nature of the land in quest—another expression of God's Kingdom in Man. Would you have the indefinite paths *always* supplemented by the shadow of the definite one—of the first influence?

A characteristic of rebellion is that its results are often deepest when the rebel breaks not from the worst to the greatest, but from the great to the greater. The youth of the rebel increases this characteristic. The innate rebellious spirit in young men is active and buoyant. They could rebel against and improve the millennium. This excess of enthusiasm at the inception of a movement causes loss of perspective, and a natural tendency to undervalue the great in that which is being taken as a base of departure. A "youthful sedition" of Emerson was his withdrawal from the communion,[o] perhaps, the

[n] William Ellery Channing (1780-1842). Preached at the Federal Street Congregational Church, Boston, from 1803. The quotations are from a discourse called "Christianity is a rational religion." For the passages, see Note 6.
[o] See "The Lord's Supper," XI, 7-29. This was a sermon delivered at the Second Church, Boston, Sept. 9, 1832, giving his reasons for discontinuing administration of the Communion, which led to his resignation from the pastorate.

most socialistic doctrine (or rather symbol) of the church—a "commune" above property or class.

Picking up an essay on religion of a rather remarkable-minded boy —perhaps with a touch of genius—written when he was still in college, and so serving as a good illustration in point, we read: "Every thinking man knows that the church is dead." But every thinking man knows that the church part of the church always has been dead— that part seen by candle-light, not Christ-light. Enthusiasm is restless, and hasn't time to see that if the church holds itself as nothing but the symbol of the greater light, it is life itself; as a symbol of a symbol, it is dead. Many of the sincerest followers of Christ never heard of Him. It is the better influence of an institution that arouses in the deep and earnest souls a feeling of rebellion to make its aims more certain. It is their very sincerity that causes these seekers for a freer vision to strike down for more fundamental, universal, and perfect truths, but with such feverish enthusiasm that they appear to over-think themselves—a subconscious way of going Godward, perhaps. The rebel of the twentieth century says: "Let us discard God, immortality, miracle—but be not untrue to ourselves." Here he, no doubt, in a sincere and exalted moment, confuses God with a name. He apparently feels that there is a separatable difference between natural and revealed religion. He mistakes the powers behind them to be fundamentally separate. In the excessive keenness of his search, he forgets that "being true to ourselves" is God, that the faintest thought of immortality is God, and that God is "miracle." Over-enthusiasm keeps one from letting a common experience of a day translate what is stirring the soul. The same inspiring force that arouses the young rebel brings, later in life, a kind of "experience-afterglow"—a realization that the soul cannot discard or limit anything. Would you have the youthful enthusiasm of rebellion, which Emerson carried beyond his youth, *always* supplemented by the shadow of experience?

Perhaps it is not the narrow-minded alone that have no interest in anything but in its relation to their personality. Is the Christian religion, to which Emerson owes embryo ideals, anything but the revelation of God in a personality—a revelation so that the narrow mind could become opened? But the tendency to over-personalize personality may also have suggested to Emerson the necessity for more universal and impersonal paths, though they be indefinite of outline and vague of ascent. Could you journey with equal benefit if they were less so? Would you have the universal always supplemented by the shadow of the personal? If this view is accepted, and we doubt that it can be by the majority, Emerson's substance could well bear a supplement, perhaps an affinity; something that will support that which some conceive he does not offer; something that will help answer Alton Locke's question: "What has Emerson for the working-man?"[p] and questions of others who look for the gangplank before the ship comes in sight; something that will supply the definite banister to the infinite, which it is said he keeps invisible; something that will point a crossroad from "his person" to "his nature"; something that may be in Thoreau or Wordsworth, or in another poet whose songs "breathe of a new morning of a higher life through a definite beauty in Nature";[q] or something that will show the birth of his ideals and hold out a background of revealed religion as a perspective to his transcendent religion—a counterpoise in his rebellion which we feel Channing or Dr. Bushnell,[r] or other saints, known and unknown, might supply.

If the arc must be completed, if there are those who would have the great, dim outlines of Emerson fulfilled, it is fortunate that there are Bushnells and Wordsworths to whom they may appeal—to say nothing of the Vedas, the Bible, or their own souls. But such possibilities and conceptions, the deeper they are received, the more they seem to reduce their need. Emerson's "circle" may be a better whole without its complement. Perhaps his "insatiable demand for unity, the need to recognize one nature in all variety of objects"[s] would have been impaired if something should make it simpler for men to find the identity they at first want in his substance. "Draw if thou canst the mystic line severing rightly his from thine, which is human,

[p] Charles Kingsley, *Alton Locke, Tailor and Poet. An Autobiography* (New York, 1850). The reference may be to a letter from Kingsley to Mrs. Ludlow (p. xx) in which Kingsley expresses an interest in Emerson.
[q] "Another poet" is probably Goethe. The allusion must be to *Letters and Social Aims,* VIII, 269: The fine influences of the morning few can explain, but all will admit. Goethe acknowledges them in the poem ["Musagetes"] in which he dislodges the nightingale from her place as Leader of the Muses.
[r] Horace Bushnell (1802-1876), theologian, Hartford, Conn.
[s] "The Sovereignty of Ethics," X, 178: I see the unity of thought and of morals running through all animated nature; . . .

which divine."ᵗ Whatever means one would use to personalize Emerson's natural revelation, whether by a vision or a board walk, the vastness of his aims and the dignity of his tolerance would doubtless cause him to accept, or at least try to accept, and use [these means] "magically as a part of his fortune."ᵘ He would modestly say, perhaps, that "the world is enlarged for him not by finding new objects, but by more affinities, and potencies than those he already has." But, indeed, is not enough manifestation already there? Is not the asking that it be made more manifest forgetting that "we are not strong by our power to penetrate, but by our relatedness?"ᵛ Will more signs create a greater sympathy? Is not our weak suggestion needed only for those content with their own hopelessness?

Others may lead others to him, but he finds his problem in making "gladness, hope, and fortitude flow from his page," rather than in arranging that our hearts be there to receive it. The first is his duty—the last ours!

II

A devotion to an end tends to undervalue the means. A power of revelation may make one more concerned about his perceptions of the soul's nature than the way of their disclosure. Emerson is more interested in what he perceives than in his expression of it. He is a creator whose intensity is consumed more with the substance of his creation than with the manner by which he shows it to others. Like Petrarch, he seems more a discoverer of beauty than an imparter of it. But these discoveries, these devotions to aims, these struggles toward the absolute—do not these in themselves impart something, if not all, of their own unity and coherence which is not received as such at first, nor is foremost in their expression? It must be remembered that truth was what Emerson was after—not strength of outline or even beauty, except insofar as they might reveal themselves naturally in his explorations towards the infinite. To think hard and deeply and to say what is thought regardless of consequences may

ᵗ These lines of verse not found.
ᵘ "Fate," *The Conduct of Life*, VI, 44: Nature magically suits the man to his fortunes. . . .
ᵛ The last two quotations are from the essay "Success." For the form in which they occur, see Note 7.

produce a first impression either of great translucence or of great
muddiness—but in the latter there may be hidden possibilities. Some
accuse Brahms' orchestration of being muddy. This may be a good
name for a first impression of it. But if it should seem less so, he
might not be saying what he thought. The mud may be a form of
sincerity which demands that the heart be translated rather than
handed around through the pit. A clearer scoring might have lowered
the thought. Carlyle told Emerson that some of his paragraphs didn't
cohere. Emerson wrote by sentences or phrases rather than by logical
sequence. His underlying plan of work seems based on the large
unity of a series of particular aspects of a subject rather than on the
continuity of its expression. As thoughts surge to his mind, he fills
the heavens with them, crowds them in, if necessary, but seldom
arranges them along the ground first. Among class-room excuses for
Emerson's imperfect coherence and lack of unity is one that remembers that his essays were made from lecture notes. His habit, often, in
lecturing was to compile his ideas as they came to him on a general
subject in scattered notes, and, when on the platform, to trust to the
mood of the occasion to assemble them. This seems a specious explanation, though true to fact. Vagueness is at times an indication
of nearness to a perfect truth. The definite glory of Bernard of
Cluny's "Celestial City"ʷ is more beautiful than true—probably.
Orderly reason does not always have to be a visible part of all great
things. Logic may possibly require that unity mean something ascend-
ing in self-evident relation to the parts and to the whole, with no
ellipsis in the ascent. But reason may permit, even demand, an
ellipsis, and genius may not need the self-evident parts. In fact, these
parts may be the "blind-spots" in the progress of unity. They may be
filled with little but repetition. "Nature loves analogy and hates repetition."ʷ¹ Botany reveals evolution, not permanence. An apparent
confusion, if lived with long enough, may become orderly. Emerson
was not writing for lazy minds, though one of the keenest of his academic friends said that he (Emerson) could not explain many of his
own pages. But why should he! He explained them when he discovered them, the moment before he spoke or wrote them. A rare
experience of a moment at daybreak, when something in nature

ʷ Title not correct. For several things Ives may have had in mind, see Note 8.
ʷ¹ Probably not a quotation. For a related passage from Emerson see Note 9.

seems to reveal all consciousness, cannot be explained at noon. Yet
it is a part of the day's unity. At evening, nature is absorbed by another experience. She dislikes to explain as much as to repeat. It is
conceivable that what is unified form to the author or composer may
of necessity be formless to his audience. A home run will cause more
unity in the grandstand than in the season's batting average. If a
composer[x] once starts to compromise, his work will begin to drag on
him. Before the end is reached, his inspiration has all gone up in
sounds pleasing to his audience, ugly to him—sacrificed for the first
acoustic—an opaque clarity—a picture painted for its hanging. Easy
unity, like easy virtue, is easier to describe when judged from its
lapses than from its constancy. When the infidel admits God is great,
he means only: "I am lazy—it is easier to talk than live." Ruskin also
says: "Suppose I like the finite curves best, who shall say which of
us is right? No one. It is simply a question of experience."[y] You may
not be able to experience a symphony, even after twenty perform-
ances. Initial coherence today may be dullness tomorrow, probably
because formal or outward unity depends so much on repetition,
sequences, antitheses, paragraphs, with inductions and summaries.
Macaulay had that kind of unity. Can you read him today? Emerson
rather goes out and shouts: "I'm thinking of the sun's glory today
and I'll let his light shine through me. I'll say any damn thing that
this inspires me with." Perhaps there are flashes of light, still in cipher,
kept there by unity, the code of which the world has not yet discovered. The unity of one sentence inspires the unity of the whole—
though its physique is as ragged as the Dolomites.[z]

Intense lights, vague shadows, great pillars in a horizon are difficult things to nail signboards to. Emerson's outward-inward qualities
make him hard to classify—but easy for some. There are many who
like to say that he—even all the Concord men—are intellectuals. Perhaps—but intellectuals who wear their brains nearer the heart than
some of their critics. It is as dangerous to determine a characteristic
by manner as by mood. Emerson is a pure intellectual to those who
prefer to take him as literally as they can. There are reformers—and
in the "form" lies their interest—who prefer to stand on the plain,

[x] MS: If a poet.
[y] "Modern Painters, IV," *Works*, VI, 327.
[z] MS: ragged as "Monta Rosa."

and then insist they see from the summit. Indolent legs supply the strength of eye for their inspiration. The intellect is never a whole. It is where the soul finds things. It is often the only track to the over-values. It appears a whole—but never becomes one, even in the stock exchange or the convent or the laboratory. In the cleverest criminal, it is but a way to a low ideal. It can never discard the other part of its duality—the soul, or the void where the soul ought to be. So why classify a quality always so relative that it is more an agency than substance—a quality that disappears when classified. "The life of the All must stream through us to make the man and the moment great."[a] A sailor with a precious cargo doesn't analyze the water.

Because Emerson had generations of Calvinistic sermons in his blood, some cataloguers would localize or provincialize him with the sternness of the old Puritan mind. They make him *that,* hold him *there.* They lean heavily on what they find of the above influence in him. They won't follow the rivers in his thought and the play of his soul. And their cousin cataloguers put him in another pigeon-hole. They label him "ascetic." They translate his outward serenity into an impression of severity. But truth keeps one from being hysterical. Is a demagogue a friend of the people because he will lie to them to make them cry and raise false hopes? A search for perfect truths throws out a beauty more spiritual than sensuous. A sombre dignity of style is often confused by under-imagination, and by surface-sentiment, with austerity. If Emerson's manner is not always beautiful in accordance with accepted standards, why not accept a few other standards? He is an ascetic, in that he refuses to compromise content with manner. But a real ascetic is an extremist who has but one height. Thus may come the confusion of one who says that Emerson carries him high, but then leaves him always at *that* height, no higher—a confusion mistaking a latent exultation for an ascetic reserve. The rules of thorough-bass can be applied to his scale of flight no more than they can to the planetary system. Jadassohn,[b] if Emerson were literally a composer, could no more analyze his harmony than a Guide-to-Boston could. A microscope might show that he uses chords of the ninth, eleventh, or the ninety-ninth, but a

[a] "Natural History of Intellect," XII, 19.
[b] Salomon Jadassohn (1831-1902), German music theorist. Various works trans. into English, 1887, 1893, 1901.

lens far different tells us they are used with different aims from those of Debussy. Emerson is definite, in that his art is based on something stronger than the amusing, or, at its best, the beguiling of a few mortals. If he uses a sensuous chord, it is not for sensual ears. His harmonies may float, if the wind blows in that direction, through a voluptuous atmosphere, but he has not Debussy's fondness for trying to blow a sensuous atmosphere from his own voluptuous cheeks. And so he is an ascetic! There is a distance between jowl and soul—and it is not measured by the fraction of an inch between Concord and Paris. On the other hand, if one thinks that his harmony contains no dramatic chords, because no theatrical sound is heard, let him listen to the finale of "Success,"[c] or of "Spiritual Laws,"[d] or to some of the poems—"Brahma"[e] or "Sursum Corda,"[f] for example. Of a truth, his codas often seem to crystallize in a dramatic though serene and sustained way the truths of his subject—they become more active and intense, but quieter and deeper.

Then there comes along another set of cataloguers. They put him down as a classicist or a romanticist or an eclectic. Because a prophet is a child of romanticism, because revelation is classic, because eclecticism quotes from eclectic Hindu philosophy, a more sympathetic cataloguer may say that Emerson inspires courage of the quieter kind, and delight of the higher kind.

The same well-bound school teacher who told the boys that Thoreau was a naturalist because he didn't like to work puts down Emerson as a "classic," and Hawthorne as a "romantic." A loud voice made this doubly *true*, and *sure* to be on the examination paper. But this teacher of "truth *and* dogma" apparently forgot that there is no such thing as "classicism or romanticism." One has but to go to the various definitions of these to know that. If you go to a classic definition you know what a true classic is, and similarly a true romantic. But if you go to both, you have an algebraic formula, $x = x$, a cancellation, an *aperçu*, and hence satisfying; if you go to all definitions you have another formula $x > x$, a destruction, another *aperçu*, and hence satisfying. Professor Beers[g] goes to the dictionary (you wouldn't think

[c] In *Society and Solitude*, VII.
[d] *Essays 1*, II.
[e] In *May-Day and Other Pieces*, IX, 170-171.
[f] *Poems*, IX, 80.
[g] Henry Augustin Beers (1847-1926), educator, Yale.

a college professor would be as reckless as that). And so he can say that "romantic" is "pertaining to the style of the Christian and popular literature of the Middle Ages"[h]—a Roman Catholic mode of salvation (not this definition, but having a definition). And so Prof. B. can say that Walter Scott is a romanticist (and Billy Phelps[i] a classic —sometimes). But for our part Dick Croker[j] is a classic and Job a romanticist. Another professor, Babbitt[k] by name, links up romanticism with Rousseau and charges against it many of man's troubles. He somehow likes to mix it up with sin. He throws saucers at it, but in a scholarly, interesting, sincere, and accurate way. He uncovers a deformed foot, gives it a name, from which we are allowed to infer that the covered foot is healthy and named "classicism." But no Christian Scientist can prove that Christ never had a stomach ache. The *Architecture of Humanism* tells us that "romanticism may be said to consist in a high development of poetic sensibility towards the remote, as such."[1] But is Plato a classic, or towards the remote? Is classicism a poor relation of time—not of man? Is a thing classic or romantic because it is or is not passed by that biologic—that indescribable stream-of-change going on in all life? Let us settle the point "for good," and say that a thing is classic if it is thought of in terms of the past and romantic if thought of in terms of the future—and a thing thought of in terms of the present is—well, that is impossible! Hence, we allow ourselves to say that Emerson is neither a classic or romantic but both—and both not only at different times in one essay, but at the same time in one sentence—in one word. And must we admit it, so is everyone. If you don't believe it, there must be some true definition you haven't seen. Chopin shows a few things that Bach forgot—but he is not eclectic, they say. Brahms shows many things that Bach did remember, so he is an eclectic, they say. Leoncavallo writes pretty verses, and Palestrina is a priest, and Confucius inspires Scriabin. A choice is freedom. Natural selection is but one of Nature's

[h] In *A History of English Romanticism.* For excerpts from what Professor Beers actually said, see Note 10.
[i] William Lyon Phelps (1865-1943), educator (Yale), and literary critic.
[j] Richard Croker (1843-1922), New York politician, leader of Tammany Hall.
[k] Irving Babbitt (1865-1933), *Rousseau and Romanticism* (Boston and New York, 1919).
[1] Geoffrey Scott, *Architecture of Humanism; A Study in the History of Taste* (London, 1914), p. 39

tunes. "All melodious poets shall be hoarse as street ballads, when once the penetrating keynote of nature and spirit is sounded—the earth-beat, sea-beat, heart-beat, which make the tune to which the sun rolls, and the globule of blood and the sap of the trees."[m]

An intuitive sense of values tends to make Emerson use social, political, and even economic phenomena as means of expression—as the accidental notes in his scale, rather than as ends, even lesser ends. In the realization that they are essential parts of the greater values, he does not confuse them with each other. He remains undisturbed except in rare instances when the lower parts invade and seek to displace the higher. He was not afraid to say that "there are laws[n] which should not be too well obeyed."[o] To him, slavery was *not* a social or a political or an economic question, nor even one of morals or of ethics, but one of universal spiritual freedom only. It mattered little what party or what platform or what law of commerce governed men. Was man governing himself? Social error and virtue were but relative.

This habit of not being hindered by using, but still going beyond, the great truths of living to the greater truths of life gave force to his influence over the materialists. Thus he seems to us more a regenerator than a reformer—more an interpreter of life's reflexes than of life's "facts," perhaps. Here he appears greater than Voltaire or Rousseau, and helped, perhaps, by the centrality of his conceptions; he could arouse the deeper spiritual and moral emotions without causing his listeners to distort their physical ones. To prove that mind is over matter, he doesn't place matter over mind. He is not like the man who, because he couldn't afford both, gave up metaphysics for an automobile, and when he ran over a man, blamed metaphysics. He would not have us get overexcited about physical disturbance, but have it accepted as a part of any progress in culture—moral, spiritual or æsthetic. If a poet retires to the mountainside, to avoid the vulgar unculture of men and their physical disturbance, so that he may better catch a nobler theme for his symphony, Emerson tells him: "Man's culture can spare nothing, wants all the material. He is to convert all impediments into instruments, all enemies into power."[p]

[m] Perhaps not a quotation. For related passages, see Note 11.
[n] Fn. in MS: The Fugitive Slave Law—Mass. [See Emerson, "The Fugitive Slave Law," XI, 203-230.]
[o] "Politics," *Essays* 2, III, 199: Good men must not obey the laws too well.
[p] "Culture," *The Conduct of Life*, VI, 158-159.

The latest product of man's culture, the aeroplane, then sails o'er the mountain, and instead of an inspiration—a spray of tobacco-juice falls on the poet. "Calm yourself, Poet!" says Emerson. "Culture will convert Furies into Muses and hells into benefit.[q] This wouldn't have befallen you if it hadn't been for the latest transcendent product of the genius of culture (we won't say that kind), a consummation of the dreams of poets, from David[r] to Tennyson." Material progress is but a means of expression. Realize that man's coarseness has its future and will also be refined in the gradual uprise. Turning the world upside down may be one of its lesser incidents. It is the cause, seldom the effect, that interests Emerson. He can help the cause—the effect must help itself. He might have said to those who talk knowingly about the cause of war—or of the last war, and who would trace it down through long vistas of cosmic, political, moral evolution and what not—he might say that the cause of it was as simple as that of any dog-fight—the "hog-mind" of the minority against the universal mind, the majority.[s] The un-courage of the former fears to believe in the innate goodness of mankind. The cause is always the same; the effect different by chance. It is as easy for a hog, even a stupid one, to step on a box of matches under a tenement with a thousand souls as under an empty bird-house. The many kindly burn up for the few; for the minority is selfish and the majority generous. The minority has ruled the world for physical reasons. The physical reasons are being removed by this "converting culture." Webster will not much longer have to grope for the mind of his constituency. The majority—the people—will need no intermediary. Governments will pass from the representative to the direct.[t] The hog-mind is the principal thing that is making this transition slow. The biggest prop to the hog-mind is pride—pride in property and the power property gives.[u] Ruskin backs this up—"it is at the bottom of all great mis-

[q] "Culture," *The Conduct of Life*, VI, 159: He [Man] will convert the Furies into Muses, and the hells into benefit. [The sentence that follows within these quotation marks is not Emerson.]
[r] MS: David (Solomon). In margin of MS: I don't know who—
[s] Ives wrote further along these lines in his essay, "The Majority." He also placed a song called "Majority" at the head of his privately printed collection, *114 Songs* (Redding, Conn., 1922).
[t] For how Ives himself tried to bring this about, see Note 12.
[u] A section of "The Majority" proposes personal property limits. See also the later reference to this idea in Chapter V, "Thoreau," p. 62.

takes; other passions do occasional good, but whenever pride puts
in its word . . . it is all over with the artist."ᵛ The hog-mind and its
handmaidens in disorder—superficial brightness, fundamental dullness, then cowardice and suspicion; all a part of the minority (the
non-people); the antithesis of everything called "soul," "spirit,"
"Christianity," "truth," "freedom"—will give way more and more to
the great primal truths: that there is more good than evil, that God
is on the side of the majority (the people), that he is not enthusiastic
about the minority (the non-people),ʷ that he has made men greater
than man, that he has made the universal mind and the over-soul
greater and a part of the individual mind and soul, that he has made
the Divine a part of all.

Again, if a picture in economics is before him, Emerson plunges
down to the things that *are* because they are *better* than they are. If
there is a row [dispute] (which there usually is between the ebb and
flood tide in the material ocean), for example, between the theory of
the present order of competition and of attractive and associated
labor, he would sympathize with Ricardo,ˣ perhaps, that labor is the
measure of value, but "embrace, as do generous minds, the proposition of labor shared by all."ʸ He would go deeper than political
economics, strain out the self-factor from both theories, and make
the measure of each pretty much the same, so that the natural (the
majority) would win, but not to the disadvantage of the minority
(the artificial) because this has disappeared—it is of the majority.
John Stuart Mill's political economy is losing value because it was
written by a mind more a banker's than a poet's. The poet knows
that there is no such thing as the perpetual law of supply and demand—perhaps not of demand and supply, or of the wage-fund, or
price-level, or increments earned or unearned—and that the existence
of personal or public property may not prove the existence of God.

Emerson seems to use the great definite interests of humanity to
express the greater, indefinite, spiritual values—to fulfill what he can
in his realms of revelation. Thus, it seems that so close a relation
exists between his content and expression, his substance and manner,

ᵛ These words are not all Ruskin's. For the passage, see Note 13.
ʷ MS: and against the minority (the non-people).
ˣ David Ricardo (1772-1823), English economist.
ʸ In "Montaigne; or, The Skeptic." See Note 14 for the passage, which includes more of this sentence than the quotation marks indicate.

that if he were more definite in the latter he would lose power in the former. Perhaps some of those occasional flashes would have been unexpressed—flashes that have gone down through the world and will flame on through the ages—flashes that approach as near the divine as Beethoven in his most inspired moments—flashes of transcendent beauty, of such universal import, that they may bring, of a sudden, some intimate personal experience, and produce the same indescribable effect that comes in rare instances to men from some common sensation.

In the early morning of a Memorial Day, a boy is awakened by martial music—a village band is marching down the street—and as the strains of Reeves' majestic *Seventh Regiment March*[z] come nearer and nearer—he seems of a sudden translated—a moment of vivid power comes, a consciousness of material nobility—an exultant something gleaming with the possibilities of this life—an assurance that nothing is impossible, and that the whole world lies at his feet. But, as the band turns the corner, at the soldiers' monument, and the march steps of the Grand Army become fainter and fainter, the boy's vision slowly vanishes—his "world" becomes less and less probable—but the experience ever lies within him in its reality.[a]

Later in life, the same boy hears the Sabbath morning bell ringing out from the white steeple at the "Center," and as it draws him to it, through the autumn fields of sumach and asters, a Gospel hymn of simple devotion comes out to him—"There's a wideness in God's mercy"[b]—an instant[c] suggestion of that Memorial Day morning comes —but the moment is of deeper import—there is no personal exultation —no intimate world vision—no magnified personal hope—and in their place a profound sense of a spiritual truth[d]—a sin within reach of forgiveness. And as the hymn voices die away, there lies at his feet— not the world,[e] but the figure of the Saviour—he sees an unfathom-

---

[z] "Second Conn. Nat. Guard March." For Ives' use of the piece in his own compositions, see Note 15.

[a] See Cowell, *Ives*, p. 27, for another description of the same or a similar occasion. The band was father George Ives' Danbury Civil War Band, and it also performed a piece by Charles, age thirteen, called "Holiday Quick Step."

[b] Text: Frederick William Faber, 1862; tune: probably the one by John Zundel, 1870.

[c] MS: suddenly (instantly) he becomes transfixed,—an instant . . . .

[d] MS: (the clearest he had ever experienced).

[e] MS: not "his" world.

able courage—an immortality for the lowest—the vastness in humility, the kindness of the human heart, man's noblest strength—and he knows that God is nothing—nothing—but love!

Whence cometh the wonder of a moment? From sources we know not. But we do know that from obscurity and from this higher Orpheus come measures of sphere melodies,* flowing in wild, native tones, ravaging the souls of men, flowing now with thousand-fold accompaniments and rich symphonies through all our hearts, modulating and divinely leading them.

III

What is character? In how far does it sustain the soul, or the soul it? Is it a part of the soul? And then—what is the soul? Plato knows, but cannot tell us. Every new-born man knows, but no one tells us. "Nature will not be disposed of easily. No power of genius has ever yet had the smallest success in explaining existence. The perfect enigma remains."ᶠ As every blind man sees the sun, so character may be the part of the soul we, the blind, can see; and then have the right to imagine that the soul is each man's share of God, and character the muscle which tries to reveal its mysteries—a kind of its first visible radiance—the right to know that it is the voice which is always calling the pragmatist a fool.

At any rate, it can be said that Emerson's character has much to do with his power upon us. Men who have known nothing of his life have borne witness to this. It is directly at the root of his substance, and affects his manner only indirectly. It gives the sincerity to the constant spiritual hopefulness we are always conscious of, and which carries with it, often, even when the expression is somber, a note of exultation in the victories of "the innate virtues" of man. And it is this, perhaps, that makes us feel his courage—not a self-courage, but a sympathetic one—courageous even to tenderness. It is the open courage of a kind heart, of not forcing opinions—a thing much needed when the cowardly, underhanded courage of the fanatic would *force* opinion. It is the courage of believing in freedom, per se, rather than of trying to force everyone to *see* that you believe in it—the courage

---

* Paraphrased from a passage in *Sartor Resartus*.ᵍ

ᶠ Inexactly quoted from Emerson, "Plato; or the Philosopher." See Note 17.
ᵍ For the passage paraphrased, see Note 16.

of the willingness to be reformed, rather than of reforming—the courage teaching that sacrifice is bravery, and force, fear—the courage of righteous indignation, of stammering eloquence, of spiritual insight, a courage ever contracting or unfolding a philosophy as it grows—a courage that would make the impossible possible. Oliver Wendell Holmes says that Emerson attempted the impossible in "The Over-Soul"[h]—"an overflow of spiritual imagination."[1] But he (Emerson) accomplished the impossible in attempting it and still leaving it impossible. A courageous struggle to satisfy, as Thoreau says, hunger rather than the palate[j]—the hunger of a lifetime sometimes by one meal. His essay on the pre-soul (which he did not write) treats of that part of the over-soul's influence on unborn ages, and attempts the impossible only when it stops attempting it.

Like all courageous souls, the higher Emerson soars, the more lowly he becomes. "Do you think the porter and the cook have no anecdotes, no experiences, no wonders for you? Everybody knows as much as the savant."[k] To some, the way to be humble is to admonish the humble, not learn from them. Carlyle would have Emerson teach by more definite signs, rather than interpret his revelations, or shall we say, preach. Admitting all the inspiration and help that *Sartor Resartus* has given, in spite of its vaudeville and tragic stages, to many young men getting under way in the life of tailor or king, we believe it can be said (but very broadly said) that Emerson, either in the first or second series of essays, taken as a whole, gives, it seems to us, greater inspiration, partly because his manner is less didactic, less personally suggestive, perhaps less clearly or obviously human than Carlyle's. How direct this inspiration is, [is] a matter of personal viewpoint, temperament, perhaps inheritance. Augustine Birrell says he does not feel it—and he seems not to, even indirectly. Apparently "a non-sequacious author" can't inspire him, for Emerson seems to him "a little thin and vague."[l] Is Emerson or the English climate to blame for this? He, Birrell, says a really great author dissipates all

[h] *Essays 1*, II, 249-278.
[1] Holmes, XI, 132: "The Over-Soul" might almost be called the over-*flow* of a spiritual imagination.
[j] *Week*, p. 400: There are two classes of men called poets. The one cultivates life, the other art, . . . one satisfies hunger, the other gratifies the palate.
[k] "Intellect," *Essays 1*, II, 308.
[l] "Emerson" in *Obiter dicta* (New York, 1893), second series, p. 241.

fears as to his staying-power (though fears for our staying-power, not Emerson's, is what we would like dissipated). Besides, around a really great author there are no fears to dissipate. "A wise author never allows his reader's mind to be at large, . . ."[m] but Emerson is not a *wise* author. His essay on prudence has nothing to do with prudence, for to be wise and prudent he must put explanation first, and let his substance dissolve because of it. "How carefully," says Birrell again, "does a really great writer, like Dr. Newman or M. Rénan, explain to you what he is going to do, and how he is going to do it!"[n] Personally we like the chance of having a hand in the "explaining." We prefer to look at flowers, but not through botany, for it seems that if we look at them alone, we see a beauty of Nature's poetry, a direct gift from the Divine, and if we look at botany alone, we see the beauty of Nature's intellect, a direct gift of the Divine; if we look at both together, we see nothing.

Thus it seems that Carlyle and Birrell would have it that courage and humility have something to do with "explanation"—and that it is not "a respect for all," a faith in the power of "innate virtue" to perceive by "relativeness rather than penetration" that causes Emerson to withhold explanation to a greater degree than many writers. Carlyle asks for more utility, and Birrell for more inspiration. But we like to believe that it is the height of Emerson's character, evidenced especially in his courage and humility, that shades its quality, rather than that its virtue is less—that it is his height that will make him more and more valuable and more and more within the reach of all— whether it be by utility, inspiration, or other needs of the human soul.

Cannot some of the most valuable kinds of utility and inspiration come from humility in its highest and purest forms? For is not the truest kind of humility a kind of glorified or transcendent democracy —the practicing it rather than the talking it—the not wanting to level all finite things, but the being willing to be leveled towards the infinite? Until humility produces that frame of mind and spirit in the artist, can his audience gain the greatest kind of utility and inspiration, which might be quite invisible at first? Emerson realizes the value of "the many"—that the law of averages has a divine source. He recognizes the various life-values *in reality*—not by reason of their

m Birrell, 244.
n Birrell, 244-245.

closeness or remoteness, but because he sympathizes with men who
live them, and the *majority* do. "The private store of reason is not
great—would that there were a public store for man," cries Pascal.
"But there is," says Emerson. "It is the universal mind, an institution
congenital with the common or over-soul." Pascal is discouraged, for
he lets himself be influenced by surface political and religious history,
which shows the struggle of the group led by an individual rather
than that of the individual led by himself—a struggle as much
privately caused as privately led. The main path of all social progress
has been spiritual rather than intellectual in character, but the many
by-paths of individual materialism, though never obliterating the
highway, have dimmed its outlines and caused travelers to confuse
the colors along the road. A more natural way of freeing the congestion in the benefits of material progress will make it less difficult for
the majority to recognize the true relation between the important
spiritual and religious values and the less important intellectual and
economic values. As the action of the intellect and universal mind
becomes more and more identical, the clearer will the relation of all
values become. But for physical reasons, the group has had to depend
upon the individual as leaders, and the leaders, with few exceptions,
restrained the universal mind—they trusted to the "private store."
But now, thanks to the lessons of evolution, which Nature has been
teaching men since and before the days of Socrates, the public store
of reason is gradually taking the place of the once-needed leader.
From the Chaldean tablet to the wireless message, this public store
has been wonderfully opened. The results of these lessons, the possibilities they are offering for ever coordinating the mind of humanity,
the culmination of this age-instruction, are seen today in many ways.
Labor federation, suffrage extension, are two instances that come to
mind among the many. In these manifestations, by reason of tradition, or the bad-habit part of tradition, the hog-mind of the few
(the minority) comes in play. The possessors of this are called
leaders, but even these "thick-skins" are beginning to see that the
movement is the leader, and that they are only clerks. Broadly speaking, the effects evidenced in the political side of history have so
much of the physical because the causes have been so much of the
physical. As a result, the leaders, for the most part, have been under-
average men, with skins thick, wits slick, and hands quick with

under-values—otherwise they would not have become leaders. But
the day of leaders, as such, is gradually closing—the people are beginning to lead themselves—the public store of reason is slowly being
opened—the common universal mind and the common over-soul is
slowly but inevitably coming into its own. "Let a man believe in
God, not in names and places and persons. Let the great soul incarnated in some poor . . . sad and simple Joan go out to service
and sweep chimneys and scrub floors . . . its effulgent day beams
cannot be muffled, . . ." and then, "to sweep and scrub will instantly
appear supreme and beautiful actions . . . and *all* people will get
brooms and mops."o Perhaps, if all of Emerson—his works and his
life—were to be swept away, and nothing of him but the record of
the following incident remained to men—the influence of his soul
would still be great.p A working woman after coming from one of
his lectures said: "I love to go to hear Emerson, not because I understand him, but because he looks as though he thought everybody
was as good as he was." Is it not the courage—the spiritual hopefulness in his humility—that makes this story possible and true? Is it not
this trait in his character that sets him above all creeds—that gives him
inspired belief in the common mind and soul? Is it not this courageous universalism that gives conviction to his prophecy, and that
makes his symphonies of revelation begin and end with nothing but
the strength and beauty of innate goodness in man, in Nature and
in God—the greatest and most inspiring theme of Concord Transcendental philosophy, as we hear it?q

And it is from such a world-compelling theme and from such
vantage ground that Emerson rises to almost perfect freedom of
action, of thought and of soul, in any direction and to any height. A
vantage ground somewhat vaster than Schelling's conception of transcendental philosophy—"a philosophy of Nature become subjective."
In Concord it *includes* the objective, and becomes subjective to
nothing but freedom and the absolute law. It is this underlying courage of the purest humility that gives Emerson that outward aspect of
serenity which is felt to so great an extent in much of his work,

o Inexactly quoted from "Spiritual Laws." See Note 18.
p MS: still be great—as is ever the influence whether it be of wide or lowly
range, of all, about whom the same can be said.
q Margin of MS: and that makes it possible for him to reveal, as few men can.

especially in his codas and perorations. And within this poised strength, we are conscious of that "original authentic fire" which Emerson missed in Shelley;[r] we are conscious of something that is not dispassionate, something that is at times almost turbulent—a kind of furious calm lying deeply in the conviction of the eventual triumph of the soul[s] and its union with God!

Let us place the transcendent Emerson where he, himself places Milton,[t] in Wordsworth's apostrophe: "Pure as the naked heavens, majestic, free, so didst thou travel on life's common way in cheerful Godliness."

The Godliness of spiritual courage and hopefulness—these fathers of faith rise to a glorified peace in the depth of his greater perorations. There is an "oracle" at the beginning of the *Fifth Symphony;* in those four notes[u] lies one of Beethoven's greatest messages. We would place its translation above the relentlessness of fate knocking at the door, above the greater human message of destiny, and strive to bring it towards the spiritual message of Emerson's revelations, even to the "common heart" of Concord—the soul of humanity knocking at the door of the divine mysteries, radiant in the faith that it *will* be opened —and the human become the divine!

[r] "Thoughts on Modern Literature," *Papers from the Dial,* XII, 186: Shelley, though a poetic mind, is never a poet. . . . imagination, the original, authentic fire of the bard, he has not.
[s] MS: soul (over man).
[t] In his essay "Milton." See Note 19.
[u] Ives uses the motive of the *Fifth Symphony* in the Concord Sonata.

II. "Hawthorne"

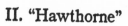

THREE

HAWTHORNE

THE substance of Hawthorne is so dripping wet with the supernatural, the phantasmal, the mystical, so surcharged with adventures, from the deeper picturesque to the illusive fantastic, that one unconsciously finds oneself thinking of him as a poet of greater imaginative impulse than Emerson or Thoreau. He was not a greater poet, possibly, than they—but a greater artist. Not only the character of his substance but the care in his manner throws his workmanship, in contrast to theirs, into a kind of bas-relief. Like Poe, he quite naturally and unconsciously reaches out over his subject to his reader. His mesmerism seeks to mesmerize us—beyond Zenobia's sister.ᵛ But he is too great an artist to show his hand in "getting his audience" as Poe and Tschaikowsky occasionally do. His intellectual muscles are too strong to let him become over-influenced, as Ravel and Stravinsky seem to be, by the morbidly fascinating—a kind of false beauty obtained by artistic monotony.ʷ However, we cannot but feel that he would weave his spell over us—as would the Grimms and Æsop. We feel as much under magic

ᵛ That is, to mesmerize us more than Zenobia's sister, Priscilla, was in *The Blithedale Romance.*
ʷ For other comments by Ives on Ravel and Stravinsky, see Note 20.

as the "Enchanted Frog." This is part of the artist's business. The
effect is a part of his art-effort in its inception. Emerson's substance,
and even his manner, has little to do with a designed effect; his
thunderbolts or delicate fragments are flashed out, regardless. They
may knock us down, or just spatter us—it matters little to him. But
Hawthorne is more considerate—that is, he is more artistic (as men
say).

Hawthorne may be more noticeably indigenous or may have more
local color, perhaps more national color, than[x] his Concord con-
temporaries. But the work of anyone who is somewhat more interested
in psychology than in transcendental philosophy will weave itself
around individuals and their personalities. If the same anyone happens to live in Salem, his work is likely to be colored by the Salem
wharves and Salem witches. If the same anyone happens to live in
the Old Manse[y] near the Concord Battle Bridge, he is likely "of a
rainy day to betake himself to the huge garret," the secrets of which
he wonders at, "but is too reverent of their dust and cobwebs to
disturb." He is likely to "bow below the shriveled canvas of an old
(Puritan) clergyman in wig and gown—the parish priest[z] of a century
ago—a friend of Whitefield."[a] He is likely to come under the spell
of this reverend ghost who haunts the Manse. And as it rains and
darkens, and the sky glooms through the dusty attic windows, he
is likely "to muse deeply and wonderingly upon the humiliating fact
that the works of man's intellect decay like those of his hands . . .
that thought grows moldy,"[b] and as the garret is in Massachusetts,
the "thought" and the "mold" are likely to be quite native. When
the same anyone puts his poetry into novels rather than essays, he is
likely to have more to say about the life around him—about the inherited mystery of the town—than a poet of philosophy is.

In Hawthorne's usual vicinity, the atmosphere was charged with
the somber errors and romance of eighteenth century New England,

[x] MS: than (some of).
[y] Ezra Ripley, D. D. (b. 1751, O. S.), minister of Concord, and step-grand-
father of Emerson, lived in the Old Manse until he died in 1841. Hawthorne
moved in with his bride in 1842.
[z] MS: parish pastor.
[a] George Whitefield (1714-1770), English religious leader. Visited the colonies
a number of times. Buried in Newburyport, Mass.
[b] The passages in quotes drawn from "The Old Manse" in Hawthorne's *Mosses
from an Old Manse.* See Note 21.

—ascetic or noble New England, as you like. A novel, of necessity, nails an art-effort down to some definite part or parts of the earth's surface; the novelist's wagon can't always be hitched to a star. To say that Hawthorne was more deeply interested than some of the other Concord writers—Emerson, for example—in the idealism peculiar to his native land (insofar as such idealism of a country can be conceived of as separate from the political) would be as unreasoning as to hold that he was more interested in social progress than Thoreau, because he was in the consular service and Thoreau was in no one's service—or that the War governor of Massachusetts was a greater patriot than Wendell Phillips,[c] who was ashamed of all political parties. Hawthorne's art was true and typically American, as is the art of all men (living in America) who believe in freedom of thought, and who live wholesome lives to prove it—whatever their means of expression.

Any comprehensive conception of Hawthorne, either in words or music, must have for its basic theme something that has to do with the influence of sin upon the conscience—something more than the Puritan conscience, but something which is permeated by it. In this relation he is wont to use what Hazlitt calls the "moral power of imagination." Hawthorne would try to spiritualize a guilty conscience. He would sing of the relentlessness of guilt, the inheritance of guilt, the shadow of guilt darkening innocent posterity. All of its sins and morbid horrors, its specters, its phantasmas, and even its hellish hopelessness, play around his pages; and vanishing between the lines are the less guilty elves of the Concord Elms which Thoreau and Old Man Alcott may have felt, but knew not as intimately as Hawthorne. There is often a pervading melancholy about Hawthorne, as Faguet[d] says of de Musset,[e] "without posture, without noise but penetrating." There is at times the mysticism and serenity of the ocean, which Jules Michelet[f] sees in its horizon rather than in its waters. There is a sensitiveness to supernatural sound waves. Hawthorne feels the mysteries, and tries to paint them rather than explain them—and here, some may say that he is wiser in a more

[c] 1811-1884. Orator, reformer, abolitionist. See Note 43.
[d] Auguste Émile Faguet (1847-1916), French literary critic.
[e] Alfred de Musset (1810-1857), French poet.
[f] Jules Michelet (1798-1874), French historian.

practical way, and, so, more artistic than Emerson. Perhaps so, but no greater in the deeper ranges and profound mysteries of the inter-related worlds of human and spiritual life.

This fundamental part of Hawthorne is not attempted in our music (the 2d movement of the series) which is but an "extended fragment" trying to suggest some of his wilder,ᵍ fantastical adventures into the half-childlike, half-fairylike phantasmal realms. It may have something to do with the children's excitement on that "frosty Berkshire morning, and the frost imagery on the enchanted hall window"; or something to do with "Feathertop," the scarecrow, and his "Looking Glass" and "the little demons dancing around his pipe bowl;"ʰ or something to do with the old hymn-tune that haunts the church and sings only to those in the churchyard to protect them from secular noises, as when the circus parade comes down Main Street; or something to do with the concert at the Stamford camp meeting, or the "Slave's Shuffle"; or something to do with the Concord he-nymph, or "The Seven Vagabonds," or "Circe's Palace," or something else in *The Wonder-Book*—not something that happens, but the way something happens; or something to do with "The Celestial Railroad," or "Phœbe's Garden,"ⁱ or something personal, which tries to be "national" suddenly at twilight, and universal suddenly at midnight; or something about the ghost of a man who never lived, or about something that never will happen, or something else that is not.

ᵍ MS: lighter but wilder.
ʰ The "frosty Berkshire morning" is perhaps a reference to the scene of *A Wonder Book* and *Tanglewood Tales;* Feathertop is a scarecrow in "Feathertop: A Moralized Legend," in *Mosses from an Old Manse;* "Looking Glass" may refer to "Monsieur du Miroir" in *Mosses;* the demons are probably those around Mother Rigby's pipe in "Feathertop."
ⁱ "The Seven Vagabonds" in *Twice-Told Tales;* "Circe's Palace" in *Tanglewood Tales;* "The Celestial Railroad" in *Mosses;* "Phœbe's Garden" must be Phœbe Pyncheon's garden in *The House of Seven Gables.* Ives derived a fantasy for piano called "The Celestial Railroad" partly from the "Hawthorne" movement of the Concord Sonata (see various references in Kirkpatrick's *Catalogue*).

III. "The Alcotts"

FOUR

"THE ALCOTTS"

If the dictagraph had been per-
fected in Bronson Alcott's time, he might now be a great writer. As
it is, he goes down as Concord's greatest talker. "Great expecter,"
say Thoreau;[j] "great feller," says Sam Staples,[k] "for talkin' big . . .
but his daughters is the gals though—always *doin'* somethin'."[1] Old
Man Alcott, however, was usually "doin' somethin'" within. An
internal grandiloquence made him melodious without; an exuberant,
irrepressible visionary, absorbed with philosophy *as* such; to him it
was a kind of transcendental business, the profits of which supported
his inner man rather than his family. Apparently his deep interest in
spiritual physics, rather than metaphysics, gave a kind of hypnotic
mellifluous effect to his voice when he sang his oracles—a manner
something of a cross between an inside pompous self-assertion and
an outside serious benevolence. But he was sincere and kindly in-
tentioned in his eagerness to extend what he could of the better
influence of the philosophic world as he saw it. In fact, there is a

[j] "Winter Visitors," *Walden,* p. 297: Great Looker! Great Expecter! to converse with whom was a New England Night's Entertainment.
[k] Identified in Note 31.
[1] Staples may not have been the spokesman. See Note. 22.

45

strong didactic streak in both father and daughter. Louisa May seldom misses a chance to bring out the moral of a homely virtue. The power of repetition was to them a natural means of illustration. It is said that the elder Alcott, while teaching school, would frequently whip himself when the scholars misbehaved, to show that the Divine Teacher—God—was pained when his children of the earth were bad. Quite often the boy next to the bad boy was punished, to show how sin involved the guiltless. And Miss Alcott is fond of working her story around so that she can better rub in a moral precept—and the moral sometimes browbeats the story. But with all the elder Alcott's vehement, inpracticable, visionary qualities, there was a sturdiness and a courage—at least, we like to think so. A Yankee boy who would cheerfully travel, in those days when distances were long and unmotored, as far from Connecticut as the Carolinas, earning his way by peddling, laying down his pack to teach school when opportunity offered, must possess a basic sturdiness. This was apparently not very evident when he got to preaching his idealism. An incident in Alcott's life helps confirm a theory—not a popular one—that men accustomed to wander around in the visionary unknown are the quickest and strongest when occasion requires ready action of the lower virtues. It often appears that a contemplative mind is more capable of action than an actively objective one. Dr. Emerson says: "It is good to know that it has been recorded of Alcott, the benign idealist, that when the Reverend Thomas Wentworth Higginson (later, a Colonel in the Northern Army), heading the rush on the United States Court House in Boston to rescue the fugitive slave, looked back for his following at the Court-room door, only the apostolic philosopher was there, cane in hand."[m] So it seems that his idealism had some substantial virtues, even if he couldn't make a living.

The daughter does not accept the father as a prototype—she seems to have but few of her father's qualities "in female." She supported the family, and at the same time enriched the lives of a large part of young America, starting off many little minds with wholesome thoughts and many little hearts with wholesome emotions. She leaves

[m] "Dr. Emerson" is Edward Waldo Emerson. The quotation is from *Henry Thoreau, As remembered by a young friend* (Boston and New York, 1917), pp. 108-109.

memory-word-pictures of healthy New England childhood days—
pictures which are turned to with affection by middle-aged children—
pictures that bear a sentiment, a leaven, that middle-aged America
needs nowadays more than we care to admit.

Concord village itself reminds one of that common virtue lying at
the height and root of all the Concord divinities. As one walks down
the broad-arched street—passing the white house of Emerson, ascetic
guard of a former prophetic beauty—he comes presently beneath the
old elms overspreading the Alcott house. It seems to stand as a kind
of homely but beautiful witness of Concord's common virtue—it
seems to bear a consciousness that its past *is living,* that the "mosses
of the Old Manse" and the hickories of Walden are not far away.
Here is the home of the "Marches"[n]—all pervaded with the trials and
happiness of the family, and telling, in a simple way, the story of "the
richness of not having." Within the house, on every side, lie re-
membrances of what imagination can do for the better amusement of
fortunate children who have to do for themselves—much-needed
lessons in these days of automatic, ready-made, easy entertainment
which deaden rather than stimulate the creative faculty. And there
sits the little old spinet piano Sophia Thoreau gave to the Alcott
children, on which Beth played the old Scotch airs, and played at
the *Fifth Symphony.*

There is a commonplace beauty about "Orchard House"—a kind
of spiritual sturdiness underlying its quaint picturesqueness—a kind
of common triad of the New England homestead, whose overtones
tell us that there must have been something æsthetic fibered in the
Puritan severity—the self-sacrificing part of the ideal—a value that
seems to stir a deeper feeling, a stronger sense of being nearer some
perfect truth than a Gothic cathedral or an Etruscan villa.[o] All
around you, under the Concord sky, there still floats the influence of
that human-faith-melody—transcendent and sentimental enough for
the enthusiast or the cynic, respectively—reflecting an innate hope,
a common interest in common things and common men—a tune the
Concord bards are ever playing while they pound away at the immensities with a Beethoven-like sublimity, and with, may we say,

[n] *Little Women.*
[o] First version in MS: Tuscan villa.

a vehemence and perseverance, for that part of greatness is not so difficult to emulate.

We dare not attempt to follow the philosophic raptures of Bronson Alcott—unless you will assume that his apotheosis will show how "practical" his vision in this world would be in the next. And so we won't try to reconcile the music sketch of the Alcotts with much besides the memory of that home under the elms—the Scotch songs and the family hymns that were sung at the end of each day—though there may be an attempt to catch something of that common sentiment (which we have tried to suggest above)—a strength of hope that never gives way to despair—a conviction in the power of the common soul which, when all is said and done, may be as typical as any theme of Concord and its Transcendentalists.

IV. "Thoreau"

FIVE

THOREAU

THOREAU was a great musician, not because he played the flute but because he did not have to go to Boston to hear "the Symphony." The rhythm of his prose, were there nothing else, would determine his value as a composer. He was divinely conscious of the enthusiasm of Nature, the emotion of her rhythms, and the harmony of her solitude. In this consciousness he sang of the submission to Nature, the religion of contemplation, and the freedom of simplicity—a philosophy distinguishing between the complexity of Nature, which teaches freedom, and the complexity of materialism, which teaches slavery. In music, in poetry, in all art, the truth as one sees it must be given in terms which bear some proportion to the inspiration. In their greatest moments, the inspiration of both Beethoven and Thoreau express profound truths and deep sentiment. But the intimate passion of it, the storm and stress of it, affected Beethoven in such a way that he could not but be ever showing it, and Thoreau, that he could not easily expose it. They were equally imbued with it, but with different results. A difference in temperament had something to do with this, together with a difference in the quality of expression between the two arts. "Who that has heard a strain of music feared lest he would speak extravagantly for-

ever," says Thoreau.[p] Perhaps music is the art of speaking extravagantly. Herbert Spencer says that some men, as for instance Mozart,
are so peculiarly sensitive to emotion that music is to them but a
continuation not only of the expression but of the actual emotion,[q]
though the theory of some more modern thinkers in the philosophy
of art doesn't always bear this out. However, there is no doubt that
in its nature music is predominantly subjective and tends to subjective
expression, and poetry more objective, tending to objective expression. Hence the poet, when his muse calls for a deeper feeling, must
invert this order, and he may be reluctant to do so, as these depths
often call for an intimate expression which the physical looks of the
words may repel. They tend to reveal the nakedness of his soul
rather than its warmth. It is not a matter of the relative value of the
aspiration, or a difference between subconsciousness and consciousness, but a difference in the arts themselves; for example, a composer
may not shrink from having the public hear his "love letter in tones,"
while a poet may feel sensitive about having everyone read his "letter
in words." When the object of the love is mankind, the sensitiveness is changed only in degree.

But the message of Thoreau, though his fervency may be incon-
stant and his human appeal not always direct, is, both in thought
and spirit, as universal as that of any man who ever wrote or sang—
as universal as it is nontemporaneous—as universal as it is free from
the measure of history, as "solitude is free from the measure of the
miles of space that intervene between man and his fellows."[r] In spite
of the fact that Henry James (who knows almost everything) says
that "Thoreau is more than provincial—that he is parochial,"[s] let us
repeat that Henry Thoreau—in respect to thought, sentiment, imagination, and soul, in respect to every element except that of place of
physical being, a thing that means so much to some—is as universal as
any personality in literature. That he said upon being shown a speci-

[p] "Conclusion," *Walden*, 357: Who has heard a strain of music feared then
lest he should speak extravagantly any more forever?
[q] Ives seems to refer here to Spencer's essay on "The Origin and Function
of Music."
[r] "Solitude," *Walden*, 150: Solitude is not measured by the miles of space that
intervene between a man and his fellows.
[s] Henry James, Jr., in *Nathaniel Hawthorne* (London, 1879), p. 94. The
passage reads: ". . . he was worse than provincial—he was parochial."

men grass from Iceland that the same species could be found in Concord is evidence of his universality, not of his parochialism. He was so universal that he did not need to travel around the world to *prove* it. "I have more of God, they more of the road. It is not worth the while to go round the world to count the cats in Zanzibar."[t] With Marcus Aurelius, if he had seen the present, he had seen all, from eternity and all time forever.

Thoreau's susceptibility to natural sounds was probably greater than that of many practical musicians. True, this appeal is mainly through the sensational element which Herbert Spencer thinks the predominant beauty of music. Thoreau seems able to weave from this source some perfect transcendental symphonies. Strains from the Orient get the best of some of the modern French music, but not of Thoreau. He seems more interested *in* than influenced *by* Oriental philosophy. He admires its ways of resignation and self-contemplation, but he doesn't contemplate himself in the same way. He often quotes from the Eastern scriptures passages which, were they his own, he would probably omit. For example, "The Vedas say, 'All intelligences awake with the morning.' "[u] This seems unworthy of "accompanying the undulations of celestial music" found on this same page, in which an "ode to morning" is sung—"the awakening to newly acquired forces and aspirations from within to a higher life than we fell asleep from . . . for *all* [italics: Ives] memorable events transpire in the morning time and in the morning atmosphere."[v] Thus it is not the whole tone scale of the Orient but the scale of a Walden morning—"music in single strains," as Emerson says—which inspired many of the polyphonies and harmonies that come to us through his poetry. Who can be forever melancholy "with Æolian music like this"?[w]

This is but one of many ways in which Thoreau looked to Nature for his greatest inspirations. In her, he found an analogy to the fundamental of Transcendentalism. The "innate goodness" of Nature

[t] One sentence is translated poetry, the other prose. See Note 23.
[u] "Where I lived," *Walden*, 99.
[v] For the passage in *Walden*, see Note 24.
[w] R. W. Emerson's essay on "Thoreau" in *Works*, X, 442: He thought the best of music was in single strains; and he found poetic suggestion in the humming of the telegraph wire. See Note 37.

is or can be a moral influence; Mother Nature, if man will but let her, will keep him straight—straight spiritually, and so morally and even mentally. If he will take her as a companion and teacher,[x] and *not* as a duty or a creed, she will give him greater thrills and teach him greater truths than man can give or teach—she will reveal mysteries that mankind has long concealed. It was the soul of Nature, not natural history, that Thoreau was after. A naturalist's mind is one predominantly scientific, more interested in the relation of a flower to other flowers than its relation to any philosophy or anyone's philosophy. A transcendent love of Nature and writing "Rhus glabra" after sumach doesn't necessarily make a naturalist. It would seem that, although thorough in observation (not very thorough according to Mr. Burroughs)[y] and with a keen perception of the specific, a naturalist—inherently—was exactly what Thoreau was *not*. He seems rather to let Nature put him under her microscope than to hold her under his. He was too fond of Nature to practice vivisection upon her. He would have found that painful, "for was he not a part with her?" But he had this trait of a naturalist, which is usually foreign to poets, even great ones: he observed acutely even things that did not particularly interest him—a useful natural gift rather than a virtue.

The study of Nature may tend to make one dogmatic but the love of Nature surely does not. Thoreau no more than Emerson could be said to have compounded doctrines. His thinking was too broad for that. If Thoreau's was a religion of Nature, as some say—and by that they mean that through Nature's influence man is brought to a deeper contemplation, to a more spiritual self-scrutiny, and thus closer to God—it had apparently no definite doctrines. Some of his theories regarding natural and social phenomena and his experiments in the art of living are certainly not doctrinal in form, and if they are in substance, it didn't disturb Thoreau and it needn't us. "In proportion as he simplifies his life, the laws of the universe will appear less complex, and solitude will not be solitude, nor poverty poverty, nor weakness weakness. If you have built castles in the air, your work need not be lost; that is where they should be. Now put the foundations

---

[x]MS: teacher, even "as a wife."

[y] John Burroughs (1837-1921), naturalist and author. *Indoor Studies*, vol. VIII of his *Writings* (Boston and New York, 1895) contains a chapter on Henry D. Thoreau which is highly critical of his abilities as a naturalist.

under them."[z] "Then we will love[a] with the license of a higher order of beings." Is that a doctrine? Perhaps. At any rate, between the lines of some such passage as this lie some of the fountain heads that water the spiritual fields of his philosophy and the seeds from which they are sown (if indeed his whole philosophy is but one spiritual garden). His experiments, social and economic, are a part of its cultivation, and for the harvest—and its transmutation—he trusts to moments of inspiration. "Only what is thought, said, or done at a certain rare coincidence is good."[b]

Thoreau's experiment at Walden was, broadly speaking, one of these moments. It stands out in the casual and popular opinion as a kind of adventure—harmless and amusing to some, significant and important to others; but its significance lies in the fact that in trying to practice an ideal he prepared his mind so that it could better bring others "into the Walden state-of-mind." He did not ask for a literal approval, or, in fact, for any approval. ". . . I would not stand between any man and his genius; . . ."[c] He would have no one adopt his manner of life, unless in doing so he adopts his own—besides, by that time "I may have found a better one."[d] But if he preached hard, he practiced harder what he preached—harder than most men.

Throughout *Walden*, a text that he is always pounding out is "Time." Time for inside work out-of-doors; preferably out-of-doors, though "you may perhaps have some pleasant, thrilling, glorious hours, even in a poor house."[e] Wherever the place—time there must be. Time to show the unnecessariness of necessities which clog up time. Time to contemplate the value of man to the universe—and of the universe to man—man's excuse for being. Time *from* the demands of social conventions. Time *from* too much labor (for some) which means too much to eat, too much to wear, too much material, too much materialism (for others). Time *from* the "hurry and waste of life." Time *from* the "St. Vitus Dance." *But*, on the other side of the

---

z "Conclusion," *Walden*, 356.

a MS: Then we will live. [For the context in which the phrase occurs, see Note 26.]

b "Conclusion," *Walden*, 363.

c "Economy," *Walden*, 81.

d For the passage, see Note 25.

e "Conclusion," *Walden*, 361.

ledger, time *for* learning that "there is no safety in stupidity alone."ᵗ Time *for* introspection. Time *for* reality. Time *for* expansion. Time *for* practicing the art, of living the art of living.

Thoreau has been criticized for practicing his policy of expansion by living in a vacuum—but he peopled that vacuum with a race of beings and established a social order there surpassing any of the precepts in social or political history. ". . . for he put some things behind and passed an invisible boundary; new, universal, and more liberal laws were around and within him, the old laws were expanded and interpreted in a more liberal sense, and he lived with the license of a higher order"ᵍ—a community in which "God was the only President" and "Thoreau not Webster was His Orator."ʰ It is hard to believe that Thoreau really refused to believe that there was any other life but his own, though he probably did think that there was not any other life besides his own for him. Living for society may not always be best accomplished by living *with* society. "Is there any virtue in a man's skin that you must touch it?"ⁱ and the "rubbing of elbows may not bring men's minds closer together";ʲ or if he were talking through a "worst seller" magazine that "had to put it over," he might say, "forty thousand souls at a ball game does not, necessarily, make baseball the highest expression of spiritual emotion." Thoreau, however, is no cynic either in character or thought, though in a side glance at himself he may have held out to be one; a "cynic in independence," possibly because of his rule laid down that "self-culture admits of no compromise."ᵏ

It is conceivable that though some of his philosophy and a good deal of his personality, in some of its manifestations, have outward colors that do not seem to harmonize, the true and intimate relations they bear each other are not affected. This peculiarity, frequently seen in his attitude towards social-economic problems, is perhaps more

ᵗ "Conclusion," *Walden*, 357: As if there were safety in stupidity alone.
ᵍ For the passage in *Walden*, see Note 26.
ʰ "Conclusion," *Walden*, 363: What are men celebrating? They are all on a committee of arrangements, and hourly expect a speech from somebody. God is only the president of the day, and Webster is his orator.
ⁱ "Solitude," *Walden*, 151: The value of a man is not in his skin, that we should touch him.
ʲ "Solitude," *Walden*, 147-148: I have found that no exertion of the legs can bring two minds much nearer to one another.
ᵏ Thoreau, in *Dial*, I, 175. Quoted from Van Doren, p. 92.

emphasized in some of his personal outbursts. "I love my friends very much, but I find that it is of no use to go to see them. I hate them commonly when I am near."[1] It is easier to see what he means than it is to forgive him for saying it. The cause of this apparent lack of harmony between philosophy and personality, as far as they can be separated, may have been due to his refusal to keep the very delicate balance which Mr. Van Doren in his *Critical Study of Thoreau* says it is necessary for a great and good man to keep between his public and private lives, between his own personality and the whole outside universe of personalities.[m] Somehow one feels that if he had kept this balance he would have lost "hitting power." Again, it seems that something of the above depends upon the degree of greatness or goodness. A very great and especially a very good man has no separate private and public life. His own personality, though not identical with outside personalities, is so clear, or can be so clear to them, that it appears identical, and, as the world progresses towards its inevitable perfection, this appearance becomes more and more a reality; for the same reason that all great men now agree—in principle but not in detail, insofar as words are able to communicate agreement—on the great fundamental truths. Someone says: "Be specific—what great fundamentals?" Freedom over slavery; the natural over the artificial; beauty over ugliness; the spiritual over the material; the goodness of man; the Godness of man; God; with all other kindred truths that have been growing in expression through the ages, eras, and civilizations—innate things which once seemed foreign to the soul of humankind. All great men—there are millions of them now—agree on these. Around the relative and the absolute value of an attribute (or quality, or whatever it may be called) is where the fight is. The relative not *from* the absolute, but *of* it—always *of* it. Geniuses—and there are millions of them—differ as to *what* is beautiful and *what* is ugly, as to *what* is right and *what* is wrong—there are many interpretations of God—but they all agree that beauty is better than ugliness and right is better than wrong, and that there is a God—all are one when they reach the essence. Every analysis of a criticism or quality of Thoreau invariably leads back and stands us against the great problems of life

[1] *Journal*, II, Vol. VIII, p. 98. Quoted from Van Doren, p. 25.
[m] Van Doren, p. 116.

and eternity. It is a fair indication of the greatness of his problems and ideals.

The unsympathetic treatment accorded Thoreau on account of the false colors that his personality apparently gave to some of his important ideas and virtues might be lessened if it were more constantly remembered that a command of his today is but a mood of yesterday and a contradiction to-morrow. He is too volatile to paint, much less to catalogue. If Thoreau did not oversay, he said nothing. He says so himself. "I desire to speak somewhere *without* bounds; like a man in a waking moment to men in their waking moments; for I am convinced that I cannot exaggerate enough even to lay the foundation of a true expression."[n] For all that, it is not safe to think that he should *never* be taken literally, as for instance in the sentence above. His extravagance at times involves him, but Thoreau never rejoices in it as Meredith seems to. He struggles against it and seems as much ashamed of being involved as the latter seems of *not* being. He seldom gets into the situation of Meredith—timidly wandering around with no clothes after stepping out of one of his "involvedensities." This habit may be a part of the novelists' license, for perhaps their inspiration is less original and less natural than that of the poets, as traits of human weakness are unnatural to or "not an innate part with human nature." Perhaps if they (novelists) had broader sources for their inspiration they would hardly need licenses, and perhaps they would hardly become novelists; for the same reason that Shakespeare might have been greater if he hadn't written plays. Some say that a true composer will never write an opera, because a truly brave man will not take a drink to keep up his courage; which is not the same thing as saying that Shakespeare is not the greatest figure in all literature; in fact, it is an attempt to say that many novels, most operas, all Shakespeares, and all brave men (and women)—(rum or no rum)—are among the noblest blessings with which God has endowed mankind—because, not being perfect, they are perfect examples pointing to that perfection which nothing yet has attained.

Thoreau's mysticism at times throws him into elusive moods—but an elusiveness held by a thread to something concrete and specific, for he had too much integrity of mind for any other kind. In these

[n] "Conclusion," *Walden*, 357.

moments, it is easier to follow his thought than to follow him. Indeed, if he were always easy to follow, after one had caught up with him, one might find that is was not Thoreau.

It is, however, with no mystic rod that he strikes at institutional life. Here again is felt the influence of the great transcendental doctrine of "innate goodness" in human nature—a reflection of the like in nature; a philosophic part which, by the way, was a more direct inheritance in Thoreau than in his brother transcendentalists. For, besides what he received from a native Unitarianism, a good part must have descended to him through his Huguenot blood from eighteenth-century French philosophy. We trace a reason here for his lack of interest in "the church." For if revealed religion is the path between God and man's spiritual part—a kind of formal causeway— Thoreau's highly developed spiritual life felt, apparently unconsciously, less need of it than most men. But he might have been more charitable towards those who do need it (and most of us do) if he had been more conscious of his freedom. Those who look today for the cause of a seeming deterioration in the influence of the church may find it in a wider development of this feeling of Thoreau's: that the need is less because there is more of the spirit of Christianity in the world today. Another cause for his attitude towards the church as an institution is one always too common among "the narrow minds" to have influenced Thoreau. He could have been more generous. He took the arc for the circle, the exception for the rule, the solitary bad example for the many good ones. His persistent emphasis on the value of "example" may excuse this lower viewpoint. "The silent influence of the example of one sincere life . . . has benefited society more than all the projects devised for its salvation."[o] He has little patience for the unpracticing preacher. "In some countries a hunting parson is no uncommon sight. Such a one might make a good shepherd's dog but is far from being the Good Shepherd."[p] It would have been interesting to have seen him handle the speculating parson who takes a good salary—more per annum than all the disciples had to sustain their bodies during their whole lives—from a metropolitan religious corporation for "speculating" on Sunday about the beauty of poverty, who preaches: "Take no thought (for your life) what ye

[o] Thoreau, quoted from Van Doren. See Note 27.
[p] "Higher Laws," *Walden*, 235.

shall eat or what ye shall drink nor yet what ye shall put on . . . lay not up for yourself treasure upon earth . . . take up thy cross and follow me"; who on Monday becomes a "speculating" disciple of another god, and by questionable investments, successful enough to get into the "press," seeks to lay up a treasure of a million dollars for his old age, as if a million dollars could keep such a man out of the poor-house. Thoreau might observe that this one good example of Christian degeneracy undoes all the acts of regeneracy of a thousand humble five-hundred-dollar country parsons; that it out-influences the "unconscious influence" of a dozen Dr. Bushnells, if there be that many; that the repentance of this man who did not "fall from grace" because he never fell into it—that this unnecessary repentance might save this man's own soul, but not necessarily the souls of the million headline readers; that repentance would put this preacher right with the powers that be in this world—and the next.[q] Thoreau might pass a remark upon this man's intimacy with God "as if he had a monopoly of the subject"—an intimacy that perhaps kept him from asking God exactly what his Son meant by the "camel," the "needle"—to say nothing of the "rich man."[r] Thoreau might have wondered how this man *nailed down* the last plank in *his* bridge to salvation by rising to sublime heights of patriotism in *his* war against materialism; but would even Thoreau be so unfeeling as to suggest to this exhorter that *his* salvation might be clinched if he would sacrifice his "income" (not himself) and "come-in" to a real Salvation Army. Or that the final triumph, the supreme happiness in casting aside this mere $10,000 or $20,000 every year, must be denied him[s]—for was he not captain of the ship—must he not stick to his passengers (in the first cabin—the very first cabin)—not that the *ship* was sinking but that *he* was . . . we will go no further. Even Thoreau would not demand sacrifice for sacrifice's sake—no, not even from Nature.

Property, from the standpoint of its influence in checking natural self-expansion and from the standpoint of personal and inherent

[q] MS: (and the next? —).

[r] MS: So intimate that he didn't feel quite like asking him exactly what "his Son" meant by the "camel"—the "needle"—to say nothing of the "rich man" —or exactly what he *really* did send his Son "down to earth for anyway."

[s] MS: —how he could not allow himself this joy and bliss—

right, is another institution that comes in for straight and cross-arm jabs—now to the stomach, now to the head, but seldom sparring for breath. For does he not say that "wherever a man goes, men will pursue him with their dirty institutions"? The influence of property, as he saw it, on morality or immorality, and how through this it may or should influence "government" is seen by the following: "I am convinced that if all men were to live as simply as I did, then thieving and robbery would be unknown. These take place only in communities where some have got more than is sufficient while others have not enough—

> Nec bella fuerunt,
> Fagimus astabat dum
> Scyphus ante dapes—

You who govern public affairs, what need have you to employ punishments? Have virtue and the people will be virtuous."[t] If Thoreau had made the first sentence read: "If all men were *like* me and were to live as simply," etc., everyone would agree with him. We may wonder here how he would account for some of the degenerate types we are told about in some of our backwoods and mountain regions. Possibly by assuming that they are an instance of perversion of the species—that the little civilizing their forbears experienced rendered these people more susceptible to the physical than to the spiritual influence of nature; in other words, if they had been purer naturists, as the Aztecs for example, they would have been purer men. Instead of turning to any theory of ours or of Thoreau for the true explanation of this condition (which is a kind of pseudo-naturalism) for its true diagnosis and permanent cure—are we not far more certain to find it in the radiant look of humility, love, and hope in the strong faces of those inspired souls who are devoting their lives with no little sacrifice to these outcasts of civilization and nature? In truth, may not mankind find the solution of its eternal problem—find it after and beyond the last, most perfect system of wealth distribution which science can ever devise, after and beyond the last sublime echo of the greatest socialistic symphonies, after and beyond every transcendent thought

[t] There are some inaccuracies and omissions in the quotation. See Note 28.

and expression—in the simple example of these Christ-inspired souls, be they Pagan, Gentile, Jew, or angel?[u]

However, underlying the practical or impractical suggestions implied in the quotation above, which is from the past paragraph of Thoreau's "Village," is the same transcendental theme of "innate goodness." For this reason, there must be no limitation except that which will free mankind from limitation, and from a perversion of this "innate" possession. And "property" may be one of the causes of this perversion—property in the two relations cited above. It is conceivable that Thoreau, to the consternation of the richest members of the Bolsheviki and Bourgeois, would propose a policy of liberation, a policy of a limited personal property right[v] on the ground that congestion of personal property tends to limit the progress of the soul (as well as the progress of the stomach)—letting the economic noise thereupon take care of itself—for dissonances are becoming beautiful —and do not the same waters that roar in a storm take care of the eventual calm? This limit of property would be determined not by the *voice* of the majority but by the *brain* of the majority under a government limited to no national boundaries.[w] "The government of the world I live in is not framed in after-dinner conversation"[x] around a table in a capital city, for there is no capital—a government of principles not parties; of a few fundamental truths and not of many political expediencies—a government conducted by virtuous leaders, for it will be led by all, for all are virtuous, as then their "innate virtue" will no more be perverted by unnatural institutions. This will not be a millennium but a practical and possible application of uncommon common sense. For is it not sense, common or otherwise, for Nature (to want) to hand back the earth to those to whom it

[u] MS: —In truth may not mankind find the solution of its eternal problem— find it after and beyond the last, most-perfect (system of) wealth-distribution than science can ever conceive—after and beyond the last sublime echo of the greatest (great) symphonies of socialistic (social) ideals—after and beyond every transcendent thought and expression—after and beyond all of these and more,—will not mankind find the answer (solution) of all life and eternity, in the simple example of (these) Christ-inspired souls—be they, Gentile, Jew or Angel!

[v] Ives applied this policy to himself. See Note 29.

[w] This is another idea about which Ives wrote a great deal. See Note 30.

[x] "Conclusion," *Walden*, 366: The government of the world I live in was not framed, like that of Britain, in after-dinner conversations over the wine.

belongs—that is, to those who have to live on it? Is it not sense that
the average brains, like the average stomachs, will act rightly if they
have an equal amount of the right kind of food to act upon, and
universal education is on the way with the right kind of food? Is it
not sense then that all grown men and women (for *all* are necessary
to work out the divine "law of averages") shall have a *direct*, not an
indirect say about the things that go on in this world?[y]

Some of these attitudes, ungenerous or radical, generous or conservative (as you will) towards institutions dear to many, have no
doubt given impressions unfavorable to Thoreau's thought and personality. One hears him called, by some who ought to know what
they say and some who ought not, a crabbed, cold-hearted, sour-faced
Yankee—a kind of a visionary sore-head—a cross-grained, egotistic
recluse — even non-hearted. But it is easier to make a statement than
prove a reputation. Thoreau may be some of these things to those
who make no distinction between these qualities and the "manner"
which often comes as a kind of by-product of an intense devotion to a
principle or ideal. He was rude and unfriendly at times, but shyness
probably had something to do with that. In spite of a certain self-
possession, he was diffident in most company. But, though he may
have been subject to those spells when words do not rise and the
mind seems wrapped in a kind of dull cloth which everyone dumbly
stares at instead of looking through, he would easily get off a rejoinder
upon occasion. When a party of visitors came to Walden and someone asked Thoreau if he found it lonely there, he replied: "Only by
your help." A remark characteristic, true, rude, if not witty. The
writer remembers hearing a schoolteacher in English literature dis-
miss Thoreau (and a half-hour lesson, in which time all of *Walden*—
its surface—was sailed over) by saying that "this author" (he called
everyone "author" from Solomon down to Dr. Parkhurst)[z] "was a
kind of a crank who styled himself a hermit-naturalist and who idled
about the woods because he didn't want to work." Some such stuff is
a common conception, though not as common as it used to be. If this

[y] See Note 12 concerning Ives' proposed amendment to the Constitution to
change the government of the United States from representative ("indirect")
to one relying on referendum ("direct"), in which the people would make all
major decisions directly by vote.
[z] Charles Henry Parkhurst (1842-1933), Presbyterian minister, writer on religious subjects, N. Y.

teacher had had more brains, it would have been a lie. The word "idled" is the hopeless part of this criticism, or, rather, of this uncritical remark. To ask this kind of a man, who plays all the "choice gems from celebrated composers" literally, always literally, and always with the loud pedal, who plays all hymns, wrong notes, right notes, games, people, and jokes literally, and with the loud pedal, who will die literally and with the loud pedal—to ask this man to smile even faintly at Thoreau's humor is like casting a pearl before a coal baron.[a] Emerson implies that there is one thing a genius must have to be a *genius*, and that is "mother-wit." "Doctor Johnson, Milton, Chaucer and Burns had it. Aunt Mary Moody Emerson has it, and can write scrap letters. Who has it need never write anything but scraps. Henry Thoreau has it."[b] His humor, though a part of this wit, is not always as spontaneous, for it is sometimes pun shape (so is Charles Lamb's)—but it is nevertheless a kind that can serenely transport us, and which we can enjoy without disturbing our neighbors. If there are those who think him cold-hearted and with but little human sympathy, let them read his letters to Emerson's little daughter, or hear Dr. Emerson tell about the Thoreau home life and the stories of his boyhood—the ministrations to a runaway slave; or let them ask old Sam Staples, the Concord sheriff[c] about him. That he "was fond of a few intimate friends, but cared not one fig for people in the mass," is a statement made in a school history and which is superficially true. He cared *too* much for the masses—too much to let his personality be "massed"—too much to be unable to realize the futility of wearing his heart on his sleeve but not of wearing his path to the shore of "Walden" for future masses to walk over, and perchance find the way to themselves. Some near-satirists are fond of telling us that Thoreau came so close to Nature that she killed him before he had discovered her whole secret. They remind us that he died with consumption but forget that he lived with consumption. And without using much charity, this can be made to excuse many of his irascible and uncongenial moods. You to whom that gaunt face seems forbidding—look into the eyes! If he seems "dry and priggish" to you,

[a] MS: blackblinded coal-baron.
[b] Quoted from E. W. Emerson, *Thoreau*, p. 109.
[c] Ives refers again to Dr. Edward Waldo Emerson's *Thoreau*. For the references and a brief note on Sam Staples, see Note 31.

Mr. Stevenson, "with little of that large unconscious geniality of the
world's heroes,"[d] follow him some spring morning to Baker Farm,
as he rambles through "pine groves . . . like temples, or like fleets
at sea, full-rigged, with wavy boughs, and rippling with light, so soft
and green and shady that the Druids would have forsaken their oaks
to worship in them." Follow him to "the cedar wood beyond Flint's
Pond, where the trees, covered with hoary blue berries, spiring
higher and higher, are fit to stand before Valhalla."[e] Follow him, but
not too closely, for you may see little if you do, as he walks "in so
pure and bright a light, gilding the withered grass and leaves, so
softly and serenely bright" that he thinks he has "never bathed in
such a golden flood." Follow him as "he saunters towards the holy
land till one day the sun shall shine more brightly than ever it has
done, perchance shine into your minds and hearts and light up your
whole lives with a great awakening, light as warm and serene and
golden as on a bankside in autumn."[f] Follow him through the golden
flood to the shore of that "holy land" where he lies dying—as men
say, dying as bravely as he lived. You may be near when his stern old
aunt in the duty of her Puritan conscience asks him: "Have you
made your peace with God"? and you may see his kindly smile as
he replies, "I did not know that we had ever quarreled."[g] Moments
like these reflect more nobility and equanimity, perhaps, than
geniality—qualities, however, more serviceable to world's heroes.

The personal trait that one who has affection for Thoreau may
find worst is a combative streak, in which he too often takes refuge.
An obstinate elusiveness, almost a "contrary cussedness"—as if he
would say (which he didn't): "If a truth about something is not as I
think it ought to be, I'll make it what I think, and it *will* be the truth
—but if you agree with me, then I begin to think it may not be the
truth." The causes of these unpleasant colors (rather than characteristics) are, too easily attributed to a lack of human sympathy, or
to the assumption that they are at least symbols of that lack, instead
of to a supersensitiveness, magnified at times by ill health, and at

[d] Quoted from Van Doren. See Note 32.
[e] "Baker Farm," *Walden*, 223.
[f] Drawn from *Excursions*. For the passage, see Note 33.
[g] This version of the story corresponds closely with the one in E. W. Emerson,
Thoreau, pp. 117-118.

times by a subconsciousness of the futility of actually living out his ideals in this life. It has been said that his brave hopes were unrealized anywhere in his career—but it is certain that they started to be realized on or about May 6, 1862,[h] and we doubt if 1920 will end their fulfillment or his career. But there were many in Concord who knew that within their village there was a tree of wondrous growth, the shadow of which—alas, too frequently—was the only part they were allowed to touch. Emerson was one of these. He was not only deeply conscious of Thoreau's rare gifts but in the *Woodland Notes*[l] pays a tribute to a side of his friend that many others missed. Emerson knew that Thoreau's sensibilities too often veiled his nobilities—that a self-cultivated stoicism, ever fortified with sarcasm, none the less securely because it seemed voluntary, covered a warmth of feeling. "His great heart, him a hermit made"[j]—a breadth of heart not easily measured, found only in the highest type of sentimentalists: the type which does not perpetually discriminate in favor of mankind. Emerson has much of this sentiment, and touches it when he sings of Nature as "the incarnation of a thought,"[k] when he generously visualizes Thoreau, "standing at the Walden shore invoking the vision of a thought as it drifts heavenward into an incarnation of Nature."[1] There is a Godlike patience in Nature,—in her mists, her trees, her mountains—as if she had a more abiding faith and a clearer vision than man of the resurrection and immortality!

There comes to memory an old yellow-papered composition of school-boy days whose peroration closed with "Poor Thoreau; he communed with nature for forty odd years, and then died." "The forty odd years"—we'll still grant that part, but he is over a hundred now, and maybe, Mr. Lowell,[m] he is more lovable, kindlier, and more radiant with human sympathy to-day, than, perchance, you were fifty years ago. It may be that he is a far stronger, a far greater, an incalculably greater force in the moral and spiritual fibre of his

[h] Date of Thoreau's death.
[1] "Woodnotes," *Poems*, IX, 43-57.
[j] "Woodnotes I," *Poems*, IX, 46: Three moons his great heart him a hermit made, / So long he roved at will the boundless shade.
[k] "Nature," *Essays* 2, III, 187-188: Nature is the incarnation of a thought, and turns to a thought again, as ice becomes water and gas.
[1] Not a quotation from Emerson. See Note 34.
[m] James Russell Lowell, "Thoreau," in *My Study Windows* (Boston, 1871).

fellow-countrymen throughout the world today than you dreamed of fifty years ago. You, James Russell Lowells! You, Robert Louis Stevensons! You, Mark Van Dorens! with your literary perception, your power of illumination, your brilliancy of expression—yea, and with your love of sincerity, you know your Thoreau—but not my Thoreau —that reassuring and true friend, who stood by me one "low" day, when the sun had gone down, long, long before sunset.[n] You may know something of the affection that heart yearned for but knew it a duty not to grasp—you may know something of the great human passions which stirred that soul—too deep for animate expression— you may know all of this—all there is to know about Thoreau . . . but you know him not—unless you love him!

And if there shall be a program for our music, let it follow his thought on an autumn day of Indian summer at Walden—a shadow of a thought at first, colored by the mist and haze over the pond:

> Low anchored cloud,
> Fountain-head and
> Source of rivers. . . .
> Dew-cloth, dream drapery—
> Drifting meadow of the air. . . .[o]

But this is momentary—the beauty of the day moves him to a certain restlessness—to aspirations more specific—an eagerness for outward action—but through it all he is conscious that it is not in keeping with the mood for this "Day." As the mists rise, there comes a clearer thought, more traditional than the first—a meditation more calm. As he stands on the side of the pleasant hill of pines and hickories in front of his cabin, he is still disturbed by a restlessness and goes down the white-pebbled and sandy eastern shore. But it seems not to lead him where the thought suggests—he climbs the path along the "bolder northern" and "western shore, with deep bays indented,"[p] and now along the railroad track, "where the Æolian harp plays."[q] But his eagerness throws him into the lithe, springy stride of the

[n] An apparent allusion to his father's unexpected death at the age of 49 in the year 1894, when Ives was a freshman at Yale.
[o] The poem is altered. See Note 35.
[p] For the passages in *Walden*, see Note 36.
[q] The allusion is to a passage in *Week*. See Note 37.

specie hunter—the naturalist—he is still aware of a restlessness—with these faster steps his rhythm is of shorter span—it is still not the "tempo" of Nature—it does not bear the mood that the genius of the day calls for—(it is too specific)— *its* nature is too external—(the introspection too buoyant)—and he knows now that he must let Nature flow through *him* and slowly—he releases his more personal desires[r] to her broader rhythm, conscious that this[s] blends more and more with the harmony of her solitude; it tells him that his search for freedom on that day, at least, lies in his submission to her, for Nature is as relentless as she is benignant. He remains in this mood, and, while outwardly still, he seems to move with the slow, almost monotonous swaying beat of this autumnal day. He is more contented with a "homely burden" and is more assured of the "broad margin to his life"; he sits in his "sunny doorway, . . . rapt in revery . . . amidst goldenrod, sandcherry, and sumach . . . in undisturbed solitude." At times, the more definite personal strivings[t] for the ideal freedom—the former more active speculations—come over him, as if he would trace a certain intensity even in his submission. "He grew in those seasons like corn in the night, and they were better than any works of the hands. They were not time subtracted from his life but so much over and above the usual allowance. He realized what the Orientals meant by contemplation and forsaking of works. The day advanced as if to light some work of his—it was morning and lo! now it is evening and nothing memorable is accomplished."[u] "The evening train has gone by, and all the restless world with it. The fishes in the pond no longer feel its rumbling, and he is more alone than ever." His meditations are interrupted only by the faint sound of the Concord bell—'tis prayer-meeting night in the village—"a melody as it were, imported into the wilderness. . . . At a distance over the woods the sound acquires a certain vibratory hum, as if the pine needles in the horizon were the strings of a harp which it swept. . . . a vibration of the universal lyre, just as the intervening atmosphere makes a distant ridge of earth interesting to the eyes by the azure tint it imparts. . . ." Part of the echo may be "the voice of

[r] MS: intimate inclinations.
[s] Crossed out in MS: pulse beat of nature.
[t] MS: more intimate (definite) personal strivings (desires).
[u] For the passage in *Walden,* see Note 38.

the wood; the same trivial words and notes sung by a wood nymph."ᵛ
It it darker—the poet's flute is heard out over the pondᵂ and Walden
hears the swan song of that "Day"—and faintly echoes. . . . Is it a
transcendental tune of Concord? 'Tis an evening when the "whole
body is one sense," . . . and before ending his day he looks out over
the clear, crystalline water of the pond and catches a glimpse of the
"shadow-thought" he saw in the morning's mist and haze—he knows
that by his final submission, he possesses the "Freedom of the Night."
He goes up the "pleasant hillside of pines, hickories," and moonlight
to his cabin, "with a strange liberty in Nature, a part of herself."ˣ

ᵛ For the passage in *Walden*, see Note 39.
ᵂ The "Thoreau" movement of the Concord Sonata has an optional passage
for flute.
ˣ "Solitude," *Walden*, 143: This is a delicious evening, when the whole body
is one sense, and imbibes delight through every pore. I go and come with a
strange liberty in Nature, a part of herself.

SIX

EPILOGUE[y]

THE futility of attempting to trace the source or primal impulse of an art inspiration may be admitted without granting that human qualities or attributes which go with personality cannot be suggested, and that artistic intuitions which parallel them cannot be reflected in music. Actually accomplishing the latter is a problem, more or less arbitrary to an open mind, more or less impossible to a prejudiced mind.[z]

That which the composer intends to represent as "high vitality" sounds like something quite different to different listeners. That which I like to think suggests Thoreau's submission to nature may, to another, seem something like Hawthorne's conception of the relentlessness of an evil conscience—and to the rest of our friends, but a series of unpleasant sounds. How far can the composer be held accountable? Beyond a certain point the responsibility is more or less undeterminable. The outside characteristics—that is, the points

[y] MS: Postlude.
[z] Condensed in AR: . . . Can human qualities or attributes which go with personality be suggested, and artistic intuitions which parallel them be reflected in music? Actually accomplishing this is a problem, more or less arbitrary to an open mind, more or less impossible to a prejudiced mind.

70

furthest away from the mergings—are obvious to mostly anyone.[a] A
child knows a strain of joy from one of sorrow. Those a little older
know the dignified from the frivolous—the "Spring Song" from the
season in which the "melancholy days have come"[b] (though is there
not a glorious hope in autumn!). But where is the definite expression
of late spring against early summer—of happiness against optimism?
A painter paints a sunset—can he paint the setting sun?

In some century to come, when the school children will whistle
popular tunes in quarter-tones—when the diatonic scale will be as
obsolete as the pentatonic is now[c]—perhaps then these borderland
experiences may be both easily expressed and readily recognized. But
maybe music was not intended to satisfy the curious definiteness of
man. Maybe it is better to hope that music may always be a transcendental language in the most extravagant sense. Possibly the
power of literally distinguishing these "shades of abstraction"—these
attributes paralleled by "artistic intuitions" (call them what you will)
—is ever to be denied man for the same reason that the beginning and
end of a circle are to be denied.

II

There may be an analogy—and on first sight it seems that there
must be—between both the state and power of artistic perceptions
and the law of perpetual change, that ever-flowing stream, partly
biological, partly cosmic, ever going on in ourselves, in nature, in all
life. This may account for the difficulty of identifying desired qualities
with the perceptions of them in expression. Many things are constantly coming into being, while others are constantly going out—
one part of the same thing is coming in while another part is going
out of existence. Perhaps this is why the above conformity in art (a
conformity which we seem naturally to look for) appears at times so
unrealizable, if not impossible. It will be assumed, to make this theory
clearer, that the "flow" or "change" does not go on in the art-product

[a] Margin of MS, printed in large capital letters: RHYTHM.
[b] The quotation marks are not ironical. See Note 40.
[c] In his essay, "Some 'Quarter-tone' Impressions," first published in *Franco-
American Music Society Quarterly Bulletin*, March, 1925, Ives relates how his
father constructed a device with twenty-four violin strings tuned at intervals
smaller than a half-tone, and tried to get his family to sing the melodies he
played on the device.

itself. (As a matter of fact it probably does, to a certain extent; a
picture or a song may gain or lose in value beyond what the painter
or composer knew by the progress and higher development in all art.
Keats may be only partially true when he says that a work of beauty
is a joy forever; a thing that is beautiful *to me* is a joy *to me,* as long
as it remains beautiful *to me;* and if it remains so as long as I live, it
is so forever—that is, forever *to me.* If he had put it this way, he
would have been tiresome, inartistic, but perhaps truer.) So we will
assume here that this change only goes on in Man and Nature, and
that this eternal process in mankind is paralleled in some way during
each temporary, personal life.

A young man, two generations ago, found an identity with his
ideals in Rossini; when an older man, in Wagner. A young man,
one generation ago, found his in Wagner, but when older, in César
Franck or Brahms. Some may say that this change may not be general,
universal, or natural, and that it may be due to a certain kind of
education, or to a certain inherited or contracted prejudice. We
cannot deny or affirm this, absolutely, nor will we try to even qualita-
tively—except to say that it will be generally admitted that Rossini,
today, does not appeal to this generation, as he did to that of our
fathers. As far as prejudice or undue influence is concerned, and as
an illustration in point, the following may be cited—to show that
training may have but little effect in this connection (at least not as
much as usually supposed), for we believe this experience to be to a
certain extent normal, or at least, not uncommon. A man remembers,
when he was a boy of about fifteen years, hearing his music-teacher
(and father), who had just returned from a performance of *Siegfried,*
say with a look of anxious surprise that somehow or other he felt
ashamed of enjoying the music as he did, for beneath it all he was
conscious of an undercurrent of make-believe—the bravery was make-
believe, the love was make-believe, the passion, the virtue, all make-
believe, as was the dragon; P. T. Barnum would have been brave
enough to have gone out and captured a live one! But that same boy
at twenty-five was listening to Wagner with enthusiasm—his reality
was real enough to inspire a devotion. The "Pries-Lied,"[d] for instance,
stirred him deeply. But when he became middle-aged—and long

[d] Same misspelling also in the MS. See the Reger anecdote on p. 88.

before the Hohenzollern hog-marched into Belgium—this music had become cloying, the melodies threadbare—a sense of something commonplace—yes—of make-believe, came. These feelings were fought against for association's sake and because of gratitude for bygone pleasures, but the former beauty and nobility were not there, and in their place stood irritating intervals[e] of descending fourths and fifths. Those once transcendent progressions, luxuriant suggestions of Debussy chords of the ninth, eleventh, etc., were becoming slimy. An unearned exultation—a sentimentality deadening something within—hides around in the music. Wagner seems less and less to measure up to the substance and reality of César Franck, Brahms, d'Indy, or even Elgar (with all his tiresomeness);[f] the wholesomeness, manliness, humility, and deep spiritual, possibly religious, feeling of these men seem missing and not made up for by his (Wagner's) manner and eloquence,[g] even if greater than theirs (which is very doubtful.)[h]

From the above we would try to prove that as this stream of change flows towards the eventual ocean of mankind's perfection, the artworks in which we identify our higher ideals come by this process to be identified with the lower ideals of those who embark after us when the stream has grown in depth. If we stop with the above experience, our theory of the effect of man's changing nature, as thus explaining artistic progress, is perhaps sustained. Thus would we show that the perpetual flow of the life stream is affected by and affects each individual riverbed of the universal watersheds. Thus would we prove that the Wagner period was normal, because we intuitively recognized whatever identity we were looking for at a certain period in our life, and the fact that it was so made the Franck period possible and then normal at a later period in our life. Thus would we assume that this is as it should be, and that it is not Wagner's content or substance or his lack of virtue—that something in us has made us flow past him and not he past us. But something blocks our theory! Something makes our hypotheses seem purely speculative if not useless. It is men like Bach and Beethoven.

[e] MS: in their place stood skeletons—irritating intervals.
[f] MS: easy-sounding tiresomeness.
[g] MS: manner and form.
[h] For Ives' reaction to Wagner after hearing a performance of *Die Götter-dämmerung* in New York, 1894, see a letter to his father in Note 41.

Is it not a matter nowadays of common impression or general
opinion (for the law of averages plays strongly in any theory relating
to human attributes) that the world's attitude towards the substance
and quality and spirit of these two men, or other men of like character, if there be such, has not been affected by the flowing stream
that has changed us? But if by the measure of this public opinion, as
well as it can be measured, Bach and Beethoven are being flowed
past—not as fast perhaps as Wagner is, but if they are being passed at
all from this deeper viewpoint—then this "change" theory holds.

Here we shall have to assume, for we haven't proved it, that artistic
intuitions can sense in music a weakening of moral strength and
vitality, and that it is sensed in relation to Wagner and not sensed in
relation to Bach and Beethoven. If, in this common opinion, there is
a particle of change toward the latter's art, our theory stands—mind
you, this admits a change in the manner, form, external expression,
etc., but not in substance. If there is no change here towards the substance of these two men, our theory not only falls but its failure
superimposes or allows us to presume a fundamental duality in music,
and in all art for that matter.

Does the progress of intrinsic beauty or truth (we assume there is
such a thing) have its exposures as well as its discoveries? Does the
non-acceptance of the foregoing theory mean that Wagner's substance and reality are lower and his manner higher—that his beauty
was not intrinsic—that he was more interested in the repose of pride
than in the truth of humility? It appears that he chose the representative instead of the spirit itself—that he chose (consciously or unconsciously, it matters not) the lower set of values in this dualism. These
are severe accusations to bring—especially when a man is a little down,
as Wagner is today. But these convictions were present some time
before he was banished from the Metropolitan.

Wagner seems to take Hugo's place in Faguet's criticism of de
Vigny[1]—that the staging to him (Hugo) was the important thing, not
the conception—that in de Vigny, the artist was inferior to the poet;
finally that Hugo and so Wagner have a certain *pauvreté de fond.*
Thus would we ungenerously make Wagner prove our sum! But it is
a sum that won't prove! The theory at its best does little more than

[1] Alfred Victor de Vigny (1797-1863).

suggest something which, if it is true at all, is a platitude, viz., that progressive growth in all life makes it more and more possible for men to separate, in an art-work, moral weakness from artistic strength.

III

Human attributes are definite enough when it comes to their description, but the expression of them or the paralleling of them in an art-process has to be, as said above, more or less arbitrary. But we believe that their expression can be[j] less vague if the basic distinction of this art-dualism is kept in mind. It is morally certain that the higher part is founded, as Sturt suggests, on something that has to do with those kinds of unselfish human interests which we call knowledge and morality—knowledge, not in the sense of erudition, but as a kind of creation or creative truth. This allows us to assume that the higher and more important value of this dualism is composed of what may be called reality, quality, spirit, or substance against the lower value of form, quantity, or manner. Of these terms, "substance" seems to us the most appropriate, cogent, and comprehensive for the higher, and "manner" for the under-value. Substance in a human-art-quality suggests the body of a conviction which has its birth in the spiritual consciousness, whose youth is nourished in the moral consciousness, and whose maturity as a result of all this growth is then represented in a mental image. This is appreciated by the intuition, and somehow translated into expression by "manner"—a process always less important than it seems, or as suggested by the foregoing (in fact we apologize for this attempted definition). So it seems that substance is too indefinite to analyze in more specific terms. It is practically indescribable. Intuitions (artistic or not?) will sense it—process, unknown. Perhaps it is an unexplained consciousness of being nearer God or being nearer the devil—of approaching truth or approaching unreality; [it is] a silent something felt in the truth of nature in Turner against the truth of art in Botticelli—or in the fine thinking of Ruskin against the fine soundings of Kipling—or in the wide expanse of Titian against the narrow expanse of Carpaccio—or in some such distinction that Pope sees between what he calls Homer's "invention" and Virgil's "judgment"; [it is] apparently an inspired

[j] AR: may be.

imagination against an artistic care—a sense of the difference, perhaps, between Dr. Bushnell's "Knowing God"[k] and knowing *about* God. A more vivid explanation or illustration may be found in the difference between Emerson and Poe. The former seems to be almost wholly substance, and the latter, manner. The measure in artistic satisfaction of Poe's manner is equal to the measure of spiritual satisfaction in Emerson's substance. The total value of each man is high, but Emerson's is higher than Poe's because substance is higher than manner—because substance leans towards optimism, and manner, pessimism. We do not know that all this is so, but we feel (or, rather, know by intuition) that it is so, in the same way we know intuitively that right is higher than wrong—though we can't always tell why a thing is right or wrong, or what is always the difference or the margin between right and wrong.

Beauty, in its common conception, has nothing to do with it (substance), unless it be granted that its outward aspect, or the expression between sensuous beauty and spiritual beauty, can be always and distinctly known, which it cannot, as the art of music is still in its infancy. On reading this over, it seems only decent that some kind of an apology be made for[l] the beginning of the preceding sentence.[m] It cannot justly be said that anything that has to do with art has nothing to do with beauty in any degree—that is, whether beauty is there or not, it [substance] has something to do with it. A casual idea of it, a kind of a first necessary physical impression, was what we had in mind. Probably nobody knows what actual beauty is—except those serious writers of humorous essays in art magazines, who accurately, but kindly, with club in hand, demonstrate for all time and men that beauty is a quadratic monomial[n]—that it *is* absolute—that it *is* relative—that it *is not* relative—that it *is not*. . . . The word "beauty" is as easy to use as the word "degenerate."[o] Both come in

[k] The titles of Bushnell sermons most resembling this are "He That Knows God Will Confess Him" in *Sermons for the New Life* (New York, 1858), and "The Immediate Knowledge of God" in *Sermons on Living Subjects* (New York, 1873).

[l] MS: —(among other things).

[m] Omitted in AR: On reading this over . . . preceding sentence.

[n] MS: that it $= \dfrac{I\,x^2 - \sqrt{b^2 + 4\,ac}}{3\,(x+y)\,2}$

[o] AR: "decadent."

handy when one does or does not agree with you. For our part, something that Roussel-Despierres says comes nearer to what we like to
think beauty is . . . "an infinite source of good . . . the love of the
beautiful . . . a constant anxiety for moral beauty."[p] Even here we
go around in a circle—a thing apparently inevitable, if one tries to
reduce art to philosophy. But personally, we prefer to go around in
a circle than around in a parallelepipedon, for it seems cleaner and
perhaps freer from mathematics; or for the same reason we prefer
Whittier to Baudelaire, a poet to a genius, or a healthy to a rotten
apple—probably not so much because it is more nutritious, but because we like its taste better: We like the beautiful and don't like
the ugly; therefore, what we like is beautiful, and what we don't like
is ugly—and hence we are glad the beautiful is not ugly, for if it were
we would like something we don't like. So having unsettled what
beauty is, let us go on.

At any rate, we are going to be arbitrary enough to claim, with no
definite qualification, that substance can be expressed in music, and
that it is the only valuable thing in it;[q] and, moreover, that in two
separate pieces of music in which the notes are almost identical, one
can be of substance with little manner, and the other can be of
manner with little substance. Substance has something to do with
character. Manner has nothing to do with it. The substance of a
tune comes from somewhere near the soul, and the manner comes
from—God knows where.

IV

The lack of interest to preserve, or ability to perceive, the fundamental divisions of this duality accounts to a large extent, we believe,
for some or many [of the] various phenomena (pleasant or unpleasant
according to the personal attitude) of modern art—and all art. It is
evidenced in many ways: the sculptors' over-insistence on the
"mold"; the outer rather than the inner subject or content of his
statue—overenthusiasm for local color—overinterest in the multi-
plicity of techniques, in the idiomatic, in the effect as shown by the

[p] François Roussel-Despierres (b. 1864). Quotation not found.
[q] AR: So having unsettled what beauty is, let us be arbitrary enough to claim,
with no definite qualification, that substance in music is the only valuable thing
in it. . . .

appreciation of an audience rather than in the effect on the ideals of the inner conscience of the artist or the composer. This lack of perceiving is too often shown by an overinterest in the material value of the effect. The pose of self-absorption which some men in the advertising business (and incidentally in the recital and composing business) put into their photographs or the portraits of themselves, while all dolled up in their purple-dressing-gowns, in their twofold wealth of golden hair, in their cissy-like postures over the piano keys—this pose of "manner" sometimes sounds out so loud that the more their music is played, the less it is heard. For does not Emerson tell them this when he says "What you are talks so loud, that I cannot hear what you say"?[r] The inescapable impression that one sometimes gets by a glance at these public-inflicted trademarks, and without having heard or seen any of their music, is that the one great underlying desire of these appearing-artists is to impress, perhaps startle and shock their audiences, and at any cost. This may have some such effect upon some of the lady-part (male or female) of their listeners, but possibly the members of the men-part, who as boys liked hockey better than birthday-parties, may feel like shocking a few of these picture-sitters with something stronger than their own "forzandos."

The insistence upon manner in its relation to local color is wider than a self-strain for effect. If local color is a natural part (that is, a part of substance), the art-effort cannot help but show its color—and it will be a true color, no matter how colored. If it is a part (even a natural part) of manner, either the color part is bound eventually to drive out the local part, or the local drive out all color. Here a process of cancellation or destruction is going on—a kind of "compromise" which destroys by deadlock—a compromise purchasing a selfish pleasure—a decadence in which art becomes first dull, then dark, then dead—though throughout this process it is outwardly very much alive —especially after it is dead. The same tendency may even be noticed if there is overinsistence upon the national in art. Substance tends to create affection; manner prejudice. The latter tends to efface the distinction between the love of both a country's virtue and vices, and the love of only the virtue. A true love of country is likely to be so big that it will embrace the virtue one sees in other countries, and in

[r] Not an actual quotation. See Note 42.

the same breath, so to speak. A composer born in America, but who has not been interested in the "cause of the Freedmen," may be so interested in "negro melodies" that he writes a symphony over them. He is conscious (perhaps only subconscious) that he wishes it to be "American music." He tries to forget that the paternal negro came from Africa. Is his music American or African? That is the great question which keeps him awake! But the sadness of it is that if he had been born in Africa, his music might have been just as American, for there is good authority that an African soul under an X-ray looks identically like an American soul. There is a futility in selecting a certain type to represent a "whole," unless the interest in the spirit of the type coincides with that of the whole. In other words, if this composer isn't as deeply interested in the "cause" as Wendell Phillips was, when he fought his way through that anti-abolitionist crowd at Faneuil Hall,[s] his music is liable to be less American than he wishes. If a middle-aged man, upon picking up the *Scottish Chiefs*, finds that his boyhood enthusiasm for the prowess and noble deeds and character of Sir William Wallace and of Bruce is still present, let him put, or try to put that glory into an overture, let him fill it chuck-full of Scotch tunes, if he will. But after all is said and sung he will find that his music is American to the core (assuming that he is an American and wishes his music to be). It will be as national in character as the heart of that Grand Army Grandfather, who read those *Cragmore Tales* of a summer evening, when that boy had brought the cows home without witching. Perhaps the memories of the old soldier, to which this man still holds tenderly, may be turned into a "strain" or a "sonata," and, though the music does not contain or even suggest any of the old war-songs, it will be as sincerely American as the subject, provided his (the composer's) interest, spirit, and character sympathize with, or intuitively coincide with that of the subject.

Again, if a man finds that the cadences of an Apache war-dance come nearest to his soul—provided he has taken pains to know enough other cadences, for eclecticism is part of his duty; sorting potatoes means a better crop next year—let him assimilate whatever he finds highest of the Indian ideal so that he can use it with the

[s] Boston, 1837. For the occasion, see Note 43.

cadences, fervently, transcendentally, inevitably, furiously, in his
symphonies, in his operas, in his whistlings on the way to work, so
that he can paint his house with them, make them a part of his
prayer-book—this is all possible and necessary, if he is confident that
they have a part in his spiritual consciousness. With this assurance,
his music will have everything it should of sincerity, nobility, strength,
and beauty, no matter how it sounds; and if, with this, he is true to
none but the highest of American ideals (that is, the ideals only that
coincide with his spiritual consciousness), his music will be true to
itself and incidentally American, and it will be so even after it is
proved that all our Indians came from Asia.

The man "born down to Babbitt's Corners" may find a deep appeal
in the simple but acute Gospel hymns of the New England "camp
meetin' " of a generation or so ago.[t] He finds in them—some of them
—a vigor, a depth of feeling, a natural-soil rhythm, a sincerity—
emphatic but inartistic—which, in spite of a vociferous sentimentality,
carries him nearer the "Christ of the people" than does the *Te Deum*
of the greatest cathedral.[u] These tunes have, for him, a truer ring than
many of those groove-made, even-measured, monotonous, non-
rhythmed, indoor-smelling, priest-taught, academic, English or neo-
English hymns (and anthems)—well-written, well-harmonized
things, well-voice-led, well-counterpointed, well corrected, and well
O.K'd, by well corrected Mus. Bac. R.F.O.G.'s[v]—personified sounds,
correct and inevitable to sight and hearing; in a word, those proper
forms of stained-glass beauty which our over-drilled mechanisms—
boy choirs—are limited to. But if the Yankee can reflect the fervency
with which "his gospels" were sung—the fervency of "Aunt Sarah,"
who scrubbed her life away for her brother's ten orphans, the fervency with which this woman, after a fourteen-hour work day on
the farm, would hitch up and drive five miles through the mud and

---

[t] See Cowell, pp. 23-24, for Ives' autobiographical notes describing outdoor
camp meetings at Redding, Conn.
[u] Kirkpatrick's *Catalogue* has a special index of tunes quoted by Ives (he was
an inveterate quoter in his music as in his prose). The index lists fifty-four
hymn-tunes, many of which were used a number of times, and in different
works. The lists given by Kirkpatrick of quotations from other classes of music
show that he drew far more heavily on hymns than on any other source.
[v] A mixture of F.R.C.O. (Fellow of the Royal College of Organists) and
F.A.G.O. (Fellow of the American Guild of Organists).

rain to "prayer meetin'," her one articulate outlet for the fullness of her unselfish soul—if he can reflect the fervency of such a spirit, he may find there a local color that will do all the world good. If his music can but catch that spirit by being a part with itself, it will come somewhere near his ideal—and it will be American, too—perhaps nearer so than that of the devotee of Indian or negro melody.ᵂ In other words, if local color, national color, any color, is a true pigment of the universal color, it is a divine quality, it is a part of substance in art—not of manner.

The preceding illustrations are but attempts to show that whatever excellence an artist sees in life, a community, in a people, or in any valuable object or experience, if sincerely and intuitively reflected in his work—his work, and so he himself, is, in a way, a reflected part of that excellence. Whether he be accepted or rejected, whether his music is always played or never played—all this has nothing to do with it; it is true or false by his own measure. If we may be permitted to leave out two words, and add a few more, a sentence of Hegel appears to sum up this idea, "The universal need for expression in art lies in man's rational impulse to exalt the inner . . . world" (*i. e.*, the highest ideals he sees in the inner life of others together with what he finds in his own life) "into a spiritual consciousness for himself."ˣ The artist *does feel* or *does not feel* that a sympathy has been approved by an artistic intuition, and, so, reflected in his work. Whether he feels this sympathy is true or not in the final analysis is a thing, probably, that no one but he (the artist) knows—but the truer he feels it, the more substance it has; or as Sturt puts it, his work "*is* art so long as he feels in doing it as true artists feel, and so long as his object is akin to the objects that true artists admire."ʸ

Dr. Griggs, in an essay on Debussy,ᶻ asks if this composer's content is worthy the manner. Perhaps so, perhaps not—Debussy himself, doubtless, could not give a positive answer. He would better know

---

ᵂ For a possible interpretation of these remarks, see Note 44.

ˣ Ives probably quotes Hegel from Sturt, p. 310. See Note 45.

ʸ Sturt, p. 328.

ᶻ John C. Griggs, "Claude Debussy," *The Yale Review*, I (1912 [Ives in a note gives 1914]). Dr. Griggs was, next to Ives' father, the earliest supporter of his music. Some references to him in Cowell are incorrect. See Note 46.

how true his feeling and sympathy was, and anyone else's personal opinion can be of but little help here.

We might offer the suggestion that Debussy's content would have been worthier his manner if he had hoed corn[a] or sold newspapers for a living, for in this way he might have gained a deeper vitality and a truer theme to sing at night and of a Sunday. Or we might say that what substance there is, is "too coherent"—it is too clearly expressed in the first thirty seconds. There you have the "whole fragment"—a translucent syllogism; but there the reality, the spirit, the substance stops,[b] and the "form," the "parfume," the "manner" shimmer right along, as the soapsuds glisten after one has finished washing. Or we might say that his substance would have been worthier if his adoration or contemplation of Nature—which is often a part of it, and which rises to great heights, as is felt, for example, in *La Mer*—had been more the quality of Thoreau's. Debussy's attitude toward Nature seems to have a kind of sensual sensuousness underlying it, while Thoreau's is a kind of spiritual sensuousness. It it rare to find a farmer or peasant whose enthusiasm for the beauty in Nature finds outward expression to compare with that of the city man who comes out for a Sunday in the country, but Thoreau is that rare country man and Debussy the city man with his week-end flights into country æsthetics. We would be inclined to say that Thoreau leaned towards substance and Debussy towards manner.

V

There comes from Concord an offer to every mind—the choice between repose and truth—and God makes the offer. "Take which you please— . . . Between these, as a pendulum, man oscillates. He in whom the love of repose predominates will accept the first creed, the first philosophy, the first political party he meets—most likely his father's."[c] He gets rest, commodity, and reputation. Here is another aspect of art-duality, but it is more drastic than ours, as it would eliminate one part or the other. A man may aim as high as Beethoven, or as high as Richard Strauss. In the former case the shot may go far below the mark—in truth, it has not been reached since that "thunder

[a] First version in MS: dug potatoes.
[b] MS: STOPS [printed in capitals].
[c] Emerson, *Essays 1*, II, 318.

storm of 1828" and there is little chance that it will be reached by anyone living today—but that matters not; the shot will never re-bound and destroy the marksman. But—in the latter case the shot may often hit the mark, but as often rebound, and harden, if not destroy, the shooter's heart—even his soul. What matters it, men say; he will then find rest, commodity, and reputation—what matters it if he find there but few perfect truths—what matters (men say); he will find there perfect media—those perfect instruments of getting in the way of perfect truths.

This choice tells why Beethoven is always modern and Strauss always mediæval—try as he may to cover it up in new bottles. He has chosen to capitalize a "talent"—he has chosen the complexity of media, the shining hardness of externals, repose, against the inner, invisible activity of truth. He has chosen the first creed, the easy creed, the philosophy of his fathers, among whom he found a half-idiot-genius (Nietzsche). His choice naturally leads him to glorify and to magnify all kinds of dull things—a stretched-out *Geigermusik*,[d] which in turn naturally leads him to windmills and human heads on silver platters.[e] Magnifying the dull into the colossal produces a kind of "comfort"— the comfort of a woman who takes more pleasure in the fit of fashion-able clothes than in a healthy body—the kind of comfort that has brought so many "adventures of baby-carriages at county fairs"[f]— "the sensation of Teddy bears, smoking their first cigarette"[g]—on the program of symphony orchestras of one hundred performers—the lure of the media—the means—not the end—but the finish. Thus the failure to perceive that thoughts and memories of childhood are too tender, and some of them too sacred, to be worn lightly on the sleeve. Life is too short for these one hundred men, to say nothing of the composer and the "dress-circle," to spend an afternoon in this way. They are but like the rest of us, and have only the expectancy of the mortality-table to survive—perhaps only this "piece." We cannot but

[d] Ives had a distasteful experience with this term, described in Cowell, p. 69. Edward Stowell, director of the orchestra of the Music School Settlement in New York, told him that Daniel Gregory Mason's Violin Sonata was better than his Second Violin Sonata because it was real *Geigermusik* ("fiddler music").
[e] *Don Quixote, Salome.*
[f] John Alden Carpenter (1876-1951), "Adventures in a Perambulator."
[g] Allusion not successfully traced.

feel that a too great desire for "repose" accounts for such phenomena.
A MS. score is brought to a concertmaster[h]—he may be a violinist—
he is kindly disposed, he looks it over, and casually fastens on a
passage: "That's bad for the fiddles—it doesn't hang just right—write
it like this, they will play it better." But that one phrase is the germ
of the whole thing. "Never mind, it will fit the hand better this way—
it will sound better." My God! What has sound got to do with music!
The waiter brings the only fresh egg he has, but the man at break-
fast sends it back because it doesn't fit his eggcup. Why can't music
go out in the same way it comes in to a man, without having to crawl
over a fence of sounds, thoraxes, catguts, wire, wood, and brass? Con-
secutive fifths are as harmless as blue laws compared with the relentless tyranny of the "media." The instrument!—there is the perennial
difficulty—there is music's limitation. Why must the scarecrow of
the keyboard—the tyrant in terms of the mechanism (be it Caruso or
a Jew's-harp)—stare into every measure? Is it the composer's fault
that man has only ten fingers? Why can't a musical thought be presented as it is born—perchance "a bastard of the slums," or a "daughter of a bishop"—and if it happens to go better later on a bass-drum
than upon a harp, get a good bass-drummer.* That music must be
heard is not essential—what it *sounds* like may not be what it *is.*
Perhaps the day is coming when music-believers will learn "that
silence is a solvent . . . that gives us leave to be universal"[1] rather
than personal.

Some fiddler was once honest or brave enough, or perhaps ignorant
enough, to say that Beethoven didn't know how to write for the
violin; that, maybe, is one of the many reasons Beethoven is not a
Vieuxtemps.[j] Another man says Beethoven's piano sonatas are not

---

* The first movement (Emerson) of the music which is the cause of all these
words was first thought of (we believe) in terms of a large orchestra; the second
(Hawthorne), in terms of a piano or a dozen pianos; the third (Alcotts), of an
organ (or piano with voice or violin); and the last (Thoreau), in terms of
strings, colored possibly with a flute or horn.

---

[h] Reber Johnson, then assistant concertmaster of the New York Symphony
Orchestra, later teacher of violin for many years at Oberlin Conservatory. The
incident is also described in autobiographical notes quoted by Cowell, pp. 68-69.
[1] Emerson, "Intellect," *Essays 1*, II, 319: Silence is a solvent that destroys personality, and gives us leave to be great and universal.
[j] Henri Vieuxtemps (1820-1881), violin virtuoso, composer of brilliant works
for the violin.

pianistic; with a little effort, perhaps, Beethoven could have become a Thalberg.[k] His symphonies are perfect truths, and perfect for the orchestra of 1820; but Mahler could have made them—possibly did make them, we will say—"more perfect," as far as their media clothes are concerned; and Beethoven is today big enough to rather like it. He is probably in the same amiable state of mind that the Jesuit priest said God was in when He looked down on the camp ground and saw the priest sleeping with a Congregational chaplain. Or in the same state of mind you'll be in when you look down and see the sexton keeping your tombstone up to date. The truth of Joachim[l] offsets the repose of Paganini and Kubelik.[mn] The repose and reputation of a successful pianist (whatever that means) who plays Chopin so cleverly that he covers up a sensuality, and in such a way that the purest-minded see nothing but sensuous beauty in it—which, by the way, doesn't disturb him as much as the size of his income-tax—the repose and fame of this man is offset by the truth and obscurity of the village organist who plays Lowell Mason[o] and Bach with such affection that he would give his life rather than lose them. The truth and courage of this organist, who risks his job to fight the prejudice of the congregation, offset the repose and large salary of a more celebrated choirmaster who holds his job by lowering his ideals, who is willing to let the organ smirk under an insipid, easy-sounding barcarolle for the offertory—who is willing to please the sentimental ears of the music committee (and its wives)—who is more willing to observe these forms of politeness than to stand up for a stronger and deeper music of simple devotion, and for a service of a spiritual unity —the kind of thing that Mr. Bossitt, who owns the biggest country place, the biggest bank, and the biggest "House of God" in town (for is it not the divine handiwork of his own pocketbook)—the kind of

[k] Sigismund Thalberg (1812-1871), piano virtuoso, composer of florid works for the piano.

[l] Joseph Joachim (1831-1907), violinist and composer, greatly respected as a player of the classics.

[m] Jan Kubelik (1880-1940), violinist whose reputation was based mainly on his technical skill. (Father of the conductor, Rafael Kubelik).

[n] MS: The truth and good of Joachim and Thiebaut offset this repose or evil of Paggani [crossed out] Paganinini and Kubelik. ["Thiebaut" is Jacques Thibaud (1880-1953), a violinist admired more for his musicality than his technical skill.]

[o] 1792-1872. American hymn composer, and eminent collector of church music.

music that this man, his wife, and *his* party (of property right in pews) can't stand because it isn't "pretty."

The doctrine of this "choice" may be extended to the distinction between literal-enthusiasm and natural-enthusiasm (right or wrong notes, good or bad tones against good or bad interpretation, good or bad sentiment), or between observation and introspection, or to the distinction between remembering and dreaming. Strauss remembers; Beethoven dreams. We see this distinction also in Goethe's confusion of the moral with the intellectual. There is no such confusion in Beethoven; to him they are one. It is told, and the story is so well known that we hesitate to repeat it here, that both these men were standing in the street one day when the Emperor drove by. Goethe, like the rest of the crowd, bowed and uncovered—but Beethoven stood bolt upright, and refused even to salute, saying: "Let him bow to us, for ours is a nobler empire." Goethe's *mind* knew this was true, but his moral courage was not instinctive.

This remembering-faculty of "repose" throws the mind in ungarded moments quite naturally towards "manner," and thus to the many things the media can do. It brings on an itching to overuse them—to be original (if anyone will tell what that is), with nothing but numbers to be original with. We are told that a conductor (of *the* orchestra) has written a symphony requiring an orchestra of one hundred and fifty men.ᵖ If his work perhaps had one hundred and fifty valuable ideas, the one hundred and fifty men might be justifiable; but as it probably contains not more than a dozen, the composer may be unconsciously ashamed of them, and glad to cover them up under a hundred and fifty men. A man may become famous because he is able to eat nineteen dinners a day, but posterity will decorate his stomach, not his brain.

Manner breeds a cussed cleverness only to be clever (a satellite of super-industrialism) and perhaps to be witty in the bargain—not the wit in mother-wit, but a kind of indoor, artificial, mental arrangement

ᵖ The italics indicate that the orchestra was the New York Philharmonic Society. The conductor-composer was Mahler, who conducted in New York in 1910, the same year that his *Symphony No. 8* ("the symphony of a thousand") was brought out in Munich. Ives attended a concert conducted by Mahler in New York (Cowell, p. 41), and Mahler went so far as to take the score of Ives' *Third Symphony* back to Europe with him, but was unable to perform it before his death in 1911 (Cowell, 131 n).

of things quickly put together which have been learned and studied. It is of the material and stays there, while humor is of the emotional, and of the approaching spiritual. Even Dukas, and perhaps other Gauls in their critical heart of hearts, may admit that "wit" in music is as impossible as "wit" at a funeral. The wit is evidence of its lack. Mark Twain could be humorous at the death of his dearest friend,[q] but in such a way as to put a blessing into the heart of the bereaved. Humor in music has the same possibilities. But its quantity has a serious effect on its quality; "inverse ratio" is a good formula to adopt here. Comedy has its part, but wit—never. Strauss is at his best in these lower rooms, but his comedy reminds us more of the physical fun of Lever[r] rather than "comedy in the Meredithian sense" as Mason suggests. Meredith is a little too deep or too subtle for Strauss, unless it be granted that cynicism is more a part of comedy than a part of refined insult. Let us also remember that Mr. Disston,[s] not Mr. Strauss, put the funny notes in the bassoon. A symphony written only to amuse and entertain is likely to amuse only the writer—and him not long after the check is cashed.

"Genius is always ascetic, and piety, and love."[t] Thus Emerson reinforces "God's offer of this choice" by a transcendental definition. The moment a famous violinist refused "to appear" until he had received his check—at that moment—*precisely*—(assuming for argument's sake that this was the first time that materialism had the ascendancy in this man's soul)—at that moment he became but a man of "talent"—incidentally, a small man and a small violinist, regardless of how perfectly he played, regardless to what heights of emotion he stirred his audience, regardless of the sublimity of his artistic and financial success.

d'Annunzio, it is told, becoming somewhat discouraged at the result of some of his Fiume adventures said: "We are the only Idealists

q Margin of MS: Chas. D. Warner. [Charles Dudley Warner (1829-1900), author and editor, Hartford, Conn. Ives may have had this story first hand, as his father-in-law, the Rev. Dr. Joseph A. Twitchell, of Hartford, was a close friend both of Warner and Mark Twain.]
r Charles James Lever (1806-1872), prolific novelist, complete works issued in 1872.
s Ives must refer to Henry Distin, head of an English firm devoted after 1849 mainly to the making of brass instruments. He may be confusing Distin with Henry Disston (1819-1878), American industrialist and inventor.
t "Prudence," *Essays* I, II, 218-219.

left." This remark may have been made in a moment of careless impulse, but if it is taken at its face value, the moment it was made—that moment—his idealism started downhill. A grasp at monopoly indicates that a sudden shift has taken place from the heights where genius may be found to the lower plains of talent. The mind of a true idealist is great enough to know that a monopoly of idealism, or of wheat, is a thing nature does not support.

A newspaper music column prints an incident (so how can we assume that it is not true?) of an American violinist[u] who called on Max Reger to tell him how much he (the American) appreciated his music. Reger gives him a hopeless look and cries: "What! a musician and not speak German!" At that moment—by the clock—regardless of how great a genius he may have been before that sentence was uttered —at that moment he became but a man of "talent." For, "the man of talent affects to call his transgressions of the laws of sense trivial and to count them nothing considered with his devotion to his art." His art never taught him prejudice, or to wear only one eye. "His art is less for every deduction from his holiness, and less for every defect of common sense."[v] And this common sense has a great deal to do with this distinguishing difference of Emerson's between genius and talent, repose and truth, and between all evidences of substance and manner in art. Manner breeds partialists. "Is America a musical nation?" If the man who is ever asking this question would sit down and think something over, he might find less interest in asking it; he might possibly remember that all nations are more musical than any nation—especially the nation that pays the most, and pays the most eagerly, for anything after it has been professionally rubber-stamped. Music may be yet unborn. Perhaps no music has ever been written or heard. Perhaps the birth of art will take place at the moment in which the last man who is willing to make a living out of art is gone and gone forever. In the history of this youthful world, the best product that human beings can boast of is probably Beethoven; but, maybe, even his art is as nothing in comparison with the future

[u] Margin of MS: Spalding [Albert Spalding, 1888-1953].
[v] "Prudence," *Essays 1,* II, 219. Ives substitutes his sentence, "His art never taught him prejudice, . . ." for Emerson's, which reads: "His art never taught him lewdness, nor the love of wine, nor the wish to reap where he had not sowed."

product of some coal-miner's soul in the forty-first century. And the
same man who is ever asking about the most musical nation is ever
discovering the most musical man of the most musical nation. When
particularly hysterical he shouts: "I have found him! Smith Grabholz, the one great American poet—at last, here is the Moses the
country has been waiting for" (of course we all know that the country
has not been waiting for anybody—and we have many Moses[w] always
with us). But the discoverer keeps right on shouting: "Here is the
one true American poetry—I pronounce it the work of a genius. I
predict for him the most brilliant career—for *his* is an art that . . .
for *his* is a soul that . . . for *his* is a . . ." and Grabholz is ruined. But
ruined not alone by this perennial discoverer of pearls in any oyster-
shell that treats him the best, but ruined by his own (Grabholz's)
talent—for genius will never let itself be discovered by "a man." Then
the world may ask: "Can the one true national 'this' or 'that' be
killed by its own discoverer?" "No," the country replies, "but each
discovery is proof of another impossibility."[x] It is a sad fact that the
one true man and the one true art will never behave as they should
except in the mind of the partialist whom God has forgotten. But this
matters little to him (the man)—his business is good (for it is easy to
sell the future in terms of the past), and there are always some who
will buy anything. The individual usually "gains" if he is willing to
but lean on manner. The evidence of this is quite widespread, for if
the discoverer happens to be in any other line of business, his sudden
discoveries would be just as important—*to him*. In fact, the theory of
substance and manner in art, and its related dualisms—repose and
truth, genius and talent, etc.—may find illustration in many, perhaps
most, of the human activities. And when examined, it (the illustration) is quite likely to show how manner is always discovering
partisans. For example, enthusiastic discoveries of the "paragon" are
common in politics—an art to some. These revelations in this profession are made easy by the pre-election discovering-leaders of the
people. And the genius who is discovered forthwith starts his speeches
of "talent"—though they are hardly that; they are hardly more than a
string of subplatitudes—square-looking, well-rigged things that almost

[w] MS: Moses's [to avoid Moseses].
[x] MS (crossed out): "No" the country replies, "but it would be if such a
thing *could* be."

everybody has seen, known, and heard since Rome or Man fell. Nevertheless these signs of perfect manner, these series of noble sentiments that the "noble" never get off, are forcibly, clearly, and persuasively handed out—eloquently, even beautifully expressed, and with such personal charm, magnetism, and strength that their profound messages speed right through the minds and hearts without as much as spattering the walls, and land right square in the middle of the listener's vanity. For all this is a part of manner, and its quality is of splendor—for manner is at times a good bluff, but substance a poor one, and knows it. The discovered-one's usual and first great outburst is probably the greatest truth that he ever utters. Fearlessly standing, he looks straight into the eyes of the populace, and with a strong ringing voice (for strong voices and strong statesmanship are inseparable), and with words far more eloquent than the following, he sings: "This honor is greater than I deserve, but duty calls me . . ." (what, not stated). "If elected, I shall be your servant . . ." (for, it is told, that he believes in modesty—that he has even boasted that he is the most modest man in the country). Thus he has the right to shout: "First, last, and forever I am for the people. I am against all bosses. I have no sympathy for politicians. I am for strict economy, liberal improvements, and justice! I am also for the—Ten Commandments" (his intuitive political sagacity keeps him from mentioning any particular one). But a sublime height is always reached in his perorations. Here we learn that he believes in *honesty* —repeat, *"honesty"*; we are even allowed to infer that he is one of the very few who know that there is such a thing; and we also learn that since he was a little boy (barefoot) his motto has been, "Do Right"— he swerves not from the right!—he believes in nothing but the right (to him—everything is right!—if it gets him elected); but cheers invariably stop this great final truth (in brackets) from rising to animate expression. Now all of these translucent axioms are true (are not axioms always true?)—as far as manner is concerned. In other words, the manner functions perfectly. But where is the divine substance? This is not there; why should it be—if it were *he* might not be there. "Substance" is not featured in this discovery. For the truth of substance is sometimes silence, sometimes ellipses—and the latter, if supplied, might turn some of the declarations above into perfect truths. For instance: "First and last and forever I am for the

people ('s votes). I'm against all bosses (against me). I have no
sympathy for (rival) politicians," etc., etc. But these tedious attempts
at comedy should stop—they're too serious; besides the illustration may
be a little hard on a few—the minority (the non-people)—though
not on the many, the majority (the people)! But even an assumed
parody may help to show what a power "manner" is for reaction
unless it is counterbalanced and then saturated by the other part of
the duality. Thus it appears that all there is to this great discovery
is that one good politician has discovered another good politician. For
manner has brought forth its usual talent; for manner cannot discover the genius who has discarded platitudes—the genius who has
devised a new and surpassing order for mankind, simple and intricate
enough, abstract and definite enough, locally impractical and universally practical enough to wipe out the need for further discoveries
of "talent," and incidentally the discoverer's own fortune and political
"manner." Furthermore, he (this genius) never will be discovered
until the majority-spirit, the common-heart, the human-oversoul, the
source of all great values, converts all talent into genius, all manner
into substance—until the direct expression of the mind and soul of the
majority, the divine right of all consciousness—social, moral, and
spiritual—discloses the one true art, and thus finally discovers the one
true leader—even *itself*. Then no leaders, no politicians, no manner,
will hold sway—and no more speeches will be heard.

The intensity today with which techniques and media are organized and used tends to throw the mind away from a "common sense"
and towards manner, and thus to resultant weak and mental[y] states;
for example, the Byronic fallacy: that one who is full of turbid feeling
about himself is qualified to be some sort of an artist. In this relation, manner also leads some to think that emotional sympathy for
self is as true a part of art as sympathy for others; and [leads some to]
a prejudice in favor of the good and bad of one personality against
the virtue of many personalities. It may be that when a poet or a
whistler becomes conscious that he is in the easy path of any particular idiom—that he is helplessly prejudiced in favor of any particular means of expression—that his manner can be catalogued as
modern or classic—that he favors a contrapuntal groove, a sound-

[y] MS: weak mental states. [Perhaps "weak and mental" resulted from dictation
of "weakened mental."]

coloring one, a sensuous one, a successful one, or a melodious one
(whatever that means)—that his interests lie in the French school or
the German school, or the school of Saturn—that he is involved in
this particular "that" or that particular "this," or in any particular
brand of emotional complexes—in a word, when he becomes conscious that his style is "his personal own," that it has monopolized a
geographical part of the world's sensibilities—then it may be that the
value of his substance is not growing, that it even may have started
on its way backwards; it may be that he is trading an inspiration for
a bad habit, and, finally, that he is reaching fame, permanence, or
some other undervalue, and that he is getting farther and farther from
a perfect truth. But, on the contrary side of the picture, it is not unreasonable to imagine that if he (this poet, composer, and laborer) is
open to all the over-values within his reach—if he stands unprotected from all the showers of the absolute which may beat upon him
—if he is willing to use or learn to use (or at least if he is not afraid
of trying to use) whatever he can of any and all lessons of the
infinite that humanity has received and thrown to man, that nature
has exposed and sacrificed, that life and death have translated—if he
accepts all and sympathizes with all, is influenced by all (whether
consciously or subconsciously, drastically or humbly, audibly or in-
audibly) whether it be all the virtue of Satan or the only evil of
Heaven—and all, even at one time, even in one chord—*then* it may
be that the value of his substance, and its value to himself, to his art,
to all art, even to the Common Soul, is growing and approaching
nearer and nearer to perfect truths—whatever they are and wherever
they may be.

Again, a certain kind of manner-over-insistence may be caused by
a group-disease germ. The over-influence by, the over-admiration of,
and the over-association with a particular artistic personality, or a
particular type or group of personalities, tends to produce equally
favorable and unfavorable symptoms, but the unfavorable ones seem
to be more contagious. Perhaps the impulsive remark of some famous
man (whose name we forget) that he loved music but hated musicians, might be followed with some good results, at least part of the
time. To see the sun rise, a man has but to get up early, and he can
always have Bach in his pocket. We hear that Mr. Smith[z] or Mr.

[z] David Stanley Smith (1877-1949). See Note 47.

Morgan, etc., *et al.*, design to establish a "course at Rome,"[a] to raise the standard of American music, (or the standard of American composers—which is it?); but possibly the more our composer accepts from his patrons "*et al.*," the less he will accept *from himself*. It may be possible that a day in a "Kansas wheat field" will do more for him than three years in Rome. It may be that many men—perhaps some of genius (if you won't admit that all are geniuses)—have been started on the downward path of subsidy by trying to write a thousand-dollar prize poem or a ten-thousand-dollar prize opera.[b] How many masterpieces have been prevented from blossoming in this way? A cocktail will make a man eat more but will not give him a healthy, normal appetite (if he had not that already). If a bishop should offer a "prize living" to the curate who will love God the hardest for fifteen days, whoever gets the prize would love God the least. Such stimulants, it strikes us, tend to industrialize art rather than develop a spiritual sturdiness—a sturdiness which Mr. Sedgwick says shows itself in a close union between spiritual life and the ordinary business of life, against spiritual feebleness, which shows itself in the separation of the two.[c] If one's spiritual sturdiness is congenital and somewhat perfect, he is not only conscious that this separation has no part in his own soul, but he does not feel its existence in others. He does not believe there is such a thing. But perfection in this respect is rare. And for the most of us, we believe, this sturdiness would be encouraged by anything that will keep or help us keep a normal balance between the spiritual life and the ordinary life.[d] If for every thousand-dollar prize a potato field be substituted, so that these candidates of Clio can dig a little in real life, perhaps dig up a natural inspiration, art's air might be a little clearer[e] —a little freer from certain traditional delusions: for instance, that

[a] The names of David Stanley Smith and J. Pierpont Morgan appear as Members of the Council of the American Academy in Rome for the years 1921-22.
[b] Horatio Parker's opera *Mona* won a ten-thousand-dollar prize and a performance at the Metropolitan Opera in 1912. His opera *Fairyland* won another ten-thousand-dollar prize offered by the National Federation of Music Clubs, and was performed at the World's Fair in Los Angeles in 1915.
[c] Henry Dwight Sedgwick, *The New American Type, and Other Essays* (Boston and New York, 1908), p. 110.
[d] Concerning the balance of spiritual life and ordinary life, see Note 48.
[e] Emerson, "New England Reformers," *Essays* 2, 245: The old English rule was, 'All summer in the field, and all winter in the study.'

free thought and free love always go to the same café—that atmosphere and diligence are synonymous. To quote Thoreau incorrectly:
"When half-Gods talk, the Gods walk!"[f] Everyone should have the
opportunity of not being over-influenced.

Again, this over-influence by and over-insistence upon manner may
finally lead some to believe that manner for manner's sake is a basis
of music. Someone is quoted as saying that "ragtime is the true
American music."[g] Anyone will admit that it is one of the many true,
natural, and, nowadays, conventional means of expression. It is an
idiom, perhaps a "set or series of colloquialisms," similar to those that
have added through centuries and through natural means some
beauty to all languages. Every language is but the evolution of slang,
and possibly the broad "A" in Harvard may have come down from
the "butcher of Southwark." To examine[h] ragtime rhythms and the
syncopations of Schumann or of Brahms seems to the writer to show
how much alike they are not.[i] Ragtime, as we hear it, is, of course, more
(but not much more) than a natural dogma[j] of shifted accents, or a
mixture of shifted and minus accents. It is something like wearing
a derby hat on the back of the head, a shuffling lilt of a happy soul
just let out of a Baptist church in old Alabama. Ragtime has its possibilities. But it does not "represent the American nation" any more
than some fine old senators represent it. Perhaps we know it now as
an ore before it has been refined into a product. It may be one of
nature's ways of giving art raw material. Time will throw its vices
away and weld its virtues into the fabric of our music. It has its
uses, as the cruet on the boarding-house table has, but to make a
meal of tomato ketchup and horse-radish, to plant a whole farm with
sunflowers, even to put a sunflower into every bouquet, would be
calling nature something worse than a politician. Mr. Daniel Gregory
Mason,[k] whose wholesome influence, by the way, is doing as much

[f] MS (crossed out): The half-Gods, talk—and the Gods work! [Probably not
Thoreau intentionally misquoted, but Emerson, "Intellect," *Essays 1*, II, 319:
The ancient sentence said, Let us be silent, for so are the Gods.]
[g] Moderwell in Mason. See Note 49.
[h] MS (crossed out): To compare.
[i] Mason (see below) cites the last movement of the Schumann *Piano Concerto*
in a discussion of ragtime (pp. 244-245).
[j] MS: a (natural) dogma (formula).
[k] 1873-1953; composer, author, professor of music at Columbia Univ.

perhaps for music in America as American music is, amusingly says: ". . . if indeed the land of Lincoln and Emerson has degenerated until nothing remains of it but a 'jerk and rattle,' then we at least are free to repudiate the false patriotism of 'My country, right or wrong,' to insist that better than bad music is no music, and to let our beloved art subside finally under the clangor of the subway gongs and automobile horns, dead, but not dishonored."[1] And so may we ask: Is it better to sing inadequately of the "leaf on Walden floating," and die "dead but not dishonored," or to sing adequately of the "cherry on the cocktail," and live forever?

VI

If anyone has been strong enough to escape these rocks—this Scylla and Charybdis—has survived these wrong choices, these under-values with their prizes, Bohemias, and heroes—is not such a one in a better position, is he not abler and freer to "declare himself" and so "to love his cause so singly that he will cleave to it, and forsake all else? What is this cause for the American composer but the utmost musical beauty that he, as an individual man, with his own qualities and defects, is capable of understanding and striving towards—for-saking all else except those types of musical beauty that come home to him," and that his spiritual conscience intuitively approves?

"It matters not one jot, provided this course of personal loyalty to a cause be steadfastly pursued, what the special characteristics of the style of the music may be to which one gives one's devotion."[m] This, if over-translated, may be made to mean what we have been trying to say: that if your interest, enthusiasm, and devotion on the side of substance and truth are of the stuff to make you so sincere that you sweat—to hell with manner and repose! Mr. Mason is responsible for too many young minds in their planting season to talk like this, to be as rough, or to go as far; but he would probably admit that, broadly speaking, some such way (i. e., constantly recognizing this ideal duality in art), though not the most profitable road for art to travel, is almost its only way out to eventual freedom and salvation. Sidney

[1] *Contemporary Composers* (New York, 1918). Mason is answering an article by Moderwell concerning ragtime, which he has cited just above this quotation. For that citation, see Note 49.

[m] The passage is somewhat paraphrased. See Note 50.

Lanier, in a letter to Bayard Taylor, writes: "I have so many fair dreams and hopes about music in these days. It is gospel whereof the people are in great need. As Christ gathered up the ten commandments and re-distilled them into the clear liquid of that wondrous eleventh—Love God utterly, and thy neighbor as thyself—so I think the time will come when music, *rightly developed* [italics: Ives] to its now-little-foreseen *grandeur* [italics: Ives] will be found to be a late revelation of all gospels in one."[n] Could the art of music, or the art of anything, have a more profound reason for being than this? A conception unlimited by the narrow names of Christian, Pagan, Jew, or Angel! A vision higher and deeper than art itself!

VII

The humblest composer will not find true humility in aiming low —he must never be timid or afraid of trying to express that which he feels is far above his power to express, any more than he should be afraid of breaking away, when necessary, from easy first sounds,[o] or afraid of admitting that those half-truths that come to him at rare intervals, are half true; for instance, that all art galleries contain masterpieces, which are nothing more than a history of art's beautiful mistakes. He should never fear of being called a highbrow—but not the kind in Prof. Brander Matthews' definition.[p] John L. Sullivan was a "highbrow" in his art. A highbrow can always whip a lowbrow.[q]

If he "truly seeks," he will "surely find" many things to sustain him. He can go to a part of Alcott's philosophy: that all occupations of man's body and soul in their diversity come from but one mind and soul! If he feels that to subscribe to all of the foregoing and then submit, though not as evidence, the work of his own hands is presumptuous, let him remember that a man is not always responsible for

[n] *Letters of Sidney Lanier,* . . . 1866-1881 (New York, **1899)**, p. 113. The letter is not in the group addressed to Bayard Taylor, but occurs five pages earlier in the group of letters called "A Poet's Musical Impressions," of which all except the first were addressed to his wife. This letter bears the heading, "Baltimore, March 12, 1875."

[o] Margin of the MS: first-easy-sounds.

[p] Probably in *The American of the Future and Other Essays.* For such a passage, see Note 51.

[q] Omitted in AR: He should never fear . . . whip a low brow.

the wart on his face, or a girl for the bloom on her cheek; and as they walk out of a Sunday for an airing, people will see them—but they must have the air. He can remember with Plotinus that in every human soul there is the ray of the celestial beauty; and therefore every human outburst may contain a partial ray. And he can believe that it is better to go to the plate and strike out than to hold the bench down—for by facing the pitcher he may then know the umpire better, and possibly see a new parabola. His presumption (if it be that) may be but a kind of courage Juvenal sings about, and no harm can then be done either side. *"Cantabit vacuus coram latrone viator."*

VIII

To divide by an arbitrary line something that cannot be divided is a process that is disturbing—to some. Perhaps our deductions are not as inevitable as they are logical, which suggests that they are not "logic." An arbitrary asumption is never fair to all any of the time, or to anyone all the time. Many will resent the abrupt separation that a theory of duality in music suggests and say that these general sub-divisions are too closely inter-related to be labeled decisively "this" or "that." There is justice in this criticism, but our answer is that it is better to be short on the long than long on the short. In such an abstruse[r] art as music, it is easy for one to point to this as "substance," and to that as "manner." Some will hold (and it is undeniable—in fact, quite obvious) that manner has a great deal to do with the beauty of substance, and that to make a too arbitrary division or dis-tinction between them is to interfere, to some extent, with an art's beauty and unity. There is a great deal of truth in this, too. But on the other hand, beauty in music is too often confused with something that lets the ears lie back in an easy chair. Many sounds that we are used to do not bother us, and for that reason we are inclined to call them beautiful. Frequently—possibly almost invariably—analytical and impersonal tests will show, we believe, that when a new or un-familiar work is accepted as beautiful on its first hearing, its funda-mental quality is one that tends to put the mind to sleep. A narcotic is not always unnecessary, but it is seldom a basis of progress—that is,

---

[r] MS (crossed out): abstract. Margin of MS: get a better word.

wholesome evolution in any creative experience. This kind of
progress has a great deal to do with beauty—at least in its deeper
emotional interests, if not in its moral values. (The above is only a
personal impression, but it is based on carefully remembered instances, during a period of about fifteen or twenty years.) Possibly
the fondness for individual utterance may throw out a skin-deep
arrangement which is readily accepted as beautiful—formulæ that
weaken rather than toughen up the musical-muscles. If the composer's sincere conception of his art and of its functions and ideals
coincides to such an extent with these groove-colored permutations
of tried-out progressions in expediency that he can arrange them over
and over again to his transcendent delight—has he or has he not
been drugged with an overdose of habit-forming sounds? And as a
result, do not the muscles of his clientele become flabbier and
flabbier until they give way altogether and find refuge only in a
seasoned opera box—where they can *see* without thinking? And unity
is, too generally conceived of, or too easily accepted as analogous to
form; and form as analogous to custom; and custom to habit. And
habit may be one of the parents of custom and form, but there are all
kinds of parents. Perhaps all unity in art, at its inception, is half-
natural and half-artificial, but time insists, or at least makes us, or
inclines to make us feel that it is all natural. It is easy for us to accept
it as such. The "unity of dress" for a man at a ball requires a collar;
yet he could dance better without it. Coherence, to a certain extent,
must bear some relation to the listener's subconscious perspective.[8]
For example, a critic has to listen to a thousand concerts[t] a year, in
which there is much repetition, not only of the same pieces, but the
same formal relations of tones, cadences, progressions, etc. There is
present a certain routine series of image-necessity-stimulants, which
he doesn't seem to need until they disappear. Instead of listening to

[8] Inserted in AR: But is this its only function? Has it not another of bringing
outer or new things into a wider coherence? Is the side of the sense of per-
spection [perspective?] which is usually the first satisfied. unduly influenced
by some things made by a narrow (though natural enough) conscious "plan
of coherence"? How much of this influence is artificial and unnecessary? If
this question could be answered (and I wouldn't want to try it), would it
explain why many musicians are apt to slide easily into the habit of taking the
"past" as a stronger criterion for the "future" than is fair to the "future"?
[t] AR: A critic, by profession and nature, or anyone who has to listen to a
hundred concerts.

music, he listens around it. And from this subconscious viewpoint, he inclines perhaps more to the thinking about than thinking in music.[u] If he could go into some other line of business for a year or so, perhaps his perspective would be more naturally normal. The unity of a sonata movement has long been associated with its form, and to a greater extent than is necessary. A first theme, a development, a second in a related key and its development, the free fantasia, the recapitulation, and so on, and over again. Mr. Richter[v] or Mr. Parker may tell us that all this is natural, for it is based on the classic-song form; but in spite of your teachers a vague feeling sometimes creeps over you that the form-nature of the song has been stretched out into deformity. Some claim for Tchaikowsky that his clarity and coherence of design is unparalleled (or some such word) in works for the orchestra. That depends, it seems to us, on how far repetition is an essential part of clarity and coherence. We know that butter comes from cream—but how long must we watch the "churning arm"! If nature is not enthusiastic about explanation, why should Tschaikowsky be? Beethoven had to churn, to some extent, to make his message carry. He had to pull the ear, hard, and in the same place and several times, for the 1790 ear was tougher than the 1890 one. But the "great Russian weeper" might have spared us. To Emerson, unity and the over-soul, or the common-heart, are synonymous. Unity is at least nearer to these than to solid geometry, though geometry may be all unity.

But to whatever unpleasantness the holding to this theory of duality brings us, we feel that there is a natural law underneath it all, and like all laws of nature, a liberal interpretation is the one nearest the truth. What part of these supplements are opposites? What part of substance is manner? What part of this duality is polarity? These questions, though not immaterial, may be disregarded if there be a sincere appreciation (intuition is always sincere) of the "divine" spirit of the thing. Enthusiasm for, and recognition of these higher over these lower values will transform a destructive iconoclasm into

---

[u] AR: For some such cause, this man may find himself more inclined to "the thinking about" than "the thinking in music,"—more to "the looking towards it" than of "the going towards it."

[v] Ernst Friedrich Eduard Richter (1808-1879), German music theorist. Various works trans. into English, 1873, 1874, 1884, 1893.

creation, and a mere devotion into consecration—a consecration which, like Amphion's music, will raise the Walls of Thebes.

IX

Assuming, and then granting, that art-activity can be transformed or led towards an eventual consecration by recognizing and using in their true relation, as much as one can, these higher and lower dual values, and that the doing so is a part if not the whole of our old problem of paralleling or approving in art the highest attributes, moral and spiritual, one sees in life—if you will grant all this, let us offer a practical suggestion—a thing that one who has imposed the foregoing should try to do just out of common decency, though it be but an attempt, perhaps, to make his speculations less speculative, and to beat off metaphysics.

All, men-bards with a divine spark, and bards without,[w] feel the need, at times, of an inspiration from without, "the breath of another soul to stir our inner flame," especially when we are in pursuit of a part of that "utmost musical beauty" that we are capable of understanding—when we are breathlessly running to catch a glimpse of that unforeseen grandeur of Mr. Lanier's dream. In this beauty and grandeur, perhaps marionettes and their souls have a part—though how great their part is, we hear, is still undetermined; but it is morally certain that, at times, a part with itself must be some of those greater contemplations that have been caught in the "World's Soul," as it were, and nourished for us there in the soil of its literature.

If an interest in and a sympathy for the thought-visions of men like Charles Kingsley, Marcus Aurelius, Whittier, Montaigne, Paul of Tarsus, Robert Browning, Pythagoras, Channing, Milton, Sophocles, Swedenborg, Thoreau, Francis of Assisi, Wordsworth, Voltaire, Garrison, Plutarch, Ruskin, Ariosto,[x] and all kindred spirits and souls of great measure from David down to Rupert Brooke—if a study of the thought of such men creates a sympathy, even a love for them

---

[w] MS: All of us,—bards with the divine spark and bards without—. [Emerson, "An Address," I, 131: The divine bards are the friends of my virtue, of my intellect, of my strength.]

[x] MS: Charles Kingsley, Marcus Aurelius, Whittier, Montaigne, Paul of Tarsus, Robert Browning, Pythagoras, Channing, Milton, Aesch [crossed out] Sophocles, Swedenborg, Thoreau, Francis of Assisi, Wordsworth, Voltaire, Garrison, Plutarch, Ruskin, and Petrarch [crossed out], Ariosto.

and their ideal-part, it is certain that this, however inadequately expressed, is nearer to what music was given man for than [is] a devotion to "Tristan's Sensual Love of Isolde," to the "Tragic Murder of a Drunken Duke," or to the sad thoughts of a bathtub when the water is being let out. It matters little here whether a man who paints a picture of a useless beautiful landscape *imperfectly* is a greater genius than the man who paints a useful bad smell *perfectly*.

It is not intended in this suggestion that inspirations coming from the higher planes should be limited to any particular thought or work, as the mind receives it. The plan, rather, embraces all that should go with an expression of the composite-value. It is of the underlying spirit, the direct unrestricted imprint of one soul on another, a portrait, not a photograph, of the personality—it is the ideal part that would be caught in this canvas. It is a sympathy for "substance," the over-value, together with a consciousness that there must be a lower value—the "Demosthenic part of the Philippics," the "Ciceronic part of the Catiline," the sublimity, against the vileness of Rousseau's *Confessions*. It is something akin to, but something more than these predominant partial tones of Hawthorne: "The grand old countenance of Homer; the shrunken and decrepit form but vivid face of Æsop; the dark presence of Dante; the wild Ariosto; Rabelais' smile of deep-wrought mirth; the profound, pathetic humor of Cervantes; the all-glorious Shakespeare; Spenser, meet guest for an allegoric structure; the severe divinity of Milton; and Bunyan, moulded of humblest clay, but instinct with celestial fire, . . ."[y]

There are communities—now partly vanished, but cherished and sacred—scattered throughout this world of ours, in which freedom of thought and soul, and even of body, have been fought for. And we believe that there ever lives in that part of the over-soul native to them the thoughts which these freedom-struggles have inspired America is not too young to have its divinities, and its place-legends. Many of those "Transcendent Thoughts" and "Visions" which had their birth beneath our Concord elms—messages that have brought salvation to many listening souls throughout the world—are still growing day by day to greater and greater beauty—are still showing clearer and clearer man's way to God!

[y] "The Hall of Fantasy," *Mosses from an Old Manse*, II, 197-198.

No true composer will take his substance from[z] another finite being—but there are times when he feels that his self-expression needs some liberation from at least a part of his own soul. At such times, shall he not better turn to those greater souls, rather than to the external, the immediate, and the "Garish Day"?

The strains of one man may fall far below the the course of those Phaetons of Concord, or of the Ægean Sea, or of Westmoreland— but the greater the distance his music falls away, the more reason that some greater man shall bring his nearer those higher spheres.†

† For an insert intended for the "Epilogue" in a second edition of the *Essays*, "if there happen to be one," see Note 52.

---

[z] MS: wholly from.

PART TWO
OTHER WRITINGS

ONE

SOME "QUARTER-TONE" IMPRESSIONS

INTRODUCTORY NOTE

Even though Ives wrote at
length concerning broad underlying concepts affecting musical style
and expression, he wrote little that dealt with technical or theoretical
problems. Rather, he coped with such problems in actual tones; if
he had a theoretical idea, he wrote an experimental piece, and there
are many of them among his manuscripts. One of the rare exceptions to his general avoidance of specific technical matters in his
writings is an article on the use of quarter-tones. The article is particularly interesting for certain autobiographical passages, and for
the insight it gives into Ives' approach to new sounds. It shows that,
in spite of the scarcity of theoretical writing in his works, Ives thought
a great deal, and read more than many composers do, about the
musical material. While he was willing to take under consideration
any possible tonal combination, intellectually, he nevertheless placed
a typical musician's reliance, in the last analysis, on the judgment of
his ear—in his case, a very sharp ear indeed. Clues to the great variety
of Ives' technique may be found in this article—one being his

willingness to at least try anything, and the other being his rejection
of any dogmatic position (e.g., "Why tonality as such should be
thrown out for good, I can't see. Why it should always be present, I
can't see").

Materials in the Collection for "Some Quarter-tone Impressions"
are:
  1. An outline and rough notes.
  2. A handwritten copy (called MS. 1).
  3. A second handwritten copy (called MS. 2).
  4. Two typed versions (the second and final one called MS. 3).

The article was published in the *Franco-American Music Society
Bulletin* (later called the *Pro Musica Quarterly*) in the issue of
March 25, 1925. The present version takes this text as a basis, but
it has been necessary to correct a few fairly serious mistakes and to
revise the punctuation and the typographical handling of references
to notes of the quarter-tone scale. A number of footnotes are based
on MSS. 1, 2, and 3.

Ives relies heavily in this article upon the *Philosophy of Music* by
William Pole (1814–1900), an engineer, composer, and an examiner
in music to the University of London. Pole was thoroughly acquainted
with the works of Helmholtz and Moritz Hauptmann, and he quotes
these authors extensively. The Helmholtz references given by Ives
in this article are surely taken from Pole's book, as they follow variants
introduced by Pole as he quotes Helmholtz. (However, Cowell says,
p. 19, that "one of Helmholtz's books was in the family library" during Ives' youth.) Pole states in his introduction (p. 7) that his references are made to "On the Sensations of Tone, by Hermann L. F.
Helmholtz. Translated by A. J. Ellis. London: Longmans, 1875."
References given in the following notes are to that edition.

SOME "QUARTER-TONE"
IMPRESSIONS

IT SEEMS probable that in the various extensions of medium (of physical material, the processes of which are continuously occurring in some department of art) the importance of the two fundamental standpoints—that having to do with natural laws, and that with aesthetical principles—is always evident.

In music it may cause a situation more interesting or troublesome, as the case may be, than in most of the other arts, with the possible exception of architecture.

By extension of medium we don't mean to imply, necessarily, new material. The selection and use of different vibration numbers in some orderly plan, as we all know, is not new in the history of music. The music of many peoples and countries, ancient and modern, is full of smaller tone divisions than we are accustomed to. The ancient Aryans apparently thrived on quarter-tones;[a] how orderly they were we won't talk about now.

But if an addition of a series of smaller tone divisions is to be added to our semi-tone system "to help round out our old souls,"

[a] The first reading in MS. 2 was "Ancient Persians." This connects the passage strongly with Pole, p. 89, which reads: "The Aryans of Persia had originally, like those of India, a liking for minute intervals of sounds, for which they divided the octave into twenty-four parts, which would be equivalent to what we should call quarter-tones, each interval being half our semi-tone." Helmholtz, pp. 430—436, discusses Arabic and Persian tonal systems.

how much of a fight will the ears have to put up? What help can be found in known laws of acoustics—the physical nature of sounds? And how far may we trust in the free play of the mind and instinct —aesthetical principles? How far will our emotional reactions, our ear-habits, our predilections, help or hinder?

To go to extremes in anything is an old-fashioned habit growing more and more useless as more and more premises of truth come before man, though to hold that music is built on unmovable, definitely known laws of tone which rule so as to limit music in all of its manifestations is better—but not much—than brushing everything aside except ecstatic ebullitions and a cigarette. Instead, why not go with Wendell Phillips (who won't join a radical party or a conservative one)[b] and assume that "everybody knows more than anybody" —that all blocs are nearer right than any bloc. Helmholtz was deeply conscious of the danger of over-assumption from any single source:

At every step we encounter differences of taste, historical and national. The boundary between consonances and dissonances has been frequently changed. Similarly scales, modes, and their modulations have undergone multifarious alterations, not merely among uncultivated or savage people, but even in those periods of the world's history and among those nations where the noblest flowers of human culture have expanded.

Hence it follows (and the proposition cannot be too vividly present to the minds of our musical theoreticians and historians) *that the system of scales, modes, and harmonic tissues does not rest solely upon unalterable natural laws, but is at least partly also the result of aesthetical principles, which have already changed, and will still further change, with the progressive development of humanity.*[c]

Dr. Pole in his *Philosophy of Music*[d] gives similar advice from another angle:

The notion most generally prevalent among musicians, and embodied most frequently in works which pretend to treat of such matters, is, that the modern forms of musical structure, from the simple diatonic scale up to the more detailed rules of harmony and counterpoint, rest on some imperative natural laws, which will not admit of violation, or scarcely of alteration. The cause of this consists chiefly in a loose and indistinct idea

[b] The same reference is made in *Essays Before a Sonata*. See p. 41.

[c] Quoted by Ives from Pole (p. 13), who puts the quotation in the form of a prose extract, but treats it very freely. For the passage from Helmholtz, see Note 53.

[d] Based on a course of lectures delivered at the Royal Institution of Great Britain, in February and March, 1877. The book was published in Boston, in 1879.

of what natural laws mean, and in a fallacious appeal to the judgment of the ear, mistaking the force of education and habit for the promptings of nature.[e]

It is necessary here, at the risk of repeating what has been said before, to point out what a great tendency there is, in theories of harmony, to rely too implicitly on the argument derived from the appeal to the ear. It is assumed that because certain harmonical forms are approved, and certain others are disapproved by our ears, there is therefore some natural reason why they should be so. But this assumption overlooks how completely we are, in this respect, subject to the influence of habit and education.

No doubt, in the simplest elements of music, the ear has been the guide; and we shall see that there are physical and physiological reasons why certain preferences should have existed. But this appeal to the ear must not be carried too far; and when the ear is appealed to to sanction complicated effects of harmony, it amounts simply to begging the question. We approve certain things, not because there is any natural *propriety* in them, but because we have been accustomed to them, and have been taught to consider them right; we disapprove certain others, not because there is any natural *impropriety* in them, but because they are strange to us, and we have been taught to consider them wrong.[f]

It will probably be centuries, at least generations, before man will discover all or even most of the value in a quarter-tone extension. And when he does, nature has plenty of other things up her sleeve. And it may be longer than we think before the ear will freely translate what it hears and instinctively arouse and amplify the spiritual consciousness.

But that needn't keep anyone from trying to find out how to use a few more of the myriads of sound waves nature has put around in the air (immune from the radio) for man to catch if he can and "perchance make himself a part with nature," as Thoreau used to say.[g]

Even in the limited and awkward way of working with quarter-tones at present, transcendent things may be felt ahead—glimpses into further fields of thought and beauty.

II

The assimilation of quarter-tones with what we have now into some reasonable and satisfactory basic plan will be, it seems to me,

[e] Unless Ives was quoting from a different version of Pole's work (none other than the 1879 version has been available), this passage has been paraphrased. See Note 54.

[f] Pole, pp. 198–199.

[g] The passage referred to occurs in *Essays Before A Sonata.* See p. 69.

along harmonic lines, with the melodic coming as a kind of collateral, simultaneously perhaps, and just as important, but very closely bound up[h] with the former—in a sense, opposite to the way our present system has developed.

Man now is a kind of melodic-harmonic-rhythmic feeling creature, and we are an occidental, equal-tempered race—sometimes. We like our melody not straight[i] but blended. We like to sing our songs on the fence,[j] but not in Greek modes with intervals out of gear with our close harmony. Old Pythagoras was strong on 5ths and 4ths[k] but not on our swipe chords[l] or even our perfect imperfect 5ths.[m]

It seems to me that a pure quarter-tone melody needs a pure quarter-tone harmony not only to back it up but to help generate it.

This idea may be due to a kind of family prejudice,[n] for my father had a weakness for quarter-tones—in fact he didn't stop even with them. He rigged up a contrivance to stretch 24 or more violin strings and tuned them up to suit the dictates of his own curiosity. He would pick out quarter-tone tunes and try to get the family to sing them, but I remember he gave that up except as a means of punishment—though we got to like some of the tunes which kept to the usual scale and had quarter-tone notes[o] thrown in. But after working for some time he became sure that some quarter-tone chords must be learned before quarter-tone melodies would make much sense and become natural to the ear, and so for the voice. He started to apply a system of bows to be released by weights, which would sustain the chords, but in this process he was suppressed by the family and a few of the neighbors. A little later on he did some experimenting with

h MS. 2: and dependent on.

i MS. 3: as we used to like our whiskey [prohibition was in effect at the time].

j The old Yale fence had been moved inside the quadrangle in 1888. When Ives was in college (1894–98), singing on the fence was one of the pleasures of undergraduate life.

k The intonation known as "Pythagorean" uses the perfect fifth and fourth as tuning intervals. Pythagorean theory is discussed in Pole, pp. 91–99.

l For a reference to "swipe chords" in one of Ives' compositions, see Note 55.

m If Ives means more by this than a simple play upon words, he means that our "imperfect" (i.e., diminished) fifths in equal temperament are perfect halves of the octave, exactly equaling in size their inversions, the augmented fourths.

n MS. 2: "for" in this case.

o MS. 2: quarter-tone runs.

glasses and bells, and got some sounds as beautiful, sometimes, as they were funny–a complex that only children are old enough to appreciate.

But I remember distinctly one impression (and this about 35 years ago). After getting used to hearing a piano piece when the upper melody, runs, etc., were filled out with quarter-tone notes (as a kind of ornamentation) when the piece was played on the piano alone there was a very keen sense of dissatisfaction–of something wanted but missing–a kind of sensation one has upon hearing a piano after a harpsichord.[p]

As I've got into family affairs, I feel like keeping on. Father had "absolute pitch," as men say. But it seemed to disturb him; he seemed half ashamed of it. "Everything is relative," he said. "Nothing but fools and taxes are absolute."

A friend who was a "thorough musician"–he had graduated from the New England Conservatory at Boston–asked him why with his sensitive ear he liked to sit down and beat out dissonances on the piano. "Well," he answered, "I may have absolute pitch, but, thank God, that piano hasn't." One afternoon, in a pouring thunderstorm, we saw him standing without hat or coat in the back garden; the church bell next door was ringing. He would rush into the house to the piano, and then back again. "I've heard a chord I've never heard before–it comes over and over but I can't seem to catch it." He stayed up most of the night trying to find it in the piano. It was soon after this that he started his quarter-tone machine.

If there is to be a quarter-tone harmonic plan, what chord system will you use?

Chords of four or more notes, as I hear it, seem to be a more natural basis than triads.[q] A triad [using quarter-tones], it seems to me, leans toward the sound or sounds that the diatonic ear expects after hearing the notes which must form some diatonic interval [the fifth, C–G]. Thus the third note [a tone halfway between E and D sharp] enters as a kind of weak compromise to the sound expected

[p] This was an unusual reaction to the harpsichord at that time. Further, see Note 56.

[q] Ives' feeling that the basic chords should have four or more notes finds support in the theories of Joseph Yasser, an advocate of a 19-tone tuning (in *A Theory of Evolving Tonality*, New York, 1932). The basic chords of Yasser's system are hexads.

—in other words, a chord out of tune.[r] While if another note is added
which will make a quarter-tone interval with either of the two notes
[C–G] which make the diatonic interval, we have a balanced chord
which, if listened to without prejudice, leans neither way, and which
seems to establish an identity of its own.

It is assumed here that the chord is a division of the octave, though
later on, perhaps, greater or lesser periods than an octave as a unit
for larger, smaller, and newer scales may come as a natural development. But this is doubtful; the octave and fifth are such unrelenting
masters in the realm of the physical nature of sounds. Yet, at that,
they may be retained in a larger or lesser scale though not as a
boundary or principal division.

As illustrating the above, strike C and G on the lower keyboard
and D sharp on the upper (having in mind a quarter-tone piano
arranged as Dr. Stoehr's,[s] Mehlin & Sons [N. Y.], is, with two keyboards, the upper tuned a quarter-tone sharp). This chord to most
ears, I imagine, sounds like a C major or C minor chord [triad], out
of tune. Add A sharp on the upper keyboard and that impression
disappears. (To save time from here on we will write [only] "quarter"
after a note in upper keyboard.) If listened to several times in succession, it gathers a kind of character of its own—neither major,
minor, nor even diminished. A chord of these intervals, it seems to
me, may form a satisfactory and reasonable basis for a fundamental
chord. It has two perfect fifths, three major thirds a quarter-tone flat,
with an augmented second a quarter-tone flat completing the octave.[t]
It gives a feeling of finality and supports reasonably well a simple
quarter-tone melody. By quarter-tone melody I mean a succession of
notes fairly evenly divided between notes in both pianos or keyboards.
If the diatonic notes[*] are taken as a general basis for a melody,
using the quarter-tones only as passing notes, suspensions, etc., the
result is not difficult for the ear to get: it is agreeable and has its

* The term "diatonic" is used throughout meaning, of course, the regular
diatonic scale with its semitones.

[r] MS. 1: A triad leans it seems to me towards the sound or sounds that the
diatonic ear expects from the two notes which of course must form some
dia[tonic] interval, and thus the third note enters as a kind of weak compromise
to the sound expected—in other words a chord out of tune.

[s] Possibly Richard Stoehr (b. 1874), Austrian theorist and composer.

[t] The interval with the octave is not an augmented second but a diminished
third (A sharp–C). For the chord, see Note 57.

uses, but broadly speaking it seems to me a kind of begging the question. It is really a diatonic melody with quarter-tone coloring and seems to demand a harmony predominantly diatonic.

Again, the chord C G E (quarter) B (quarter) seems to me stronger in itself than the one we have outlined above, but the narrow interval B (quarter) with the octave makes it rather impracticable, especially in inversions.[u]

Another chord which might do as a fundamental is C E G (quarter) A sharp (quarter), but it appears to me that the assertiveness of the major third at the bottom throws the mind into a kind of diatonic expectancy which the upper intervals resist.[v] Besides it has no fifth —that inexorable thing—a part of the natural laws which apparently no aesthetic principle has yet beaten out. The fifth seems to say, "You can't get away from the fact that I am boss of the overtones— the first *real* partial. I have the octaves to walk on. If I'm not land, I'm sea, and you can't travel around the world without me." He forgot the airplane.

However, some day, perhaps, an Edison, a Dempsey, or an Einstein will or will not suppress him with a blow from a new natural law.

There is a little more choice if a secondary chord corollary to the fundamental is to be found. The chord in itself, I think, should give a feeling of less finality than the first. It should be absorbed readily by the fundamental, it should have lesser[w] intervals, and, in general, a contrasting character, and a note in common [with the primary chord], though I don't know that this is so important; it depends on the direction of the general motion or melody.

A chord of five notes of equal five-quarter-tone [i.e., minor thirds a quarter-tone flat] intervals (except the interval completing the octave) seems to meet these requirements.[x] This chord has a fifth, and if the second note making the first five-quarter interval is thrown up an octave, the chord has a more malleable sound and is in a more useful form—that is, considering it as above in the first position and not an inversion.[y]

[u] The narrow interval is B (quarter)–C. For the chord, see Note 58.
[v] For the chord, see Note 59.
[w] MS. 1: shorter.
[x] MS. 1: It appears to me that a chord of five notes—all of intervals of five quarter-tones (except the interval completing the octave) meets these requirements.
[y] For the chord, see Note 60.

These chords[z] stand up only fairly well when measured by the ratio of vibration numbers or the difference of overtone vibrations—"beats."[a] For instance, the interval of the quarter-tone flat major third[b] in the fundamental [chord] works out as follows:

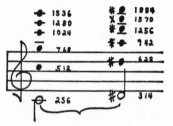

Differences between vibration numbers (difference tones) of adjacent partials 1 to 6 when a major third a quarter-tone flat (C–D sharp) is sounded: C–D sharp, 58; c–D sharp, 198; c–d sharp, 116; d sharp–g, 140; g–a sharp, 174; a sharp–cc, 82; cc–dd sharp, 232; dd sharp–ee, 24; ee–ff double sharp, 290; ff double sharp–gg, 34; gg–aa sharp, 348.

It has seemed to me that the value of measuring "roughness" is relative. I can't see why a great deal doesn't depend on how hard the notes are struck (their amplitude) or on the instruments playing them. The average ear feels the fundamental primarily and thinks in its terms. But as the effect of the vibration numbers of the fundamental is so closely bound up with those of the overtones—that is, the vibrations of all the partials as a sounding unit—on the whole the "general difference" is the safest thing to measure by. Still I don't see how one can always measure by vibrations he doesn't always hear.

These two chords outlined above might be termed major and minor

[z] MS. 2: (especially the first).

[a] The method is that of Helmholtz (Chapter X, "Beats of the Upper Partial Tones"). But the form of Ives' musical diagram (see below, where it appears in a somewhat revised shape) connects it to the discussion and illustrations in Pole, pp. 211-219.

[b] The printed article and the typescript read: "the interval of the major quarter flat triads." MS. 2 reads: "traids." The passage is not contained in MS. 1. The diagram given shows clearly that there is an error, the word "triad" having been used instead of "third." Since nothing but confusion could result from retaining this sentence in the text, it has been revised and corrected.

—more because their intervals are larger and smaller than because they carry the usual feeling between our diatonic major and minor chords, and partly because the chords of five-quarter-tone intervals offer possibilities for a minor or lesser scale which I won't try to go into now. There is also a chord—nine, five, five—which might do as a kind of third and subsidiary chord. It is comparatively weak-sounding, and therefore pliable, but its vibration measurements are all out of whack.[c]

To say that the above plan is of any certain value or of much security would be assuring something that cannot be assured, but it seems to me to give one reasonable and fairly satisfactory working basis. These primary chords, with their twenty-four possible locations and a melodic option of twenty-four notes in each octave, offer combinations and permutations that won't do our music any harm. A thing that has impressed me in trying out the chords used in this plan is that they may be played quite continuously without holding you up, as a repetition of diatonic chords seems to do. This is due, quite probably, to the ear's doing a certain amount of adjusting rather than "accepting on habit." In this connection, it may not be out of place here to refer to something that has been bearing itself in on me for much longer than a few years: the drag of repetition in many phases of art.

In a movement of music, a structure built primarily on a progression of chords not necessarily the same but of the same relative intervals seems more and more to hold up that organic flow which we feel the need of—it halts us so severely that a resort to other material is almost forced on us. As an instance, we may go perhaps to a series of chords, each different, occurring in cyclic repetition.[d] The process of finding whatever one feels is wanted in each case is mostly instinctive, but that there are underlying laws is evidenced by the fact that they may be traced in a general way after the notes are written down. As an example, it appears (but not always) that the greater the number of intervals [in the chord], the less is the movement of change, and that it takes place in the inner parts to a greater extent

[c] Counted upwards from the bass, this chord would be C-D-A-E. But there is no indication as to which notes belong on the upper (quarter-tone sharp) keyboard.

[d] MS. 2: a series of chords each different which do not repeat except as the cycle repeats and then not literally.

than in the outer; the converse seems true in a series of chords of fewer intervals. And it is not difficult to trace various underlying relations between the series themselves and the whole from different standpoints—for instance to the general motion, whether this be shown mostly in a single melodic trend, as in a song, or in a mass-melodic one in some other form.

Now all this may be obviated for a while—perhaps—by the fresh interval combinations the quarter-tone system may offer. Thus a few chords which one may like to live with for a while, with their many places of location, possibilities of combination, etc., may furnish something—I don't know exactly what, but something that many feel the need of today. This is all speculation on my part. I only hope for the best.[e]

III

A contribution of quarter-tones to rhythm may be in their ability to relieve the monotony of literal repetition.

A shift to a quarter-tone chord or tonality seems to drive in on the ear in a way somewhat similar to that of percussion instruments: and they may vary with the bass on the pulses. In a rhythmic cycle or series of uneven periods, pure quarter-tone chords alone or in a short phrase of definite tonality, used alternatively with the same in pure diatonic intervals, etc., seem to clarify the general rhythmic scheme. The quarter-tone family, like most other families, has a sense of humor. But that's a rather dangerous thing to refer to; it depends as much on where the catcher's mitt is as on the pitcher's curves.

IV

From a purely sensuous side, it seems to me that the extension of diatonic chords upward into quarter-tones offers possibilities. For instance, an augmented major triad in the normal scale and another based a whole tone higher or lower in the octave above (quarter keyboard) gives a feeling and color which, it seems to me, is not found in any combination of diatonic intervals.

An interesting effect (the manner of which is more physiological[f]

---

[e] For a paragraph which did not appear in the published article, see Note 61.
[f] This word is clearly written, "physicological" in MS. 2. While it could be a deliberate coinage out of "physiological" and "psychological," in MS. 1 it is clearly written, "physiological."

than musical) may be obtained by striking a chord on both pianos, made of a series of whole-tone triads[g] on, say, C C♯ D D♯, distributing them upward through three or four octaves. In this way all the twenty-four tones are caught, and in a chord not especially harsh. If the pedal is held, as the sounds die away, a composite is heard in rhythmic waves similar to the sounds one hears on putting the ear close to a telegraph pole in a high wind—"the music of the universal harp," as Thoreau calls it.[h] Perhaps he caught some of the composite resultants which other ears don't catch. If he did, his inspiration from natural sounds probably reached its zenith—for is not the simple resultant[i] one of the most wonderful and mysterious things in nature?

V

How quarter-tones will affect tonality, how they will help work out satisfactory polytonal and atonal[j] systems, involves so many considerations that I won't venture to say much about it—I've ventured too much already. But it strikes me that a great deal depends on whether or not satisfactory scales can be developed. If they can, listeners in future generations may enjoy or curse, as the case may be, tonalities a little longer. But quarter-tones or no quarter-tones, why tonality as such should be thrown out for good, I can't see. Why it should be always present, I can't see. It depends, it seems to me, a good deal—as clothes depend on the thermometer—on what one is trying to do, and on the state of mind, the time of day or other accidents of life.[k]

VI

In closing may I allude to two or three things or impressions that may be called "aural illusions."

With G B D in the bass, as a dominant, the interval C down to B (quarter) seems shorter than the same interval going up with the

---

[g] That is, triads constructed from the whole-tone scale (augmented triads). Ives uses these chords in the first of his three pieces for quarter-tone piano ("Largo").
[h] See Note 37 concerning such passages in Thoreau.
[i] That is, a difference tone.
[j] MS. 2 has no reference to "polytonal systems," but only to "atonal systems."
[k] For a passage quoting Pole which was in the typescript but not in the printed article, see Note 62.

tonic C E G in the bass. I've tried it several times on different days, some time apart, and I get the same impression.

A resolution upward—for instance in a chord holding C and E and sending F sharp quarter to G—sounds more satisfactory than similarly resolving A flat (quarter) down to G.

Both impressions are the opposite to those from similar resolutions, in the diatonic system. Helmholtz explains that a resolution downward seems more satisfactory than the upward because there is less resistance; it sinks easily into its place, requiring less physical effort (having the human voice particularly in mind).[1] Perhaps the converse is true in quarter-tones: that an upward progression requiring more of an effort drives the quarter interval into the mind and gives it an identity or character which the ear, not as accustomed to quarter intervals as the diatonic, must feel before it is lost again in the final chord.

Again it seems to me that parallel motion (in the quarter-tone system) is just as agreeable as opposite motion, and that the need of passing notes is felt less.[m]

This may be because the ear, as it gradually identifies the character of a chord to which it is more or less unaccustomed, feels disturbed in having that character changed, and because the passing notes, except in triads, usually have to go against quarter-tone intervals, and the ear is not ready for this abrupt dissonance. However, it is probably only a question of time till the ear will accept this seeming disturbance.

Inversions of quarter-tone chords do not seem as different in character as those [of] purely diatonic [chords]. It is usually admitted that the first position [uninverted] of a major triad, for instance, is stronger than the second [first inversion], and the third [second inversion], stronger than the second but weaker than the first. I don't seem to sense that difference in quarter-tone chord inversions, even in chords of uneven intervals with a tonality strongly in mind.

[1] Helmholtz, p. 550, reads: "Heightened pitch always gives us involuntarily the impression of greater effort, because we have continually to exert our voice in order to reach the high tones." The same passage is mentioned in Pole, p. 275.

[m] MS. 1: Does this mean that contrapuntal feeling will be lessened by a quarter-tone system. I hope not.

In this, as in the other reactions, it is quite probably my ear and not the system that is at fault.

All of the above are but personal opinions and impressions. How wrong they may seem to me in a few years or hours, I don't like to think, so I'm getting ready to say with the man who went to the horse race: "What I expected didn't happen and I didn't expect it would."

VII

Of the three short pieces that I've composed with the use of quarter-tones, the first and last were originally intended for a quarter-tone piano, two keyboards, and for one player.

The first movement, *Largo*, is primarily diatonic, using quarter-tones as passing notes or suspensions and quarter-tone chords as extensions or variants, though the middle section is of quarter-tone chord extensions.

The second movement, *Allegro*, for two pianos, one tuned a quarter-tone sharp is mostly made of rhythms contrasted or "split" between the two pianos. From a pure quarter-tone harmonic standpoint it doesn't amount to much.

The last is a "Chorale" played by two pianos as it stands written for one piano; there is very little doubling. It attempts to work along the pure quarter-tone harmonic lines outlined in the second section of this paper, and is based principally on a primary and secondary chord. A *cantus firmus*, taken by the upper voice in the coda, is made of a phrase in quarter-tones going to one in half-tones and ending in whole tones, while the harmonic plan remains throughout on a quarter-tone basis.[n]

[n] The last four paragraphs, describing the quarter-tone pieces, were given as an editor's note in the published version.

TWO

POSTFACE TO 114 SONGS

INTRODUCTORY NOTE

SOMETIME in the first half of 1920, Ives jotted down a schedule of "things to be done" on the back of a page from an early draft of the "Postface" to *114 Songs*, which reads as follows:

1. Article for Eastern Underwriter "Small Policies" (by Aug. 1).
2. Prefaces & Sonata[p] for Schirmer (by July 25).
3. Finish and copy "Circus Day Band" (as soon as possible).
4. After 1 & 2 are finish work daily on correcting "Majority."
5. Score #3 N. E. Holidays "4th of July" (anytime before Oct. 1).
6. (correct) Presentation, Torts (Insurance).
7. Send "20 Amendment" paper to magazines[q] (anytime).

---

[p] The first edition of the Concord Sonata. (The "prefaces" were excerpts from *Essays Before A Sonata*.)

[q] Ives sent the paper to the *Atlantic Monthly* on May 26, 1920, and two weeks later he sent it to *The Outlook*.

8. Address list for "Musical Courier" of names to send sonata (after Oct. or Nov.).
9. Select & correct 25 or 30ʳ songs for printing—also set English words for some of the German (Oct. or Nov.).

This schedule is a valuable summary of Ives' projects during a crucial period in his life. The last item ("Select & correct 25 or 30 songs") was not taken care of in October or November of 1920 as Ives had hoped, but in 1922, when the number of songs had grown to one hundred and fourteen. The collection was privately printed at Ives' expense by G. Schirmer of New York. While the volume has no preface, there are a number of footnotes for individual songs. What in most books would have been a preface—a general description of the contents, and an exposition of the composer's point of view—turns up modestly at the very end, as a "postface," so to speak (the text has no caption, nor is it mentioned in the index).

The "Postface" of *114 Songs* is one of Ives' most intriguing bits of prose. Its nervous loquaciousness, its not-too-subtle humor, and its bewildering syntax all would appear to cover the same sort of bashfulness Ives displayed at the age of thirteen, when he remained in the back yard playing handball against the barn door while his father's band marched past the house playing his "Holiday Quickstep" (see Cowell, p. 27). Ives' adaptation of "The Danbury News Man's" introduction to *Life in Danbury* ("I have not written a book at all—I have merely cleaned house"), while possibly a true description of the act of assembling the contents, is deceptively casual. It is now generally agreed that his song collection is the richest one of its kind by an American composer.

The materials for the "Postface" in the Collection are:
1. A number of rough notes and jottings (it is on the back of one of these pages that Ives' schedule is found).
2. A manuscript which can be designated as the first real draft.
3. A second and final manuscript.
4. A carbon of the typescript (p. 1 is missing) made from the final manuscript (Item 3).

ʳ Eventually, *114 Songs* (1922).

The version printed in the volume of 114 *Songs* follows the final manuscript and typed copy quite faithfully. That version has been used here except for the punctuation, which has been revised slightly. A few small mistakes have been corrected on the basis of the manuscripts, and occasional variants have been noted. Items 2 and 3 above have been called respectively (in the Notes) MS. 1 and MS. 2.

POSTFACE TO 114 SONGS

GREEK philosophers, ward-politicians, unmasked laymen, and others, have a saying that bad habits and bad gardens grow to the "unintendedables";[t] whether these are a kind of "daucus carota,"[u] "men," "jails," or "mechanistic theories of life" is not known—but the statement is probably or probably not true. The printing of this collection was undertaken primarily in order to have a few clear copies that could be sent to friends who from time to time have been interested enough to ask for copies of some of the songs, but the job has grown into something different; it contains plenty of songs which have not been and will not be asked for. It stands now, if it stands for anything, as a kind of "buffer state"—an opportunity for evading a question somewhat embarrassing to answer: "Why do you write so much ——— which no one ever sees?"[v] There are several good reasons, none of which are worth recording.

Another, but unconvincing, reason for not asking publishers to risk their capital or singers their reputation may be charged to a theory (perhaps it is little more than a notion, for many do not agree with it—to be more exact, a man did agree with it once; he had something to sell—a book, as I remember, called, "The Truth about

t This word in MS. 2 was originally "unintentionables." It was crossed out and "unintendedables" was written in above the line. In the margin, the word "intendedables" is written.

u *Daucus Carota*, in wild form, a weed; cultivated, the root is the carrot.

v MS. 2: (most of our friends are too polite to add—"ever hears"?).

123

Something," or "How to write Music while Shaving!") Be that as it may, our theory has a name: it is, "the balance of values," or "the circle of sources" (in these days of chameleon-like efficiency every whim must be classified under a scientific-sounding name to save it from investigation). It stands something like this: that an interest in any art-activity from poetry to baseball is better, broadly speaking, if held as a part of life, or *of* a life, than if it sets itself up as a whole —a condition verging, perhaps, toward a monopoly or, possibly, a kind of atrophy of the other important values, and hence reacting unfavorably upon itself. In the former condition, this interest, this instinctive impulse, this desire to pass from "minor to major," this artistic intuition, or whatever you call it, may have a better chance to be more natural, more comprehensive, perhaps, freer, and so more tolerant—it may develop more muscle in the hind legs and so find a broader vantage ground for jumping to the top of a fence, and more interest in looking around, if it happens to get there.

Now all this may not be so; the writer certainly cannot and does not try to prove it so by his own experience, but he likes to think the theory works out somewhat in this way. To illustrate further (and to become more involved): if this interest, and everyone has it, is a component of the ordinary life, if it is free primarily to play the part of the, or a, reflex, subconscious-expression, or something of that sort, in relation to some fundamental share in the common work of the world, as things go, is it nearer to what nature intended it should be, than if, as suggested above, it sets itself up as a whole—not a dominant value only, but a complete one? If a fiddler or poet does nothing all day long but enjoy the luxury and drudgery of fiddling or dreaming, with or without meals, does he or does he not, for this reason, have anything valuable to express?—or is whatever he thinks he has to express less valuable than he thinks?

This is a question which each man must answer for himself. It depends, to a great extent, on what a man nails up on his dashboard as "valuable." Does not the sinking back into the soft state of mind (or possibly a non-state of mind) that may accept "art for art's sake" tend to shrink rather than toughen up the hitting muscles—and incidentally those of the umpire or the grandstand, if there be one? To quote from a book that is not read,[w] "Is not beauty in music too often confused with something which lets the ears lie back in an easy-chair? Many sounds that we are used to do not bother us, and for that reason are we not too easily inclined to call them beautiful? . . . Possibly the fondness for personal expression—the kind in which self-indulgence dresses up and miscalls itself freedom—may throw out a skin-deep arrangement, which is readily accepted at first as beautiful—formulae that weaken rather than toughen the musical-muscles. If a composer's conception of his art, its functions and ideals, even if sincere,[x] coincides to such an extent with these groove-colored permutations of tried-out progressions in expediency so that he can arrange them over and over again to his delight—has he or has he not been drugged with an overdose of habit-forming sounds? And as a result do not the muscles of his clientele become flabbier and flabbier until they give way altogether and find refuge only in exciting platitudes—even the sensual outbursts of an emasculated rubber-stamp, a 'Zaza,' a 'Salome' or some other money-getting costume of effeminate manhood? In many cases probably not, but there is this tendency."

If the interest under discussion is the whole, and the owner is willing to let it rest as the whole, will it not produce something less vital than the ideal which underlies, or which did underlie it? And is the resultant work from this interest as free as it should be from a certain influence of reaction which is brought on by, or at least is closely related to, the artist's over-anxiety about its effect upon others?

And to this, also, no general answer must be given—each man will answer it for himself, if he feels like answering questions. The whole matter is but one of the personal conviction. For, as Mr. Sedgwick says in his helpful and inspiring little book about Dante,[y] "in judging human conduct"—and the manner in which an interest in art is used has to do with human conduct—"we are dealing with subtle mysteries of motives, impulses, feelings, thoughts that shift, meet, combine and separate like clouds."

[w] The "book that is not read" is *Essays Before A Sonata,* and the passages may be found on pp. 97–98. The quotation is free.
[x] MS: (as far as his idea of sincerity goes).
[y] Henry Dwight Sedgwick, *Dante: An Elementary Book for Those Who Seek in the Great Poet the Teacher of Spiritual Life* (New Haven, 1918), p. 38.

Every normal man—that is, every uncivilized or civilized human being not of defective mentality, moral sense, etc.—has, in some degree, creative insight (an unpopular statement) and an interest, desire and ability to express it (another unpopular statement). There are many, too many, who think they have none of it, and stop with the thought, or before the thought. There are a few who think (and encourage others to think) that they and they only have this insight, interest, etc., and that (as a kind of collateral security) they and they only know how to give true expression to it, etc. But in every human soul there is a ray of celestial beauty (Plotinus[z] admits that), and a spark of genius (nobody admits that).

If this is so, and if one of the greatest sources of strength, one of the greatest joys and deepest pleasures of men is giving rein to it in some way, why should not everyone instead of a few be encouraged and feel justified in encouraging everyone, including himself, to make this a part of every one's life, and his life—a value that will supplement the other values and help round out the substance of the soul?

Condorcet,[a] in his attitude towards history; Dryden, perhaps, when he sings, ". . . from heavenly harmony, This universal frame began. . . . The diapason closing full in man";[b] more certainly Emerson in the "Over-soul" and [in the idea of the] "common-heart" seem to lend strength to the thought that this germ-plasm of creative art interest and work is universal, and that its selection theory is based on any condition that has to do with universal encouragement. Encouragement here is taken in the broad sense of something akin to unprejudiced and intelligent examination, to sympathy and unconscious influence—a thing felt rather than seen. The problem of direct encouragement is more complex and exciting but not as fundamental or important. It seems to the writer that the attempts to stimulate interest by elaborate systems of contests, prizes, etc., are a little overdone nowadays. Something of real benefit to art may be accomplished

[z] Concerning this reference to Plotinus and one in *Essays Before A Sonata*, see Note 63.

[a] M. J. A. N. Caritat, Marquis de Condorcet (1743–1794). The attitude Ives refers to is that shown in his *Esquisse d'un tableau historique des progrès de l'esprit humain*. The work attempts to show the continuous progress of the human race on the path to ultimate perfection.

[b] John Dryden, "A Song for St. Cecilia's Day, 1687."

in this way, but perhaps the prizes may do the donors more good than the donatees. Possibly the pleasure and satisfaction of the former in having done what they consider a good deed may be far greater than the improvement in the quality of the latter's work. In fact, the process may have an enervating effect upon the latter—it may produce more Roderick Hudsons[c] than Beethovens. Perhaps something of greater value could be caught without this kind of bait.[d] Perhaps the chief value of the plan to establish a "course at Rome" to raise the standard of American music (or the standard of American composers—which is it?) may be in finding a man strong enough to survive it. To see the sunrise a man has but to get up early, and he can always have Bach in his pocket. For the amount of a month's wages, a grocery-clerk can receive "personal instruction" from Beethoven and other living "conservatories." Possibly, the more our composer accepts from his patrons, "et al.," the less he will accept from himself. It may be possible that a month in a "Kansas wheat field" will do more for him than three years in Rome. It may be that many men—perhaps some of genius (if you won't admit that all are geniuses)—have been started on the downward path of subsidy by trying to write a thousand-dollar prize poem or a ten-thousand-dollar prize opera. How many masterpieces have been prevented from blossoming in this way? A cocktail will make a man eat more but will not give him a healthy, normal appetite (if he had not that already). If a bishop should offer a "prize living" to the curate who will love God the hardest for fifteen days, whoever gets the prize would love God the least—probably. Such stimulants, it strikes us, tend to industrialize art rather than develop a spiritual sturdiness—a sturdiness which Mr. Sedgwick says shows itself in a close union between spiritual life and the ordinary business of life, against spiritual feebleness, which shows itself in the separation of the two. And for the most of us, we believe, this sturdiness would be encouraged by anything that will keep or help us keep a normal balance between the spiritual life and the ordinary life. If for every thousand dollar prize a potato field be substituted, so that these candidates of Clio can dig a little in real life, perchance

[c] Weak-charactered artist who studied abroad, in Henry James' novel, *Roderick Hudson* (1876).

[d] The remainder of this paragraph, excepting the last sentence, is from *Essays Before A Sonata*, pp. 92–94.

dig up a natural inspiration, art's air might be a little clearer—a little freer from certain traditional delusions: for instance, that free thought and free love always go to the same café—that atmosphere and diligence are synonymous. To quote Thoreau incorrectly: "When half-Gods talk, the Gods walk!"[e] Everyone should have the opportunity of not being over-influenced. But these unpopular convictions should stop—"On ne donne rien si liberalement que ses conseils."

A necessary *part* of this *part* of progressive evolution (for they tell us now that evolution is not always progressive) is that every one should be as free as possible to encourage every one, including himself, to work and to be willing to work where this interest directs, "to stand and be willing to stand unprotected from all the showers of the absolute which may beat upon him, to use or learn to use, or at least to be unafraid of trying to use, whatever he can of any and all lessons of the infinite which humanity has received and thrown to him, that nature has exposed and sacrificed for him, that life and death have translated for him,"[t] *until* the products of his labor shall beat around and through his ordinary work—shall strengthen, widen, and deepen all his senses, aspirations, or whatever the innate power and impulses may be called, which God has given man.

Everything from a mule to an oak which nature has given life has a right to that life, and a right to throw into that life all the values it can. Whether they be approved by a human mind or seen with a human eye is no concern of that right. The right of a tree, wherever it stands, is to grow as strong and as beautiful as it can whether seen or unseen, whether made immortal by a Turner, or translated into a part of Seraphic architecture or a kitchen table. The instinctive and progressive interest of every man in art, we are willing to affirm with no qualification, will go on and on, ever fulfilling hopes, ever building new ones, ever opening new horizons, until the day will come when every man while digging his potatoes will breathe his own epics, his own symphonies (operas, if he likes it); and as he sits of an evening in his backyard and shirt sleeves smoking his pipe and watching his brave children in *their* fun of building *their* themes for *their* sonatas

[e] See the reference on p. 94. Still another source for this "misquote" is Emerson's poem, "Give All To Love," (IX, 85) which reads: "When half-gods go,/The gods arrive."
[t] Freely quoted from *Essays Before A Sonata*, p. 92.

of *their* life, he will look up over the mountains and see his visions in
their reality, will hear the transcendental strains of the day's symphony resounding in their many choirs, and in all their perfection,
through the west wind and the tree tops!

It was not Mark Twain but the "Danbury News Man"[g] who
became convinced that a man never knows his vices and virtues until
that great and solemn event, that first sunny day in spring when he
wants to go fishing, but stays home and *helps* his wife clean house.
As he lies on his back under the bed—under all the beds—with nothing beneath him but tacks and his past life, with his soul (to say
nothing of his vision) full of that glorious dust of mortals and carpets,
with his fingertips rosy with the caresses of his mother-in-law's ham-
mer (her annual argument)—as he lies there taking orders from the
hired girl, a sudden and tremendous vocabulary comes to him. Its
power is omnipotent, it consumes everything—but the rubbish heap.
Before it his virtues quail, hesitate, and crawl carefully out of the
cellar window; his vices—even they go back on him, even they can't
stand this—he sees them march with stately grace (and others) out
of the front door. At this moment there comes a whisper, the still
small voice of a "parent on his father's side"—"Vices and Virtues!
Vices and Virtues! they ain't no sech things—but there's a tarnal lot
of 'em." Wedged in between the sewing machine and the future, he
examines himself, as every man in his position should do:[h] "What
has brought me to this? Where am I? Why do I do this?" "These are
natural inquiries. They have assailed thousands before our day; they
will afflict thousands in years to come. And probably there is no form
of interrogation so loaded with subtle torture—unless it is to be asked
for a light in a strange depot by a man you've just selected out of

[g] James Montgomery Bailey (1841–1894), founder and owner of the *Danbury News*, writer of humorous sketches which made his newspaper famous.
Since Ives was born in Danbury and lived there until he came to school and
college in New Haven (1893), he must have read a great deal of Bailey's
writing.

[h] The above passage is probably from a newspaper sketch by Bailey. The
passage which follows in quotes is from the introduction to *Life in Danbury:
Being a Brief but Comprehensive Record of the Doings of a Remarkable
People, Under More Remarkable Circumstances, and Chronicled in a Most
Remarkable Manner by the Author*, James M. Bailey, "The Danbury News
Man" (Boston, 1873). The quotation is adapted to some extent. For the pas-
sage, see Note 64.

seventeen thousand as the one man the most likely to have a match. Various authors have various reasons for bringing out a book, and this reason may or may not be the reason they give to the world; I know not, and care not. It is not for me to judge the world unless I am elected. It is a matter which lies between the composer and his own conscience, and I know of no place where it is less likely to be crowded. . . . Some have written a book for money; I have not. Some for fame; I have not. Some for love; I have not. Some for kindlings; I have not. I have not written a book for any of these reasons or for all of them together. In fact, gentle borrower, I have not written a book at all"—I have merely cleaned house. All that is left is out on the clothes line; but it's good for a man's vanity to have the neighbors see *him*—on the clothes line.

For some such or different reason, through some such or different process, this volume, this package of paper, uncollectable notes, marks of respect and expression, is now thrown, so to speak, at the music fraternity, who for this reason will feel free to dodge it on its way—perhaps to the waste basket. It is submitted as much or more in the chance that some points for the better education of the composer may be thrown back at him than that any of the points the music may contain may be valuable to the recipient.

Some of the songs in this book, particularly among the later ones, cannot be sung,[1] and if they could, perhaps might prefer, if they had a say, to remain as they are; that is, "in the leaf"—and that they will remain in this peaceful state is more than presumable. An excuse (if none of the above are good enough) for their existence which suggests itself at this point is that a song has a *few* rights, the same as other ordinary citizens. If it feels like walking along the left-hand side of the street, passing the door of physiology or sitting on the curb, why not let it? If it feels like kicking over an ash can, a poet's castle, or the prosodic law, will you stop it? Must it always be a polite triad, a "breve gaudium," a ribbon to match the voice? Should it not be free at times from the dominion of the thorax, the diaphragm, the ear, and other points of interest? If it wants to beat around in the valley, to throw stones up the pyramids, or to sleep in the park, should it not have some immunity from a Nemesis, a Rameses, or a policeman? Should it not have a chance to sing to itself,

[1] MS. 2: (by celebrated opera singers).

if it can sing?—to enjoy itself without making a bow, if it can't make a bow?—to swim around in any ocean, if it can swim, without having to swallow "hook and bait," or being sunk by an operatic greyhound? If it happens to feel like trying to fly where humans cannot fly, to sing what cannot be sung, to walk in a cave on all fours, or to tighten up its girth in blind hope and faith and try to scale mountains that are not, who shall stop it?

—In short, must a song
always be a song!

LETTER TO THE SUN

The NY Ev Sun   Sep 10

Gentlemen:

This is to supplement my telegram to you of Sep 2, requesting that the enclosed article (of Aug 29) which was printed without my request, desire, or knowledge, be not inserted again. It strikes me, that it would have been decent of you, if, before giving me this undesired publicity you had written and found out if there were more copies of the book, etc. I cannot afford to supply a public demand that "The Sun" might create—even if this were desirable (for the public!). If I'd intended to play the role of public-benefactor to your readers, I'd offer to distribute Schubert's songs—not mine.

Your Editorial (or Literary) dept. a while ago, kindly gave me permission to use words to No. 19, p. 43, No. 25, p. 59, No. 103, p. 240;[1] and the book was sent to show that proper acknowledgment of the curtesy had been made in it. It was not sent for public comment or to be reviewed,—though I'm glad of all the thoughtful, frank & constructive criticism I can get,—*I'm not looking for publicity.*

The idea in getting the book out was primarily to have clear copies that could be sent to friends and some musicians who might be interested. The offer to send complimentary copies to anyone was made in an inconspicuous place at the back of the book, and only in the thought there might be a few who having seen the book might be interested enough to want a copy—if there were any left over.

[1] The songs were: "The Greatest Man" (Anne Collins), "Ann Street" (Maurice Morris), and "The White Gulls" (from the Russian by Maurice Morris).

132

To those to whom I cannot send copies I shall write and explain the situation as best I can,—(as soon as I can get a week off!):

Please see that this notice is not printed again—nor is there the need of publishing this letter; just let the matter drop.

Yours truly,

Chas. E. Ives

In looking over, again, some (of the hundreds) of letters that came in answer to your notice, there seems to be a sincere interest in the poets mentioned, particularly Wordsworth, Whittier and Shelley. I'm almost tempted (and if possible I shall do so) to have another edition printed of some of the songs of more general interest, particularly those to the verses of the poets referred to, and sent to those who have written. It would help me out of the somewhat embarrasing position you have placed me in——an effort to keep good faith at least ——*but please give me no more publicity!*

C.E.I.

THREE

STAND BY THE PRESIDENT
AND THE PEOPLE

INTRODUCTORY NOTE

O N AUGUST 29, 1916, a Council of National Defense was established under the Army Appropriation Act. The Council consisted of the Secretary of War and five other cabinet members. It was to coordinate national resources and industry in the interest of security. Following the entry of the United States into World War I on April 6, 1917, the Council established on July 28 a War Industries Board to act as a clearing agency and to stimulate production and reduce waste. It was probably in reaction to the establishment of this board that Ives wrote a document called *Stand By the President and the People.*

The materials for this document in the Collection are a typescript and a carbon copy. The carbon copy has a note at the top of the first page which reads: "from letter in Safe, 38 Nassau, Aug. 6–1917." The address was that of Ives and Myrick, managers of the Mutual Life Insurance Company of New York, from February 1, 1914, to

April 30, 1923.[k] The face copy contains penciled corrections and some marginal additions. The additions are quite illegible, but the corrections have been utilized in the present version.

[k] Addresses are more frequent than dates in Ives' manuscripts, therefore they assume great importance in establishing a chronology. Kirkpatrick's *Catalogue* contains three pages of addresses for which he has supplied dates.

STAND BY THE PRESIDENT
AND THE PEOPLE

PROPERTY, in the name of efficiency, is trying to get control of the war machinery, and so more effectively establish itself in control of this country.

This is a war for democracy. It must be fought by democracy. It can be won only by democracy. President Wilson has done more than any other President to voice the sentiments of the people rather than of politicians. He has been quick to sense the great change that is going on throughout the world, the resentment and the growing social consciousness among the proletariat the world over against the medieval idea of government by property, carried to its most brutal extreme by the Hohenzollerns, but still hung to by some of the reactionaries of this country. There are a great number of these men in the United States Senate and some in Congress. These men feel safe in the exploitation of the interest of the large property of this country, because our government is one of representation. However reactionary their attitude, or political the cause, they point to the fact that this government is a representative government. It is only in theory.

The present state of communication, transportation, and education makes a change from representative to direct government possible. Fundamental questions can be put before the whole people, and the whole people can be trusted to act intelligently. The question of war, the question of peace terms, the question of free trade, the question of prohibition, are matters that should not stand in the hands of a group made up of corporation lawyers, and the type of men that now dominate the United States Senate.

It is time the people had something to say about the cause of all war: the greed for personal property. It is time the people had something to say about the limitation of personal property. It can't be done by taxation. The time has almost come when no man who has personal property to the amount of, say, $100,000 should have any active part in a government by the people.

Here are a few samples of the men who have a great deal too much to say regarding the people's government:

Root[1] $15,000,000.

Hurd[m]   3,000,000.

Wadsworth[n]   4,000,000.

Penrose[o]   5,000,000.

Roosevelt[p]—inherited an easy living. Never made a cent for himself in any legitimate business outside of politics.

Senator Fall[q]—who wanted war with Mexico, and owns $1,000,000 in Mexican mines.

Hearst[r]—who wanted war with Mexico, and owns $1,000,000 of Mexican property.

Shall we stick by the President and fight this war out in a democratic way, even if less efficient, or shall we let the country slide back and stay in control of property? Again we ask, who are the truer patriots: the sons of prominent politicians and friends of the

[1] Elihu Root (1845–1937), lawyer and politician. Nobel Peace Prize, 1912.

[m] Possibly Richard Melancthon Hurd (1865–1941). See Note 65.

[n] James Wolcott Wadsworth, Jr. (1877–1952), U. S. Senator from N. Y., 1915–21. Classmate of Ives at Yale ('98).

[o] Boies Penrose (1860–1921), U. S. Senator from Pennsylvania.

[p] Franklin Delano Roosevelt, then Assistant Secretary of the Navy.

[q] Albert Bacon Fall (1861–1944), U. S. Senator at the time. Further, see Note 66.

[r] The publisher, William Randolph Hearst (1863–1951), who inherited land and mines from his father, U. S. Senator from California, 1886–1893. Opposed to U. S. entry into World War I, and to the League of Nations.

rich who can afford to rush to Plattsburg[s] in order to get preferred commissions in the Army, rather than those who waited for the draft? The sons of the rich who are appointed on the staff of General Pershing, one hundred miles from the front, with one chance out of eighty of being killed, or the poor boy who has to wait for the draft and go in the trenches, with four chances out of ten of being killed?

It is time the people had something to say about war, about peace, and about property.

[s] A military training camp for civilians was established at Plattsburg, N. Y., in 1915, as a part of the "preparedness movement."

FOUR

THE MAJORITY

INTRODUCTORY NOTE

IVES' LARGEST single essay, "The Majority," was produced in that crucial period, 1919-1920, when he was attempting to get some of his major musical works into print, attempting to do something in his own way to correct the conditions which had led the world into the catastrophe of 1914, and, at the same time, continuing his creative efforts in the field of life insurance. Many of the ideas in "The Majority" were, however, of earlier origin. The MS provides a clue as to how early; a marginal note in the first section reads: "These questions were written before the war . . ." Another clue which indicates that the ideas were in genesis sometime before the final working out of the essay is found among miscellaneous papers in the Collection. On a letter sent to Ives on January 1, 1916, soliciting a contribution to a playground program, Ives jotted the following note: "If every man's moral consciousness told him that it was a social crime for him to hold & enjoy a personal property right of over $100,000, all children would have a natural & hence more adequate opportunities in all undertakings without your help——C. E. I." Limiting property rights of individuals is one of the main ideas expounded in "The Majority." Other references in the essay indicate the years 1919 and 1920 as the time of writing. In the final section, a reference is made to the 1919 Senate, and to the "recent" discussions of the League of Nations (these took place in the summer of 1919). But at a previous point in the essay a sentence scribbled in as a correction makes a reference to the cost of a 1920 pair of shoes.

Here is a list of materials in the Collection relating directly to "The Majority":

1. An early incomplete draft. Twenty-one pages, with mixed numbering.

2. A clearer and more complete draft, of which page 8 and pages 20–40 remain. This version uses (partially) the form of a dialogue between "George† and his wife." Some of the pages were renumbered, the original numbers exceeding 100, which suggests that there may have been an earlier, much larger form of "The Majority," or a different larger essay which contained some of the same material.

3. A complete MS, pages 1 to 84 (with a number of inserts on separate pages), from which the typed version was made. This manuscript, too, contains renumbered pages (in one case with numbers 201–208), lending further support to the speculation that "The Majority" either existed in a larger form, or absorbed parts of an earlier, larger essay.

4. A five-page MS marked as an insert for "p. 45, line 8, or later?" This insert was kept separate from the main MS. (Item 3 above), and was not included in the typed version.

5. A carbon of the typed version, marked "uncorrected" in Ives' hand on the thirty-eighth actual page (the typist numbered each group·of pages as they came from Ives, beginning with number one).

The Collection also contains pages which appear to date from the 'thirties (judging from the handwriting and the paper used) that deal with the idea of "limited property rights," but they do not seem to contribute anything really new to the discussion in the formal essay.

The MS (Item 3 above) has a marginal note on page 47 which reads: "Insert while dictating to Miss [name illegible]." That some

† "George" in Ives' writings is the personification of the average man.

of the typescript (Item 4) was done from dictation provides the only explanation for some of the errors in the uncorrected carbon, such as the following: "loss" for "laws"; "inner qualities" for "inequalities"; "fiscal" for "physical"; "Bathome" for "Beethoven." Other errors seem to have resulted from misreading Ives' handwriting, such as "Karus" for "Kaisers," or "cheaper" for "deeper." On the other hand, the typescript corrects a number of misspellings present in the MS, and the punctuation is revised for the better.

To print the typed version as it is, preserving all its mistakes and giving MS readings in footnotes, would be unduly honoring a typist who read Ives' handwriting poorly, could not understand his speech, and obviously had little idea of the content.

To print the MS as it is, giving the changes in the typed version in footnotes, would mean replacing the typist's misreadings with Ives' misspellings and half-done punctuation (both matters in which he was accustomed to relying on secretarial help, better or worse).

Since neither of the two main sources is sufficiently accurate to stand as it is (in the manner that the 1920 book stood as the basic text for *Essays Before A Sonata*), and a complete published collation of the two would be unjustified by the nature of the material, the version given here is basically the carbon copy corrected against the MS. Both versions are given, by means of notes, only when there is doubt as to the meaning or when some new insight is gained. While the typed copy corrects spellings of the MS and adjusts the grammar to some extent, further efforts in that direction have been made in this edition, although never to the point of reshaping sentences, as the typist seems to have done in some instances. Words (except for articles and conjunctions) inserted by the editor are in square brackets. In other respects, the editorial treatment corresponds to that adopted for *Essays Before A Sonata*.

THE MAJORITY

W HO are going to run things in this country—in this world, for that matter? A few millionaires, a few anarchists, a few capitalists, a few party-leaders, a few labor-leaders, a few political-leaders, a few "hystericals," a few conservatives, a few agitators, a few cranks,[u] a few this, a few that, or Y O U ! —the Majority—the People?

If some such question could be branded in the horizon, would it penetrate the hog-mind, the self-will of the Minority (the Non-People)?

These minority undervalues—personified partisans of the relative, never of the absolute—of the immediate over-obvious and external, never of the fundamental—of the search for commodity, never perfect truths—these party-digits are interested in the effect, seldom in the cause—in processes that tend away from the universal and towards the personal. If they are interested in saving mankind they are more interested in saving it in their own personal, exclusive way. They are sometimes even exclusive enough to call in the world's greatest idiot—"Brute Force"—who at first dumbly makes a big effort in their favor and then as dumbly exterminates them and their cause. The uncourage of these dull-values fears to trust men. It compromises with Nature's weaker side—Man. They are too timid to believe in the predominance of innate virtue. They feel easier in the protection which the inactivity of permanence temporarily gives.

[u] MS: a few nice old ladies, a few self-sufficient reformers, a few holier than thou know it alls.

142

Hence the many have suffered for the few—even the few who champion the many. The open mind of the Majority (the People) has been to a great extent over-supervised by the timidity of the closed mind of the Minority (the Non-People); for the Minority is selfish and the Majority[v] is generous. The Minority, broadly speaking, has ruled the world, necessarily, for physical reasons. These physical reasons, it appears, are fast being removed. Universal education is a substantial co-worker in this process, as is that "converting culture" which is transforming the complex simple truths of nature into a better material and spiritual foundation for human nature to build upon. The "Websters" will but little longer have to grope for the mind of their constituency.[w] The Majority will need no intermediary. The many are autogenerating a collective-personal social consciousness. Their governments, by natural processes, are passing from the indirect to the direct; it doesn't take a biologist to observe this tendency. The hog-mind of the Minority is one of the counter forces, perhaps the principal counter force, that is making this transition slow. The two strongest props in the scaffolding sustaining the hog-mind are: first, the lack of an efficient organism for better assimilating, clarifying, and then separating the detail from the fundamental, the secondary from the vital, and presenting the resulting premises to better co-ordinate the public mind; [and, second,] the other prop is pride—the pride that stops men from giving in after their conscience tells them that they are wrong—the pride that begets a cowardly courage: the fear of being misunderstood (a great mass disease)—the pride of accumulating more property per capita or per family unit than is "reasonably necessary" (two words which describe something easier to write down than to determine)—and lastly, the pride in the power which a personal ownership of surplus property gives. Ruskin backs this up: "Pride is at the bottom of all great mistakes. Other passions do occasional good, but when pride puts in its word it is all over with the user."[x] But, it appears, the hog-mind

---

[v] The MS reads dogmatically throughout, "the majority (the people)." The term "majority" is distinguished in this edition by the use of upper case M, and the parenthetical "the people" is omitted except in instances where it is needed for clarity.

[w] The preceding sentences relate to *Essays Before A Sonata*, p. 28.

[x] The same passage from Ruskin is also quoted freely in *Essays Before A Sonata*. For the source, see Note 13.

and its handmaidens in disorder—superficial brightness, surface or gallery thinking, fundamental dullness; then suspicion, cowardice, and fear; and finally "weapon-grabbing" (all a part of the Minority, the Non-People, the antithesis of everything called Soul, Spirit, Christianity, Truth, Freedom)—all this is retreating more and more in face of the great primal truths: that there is more good than evil, that God is on the side of the Majority, that He is not particularly enthusiastic about the Minority, that He has made Men greater than Man, that He has made the Common Heart, the Universal Mind, and the Over-soul greater than the individual heart, mind, and soul, and the predominant part of each. The Majority should have the opportunity of not being over-influenced. Natural premises—series of clearly presented facts, exhibits that show the roots of the plant—are the things to be sought. It is such nourishing food as this, not stimulants, that the Majority Mind needs. The Majority has a right to fully use its discretion, its digestive apparatus. Possibly the Majority knows how to use it naturally, more instinctively, more accurately, and in normal ways more conducive to the better health of the body-politic than the average leader thinks. If there is a storm, which there usually is at ebb and flood tide in the material ocean, possibly the Majority can pilot themselves through it better than the Minority thinks. For example, [in regard to the open question] between the theory of the present order of competition and of attractive and associated labor, it is reasonable to believe that, after the premises have found a way for adequate presentation, the Universal Mind, the Majority will sense a safer course than the Minority. The former, we believe, would come pretty near sympathizing with Ricardo that labor is the measure of value, but would "embrace as do generous minds the proposition of labor shared by all."[7] The Majority Mind quite probably would learn to go deeper than political economics and strain out the selfish factor in both theories, making a measure of each very much the same. Appeals to the Universal Mind will eventually, if not at first, tend to throw the artificial back towards the natural, but not to the disadvantage of the Minority, the artificial, because it [the Minority, the artificial] would then be of the Majority.

[7] A footnote in the MS reads: " 'Society and Solitude'—Emerson." This is not the source. See *Essays Before A Sonata*, p. 29, for the source and a parallel passage.

John Stuart Mill's political economy is losing value because it was written by a mind more a banker in substance than a practical idealist —by a Minority logic rather than a Majority reason. The latter [Majority reason] knows that there is no such thing as the perpetual law of supply and demand—perhaps not even of demand and supply —or of the wage-fund or price-level or increments earned or unearned, and that the existence of personal or public property may not prove the existence of God. But, more seriously, the Universal Mind knows, perhaps subconsciously, that there is no such thing as Capital and Labor; or, rather, to be still more serious, that there is no distinct difference between Capital and Labor—that they are but particles of the same part of Nature, particles changed by time or place, capital [which is] stored-up energy of past labor—that Labor is the muscle-part of Man and Capital the shovel-part—that somehow the kinetic energy in the shovel-part becomes potential when acted upon by the muscle part—and so more industry becomes possible, and so Man presumably enjoys life more, has a better chance to develop in many directions, and so forth. "Then what causes all the row?" asks a voice from the Majority (the People). The Majority Mind may reply that because some men, after the first job was over ages ago when Man first started to talk, either didn't think very far ahead and so threw their shovels away, or lost them through carelessness or misfortune—that perhaps the Minority (the Non-People) attacked a few of the Majority (the People) and stole their shovels. Or perhaps some of the group, for some good or poor reason, had never made their shovels ("capital"). At any rate, on the next job the no-shovel men had to take time off to build more shovels or to borrow from the plus-shovel men and pay by working for them ("interest"). So, to make a long story shorter, as time went on some men had many more shovels than they needed and many had none. Now, the process that causes this situation or condition is partly natural and partly artificial —that is, the thrift, mental effort and the industrious part of human nature is rewarded by Nature with a greater margin of comfort than the careless, the mentally and physically lazy part. But the Minority, the artificial, has inclined to start in where Nature leaves off, and to over-reward the "fittest," broadly speaking, and over-penalize the under- or less fit. So the Majority Mind sees that it is not Capital and Labor (the "shovel" and "muscle") in themselves that cause the row—it is the over-ownership by a per capita measure, the over-ownership of either one [Capital or Labor] that causes the trouble. And these arguments of the Majority Mind lead us to say that Nature may be willing for one man who has done well to possess a dozen shovels or so for the use of his family and for a rainy day. But when he wants to get hold of nine hundred and eighty-eight of every thousand, it is a desire and process that Nature, we believe, looks on as unnatural. At least she does not give a few fish most of the ocean, or the biggest part of the earth very little sunlight and the smallest part most of the light. Nature has her occasional favorites, but she plays no permanent super-favorites. She may believe that if the men who lost their shovels should each get another chance, it would be found, perhaps, that a reversion for reason of this age-experience to a higher specie of innate virtue has occurred. Perhaps Nature has even encouraged the artificial. We know little, perhaps nothing, even after all biology can tell us, of Nature's reasons for her discipline. The Universal Mind (the People) hears shouts on all sides from minority groups. The scientist has his conviction. The Socialist has his pet scheme. The captain of industry has his big plan. The Soviet enthusiast has his. The single-taxer, his remedy (perhaps the most natural of all). The syndicalist has his pet cure: for example, he wants all the shovel-makers to get together and manage all the shovel business. Now, this plan *may* be valuable to society, and if it is it will be valuable to the shovel-making group. But if it is an economic fallacy, it will be no more valuable to the shovel group than to the total group (society). But shall this plan or that plan be tried out? Yes, *if* you, the Majority (the People), after knowing all there is to know about it, *say so.* But the syndicalist or some of the other groups perhaps don't worry about getting the consent of the Majority. In fact, some of them may say, "What is the use of the State?" which is the same thing as saying what is the use of the ocean, or of food or of air or of human beings or the law of gravitation, or even its modern apotheosis. In fact, a State *is* a law of gravitation. It is a part of Nature as much as the child is of the mother. But some of these minority groups or their leaders haven't learned it, and they say their conscience doesn't approve of the State. A man's conscience may not approve of a tornado so sincerely that he puts his body in front of it and tries to stop it. But the Majority may suggest that his conscience would be better off if he gave his mind a little more attention. The thing Nietzsche or the Hapsburgs or the Caesars called "State" was for the most part but an artificial product of the hog-mind, the Minority (the Non-People). If there were three men living in the year 500,000 B.C., a State existed. It is the influence of the Universal Mind. It is the consciousness in the individual soul that there is a common or over-soul. It may be only embryonic in form, or it may be of a rare maturity of form, latent or active insofar as its functioning power is considered. Darwin found that inanimate life was governed by its "State"—natural selection (the Majority influence). Thus it [the State] appears when a man thinks he has struck on the one way of righting human wrongs by having each group manage its own activity as a separate unit, whether large or small (a theory which probably ought to be tried out sometime by all groups simultaneously). But when at the same time his plan leaves out of consideration all the other groups—the State, the Majority, the People, the sum of the consciousness of all workers— he thinks only half-way and quits, and the success of his particular group will only be spasmodic.

There isn't such a thing as the proletariat *until* it registers its consciousness. One group has no moral right to expression, or at least no social value in its expression, unless it is a part of the Universal Consciousness and acts with the consent of the Majority. Without this majority consent any action is but continuing in another way the evils of what may be called capitalism (that is, in its perverted sense popular today) or some other kind of minority influence.

It is easy to see what would happen among the groups if each should try to disregard the majority consciousness (that is, all groups), or if there were no way to register and enforce it. Suppose that the automobile and aeroplane put the railroads out of business, but that the steel workers are getting so rich that some of the cleverer laborers are becoming millionaires. Suppose they won't give or lend to or let the railroad men come into their business. Their business then becomes a monopoly, a trust, the surplus of which goes to none but themselves, except in so far as they spend it. What does the unfortunate railroad worker care whether the slicker steel laborer or the slicker Capitalist makes a million out of a monopoly? He's just as miserable. Even the most enthusiastic labor leader in charge of the railroad workers can't make a strike pay wages, if the public uses the railroads but little. He might call a strike to make the public abolish the automobile and buy railroad tickets—but where would the automobile workers be then? It is not the "closed shop" that makes the trouble, but the closed mind.

Again, assume that the syndicalist has accomplished the physically impossible, and has established a nature-anomaly, and has discarded the State (the Majority, the People). Who or what has the railroad man to appeal to? None of the successful groups will take him in; he of necessity then becomes the lowest group, financially speaking—perhaps a pauper class—and in the same way that the poor class usually have become what they are: fundamentally through little fault of their own.

But suppose that the steel group realizes that it has been more fortunate than the other groups, and agrees that all surplus (per group and per man, over a certain amount) be divided among the other groups—then they establish a "State," and that group which has the surplus eventually becomes the government, and a capitalistic capitol at that. From such a transition, things would probably go on again about as they have since the days of the feudal barons. The quicker witted, the less sensitive, the hog-minded ones of the various worker groups would push themselves forward and the term "leader" would be given them. Eventually, then, these [people] would become what are called "Capitalists." In fact, in some such way did the evils of feudalism, monarchism, capitalism, start. Things will go on in the same old way until the Universal Mind, the Majority Consciousness, asserts itself again and makes some better arrangement. Mankind will go around in a centerless circle—the wheel of hopeless permutations—until it finds the majority hub and hence easier riding.

Again, if the Communist begins to shout (not the reasonable kind partial to government ownership of public utilities and general socialization of some industries but the Communist in the essence, the furious but partial thinker who shouts: "Away with all group workers, personal occupations, and shoe horns and individual cigars! Make the State the great public grab-bag from which everybody can grab anything and nothing; make every man a perfectly free, nailed picket in the fence around the common burying ground!"—the primeval

doctrine of living that the old Peruvians had, or our Apaches had—
a kind of communism you notice in a flock of sheep), we are inclined to think that the open Universal Mind, the Majority (the
People), may begin to feel that this fellow's idea is rather an
emasculated one—that human nature, if it is forced to, may grow
down to this in a thousand years or so, but that a sudden amount of
perfect equality today thrown on the world would bring in its wake
an equal amount of perfect melancholy—for is there anything as discouraging to man as the right not to be himself? We imagine the
Majority may curiously look about for prototypes of this kind of
organism and find that there are several. In a mutual life insurance
company they find perhaps one example of "no-property-ahead-
labor": here there is no capital stock, no private ownership. But
though, on the other hand, the product is well manufactured—that
is, highly serviceable to the public—are they able to find an enthusiastic insurance clerk? And the Majority may not warm up to the
idea of becoming mutual community clerks for eternity. And among
the many Majority-thinkers there may arise a popular conjecture
that, somehow, if everybody has nothing, somebody must be trying
to get everything. They may remember some of the enthusiastic experiments in New England of over half a century ago. "Brook Farm"[z]
caused many chronic visionaries (every town had one) to organize
similar experiments. In one town, so the story goes, one "incessant
talker" (therein lay his "labor"), started a "Perfect Equality Settlement." There was to be no money used in its workings—only natural
exchange of equal labor. The leader (the most incessant talker) had
charge of the chicken department, the chickens personally being the
nearest practical exponents of the plan. After the settlement had
ended in broken equality, pledges, heads and perfect rows [quarrels],
it was found that the leader had apparently been so distressed at the
sight of money that he hid all he could get from the chicken department at night under the chickenhouse floor.

The Universal Mind will probably admit that this incident doesn't
necessarily prove that all commonist[a] theories are wrong. In fact,

[z] The labor-sharing farm and educational community of the Transcendentalists at West Roxbury, Mass. Founded by the Rev. George Ripley in 1841, and
sold (after a fire) at auction in 1849.

[a] This coinage is perhaps deliberate. In the MS "communist" was written
first and then deleted.

sincere thought and ideals have some value in them. And in this connection, it may be asked, "Who, next to 'Brute-Force,' is the world's greatest organic idiot? The one who sees no good in the new, or the one who sees no good in the old, or the one who sees no good in anything?" But this incident may tend to prove that the theory is wrong which accepts leaders as such and as essentials. A premonition may come to the Majority that, when they learn to better adjust their own destinies, somehow the hiding of money under chicken house floors will be a futile and uninteresting pastime, and as unnecessary as croquet.

But it is more than a premonition which tells the Universal Mind that, in the present state of world social-fabric development and consciousness, any plan, no matter how sincerely inspired, that takes everything away from everybody, or gives to any one or to any group an over-surplus with its corollary "over-power," cannot co-exist with and cannot stand up against the simplest laws of evolution and any progress in human nature—that it is "like unto the grass that withereth and as the flower thereof that falleth away," in spite of the fact that in expression the Majority Mind has grown little more than from the negative to the vague in the last few centuries. No group has been able to disregard the Majority Mind completely but for a short period, or incompletely for a long period. The Hohenzollern stunned it temporarily; it is now apparently discarded or inactive, or at least unexpressive, in Russia, but there it has never been fairly well awake. In the partial or temporary social chaos in many places today, it is fairly well asleep. But until the three last men of this world die, the divinely inspired Majority influence will guide mankind, we believe, more and more completely, and, with fewer and fewer lapses, lead it to eventual perfection. It will always be the compelling force, the social over-soul, the moral solution of every problem of the man-relation, whether measured in terms of the community, of the country, or of the world. The group pragmatists, the group Capitalists, the group syndicalists, the group naturalists, the group Socialists—all groups from the worst to the best of the Minority are powerless, inherently, because minoritily powerless to stand against this world molecular force. And, as this majority personality, this collective organism becomes more and more conscious of its mission, it becomes more and more dependable.

Do you think the world would gain nothing in material, moral and spiritual grace if it were confronted tomorrow with a certain miracle? And suppose the miracle were this: that all governments throughout the world, and all organizations or disorganizations posing as governments, should simultaneously realize the possibilities that lie in a more liberal interpretation of the underlying laws of Nature, or the futility of opposing them, if only by acts of omission—that, synchronically, they (all governments) put before all grown men and women (assuming they all can read and write) some such questionnaire as the following:

I. Do you or do you not desire your government to so organize itself that it can better register the Majority Mind so that the expression of this can be made a fundamental of all government procedure?[b]

II. Do you or do you not agree to have to employ no army or navy now and forever if the Majority (the People) of all other countries agree to the same?

III. Do you or do you not agree to free unrestricted intercourse in all transactions and relations between men, whether they be, in nature, commercial, industrial, racial, or religious, or whether they be something that has to do with the sciences, with art, or with any product of the labor of man's body, mind or soul?[c]

IV. Do you or do you not desire your government to undertake to formulate a plan or plans for your serious consideration, the underlying purpose of which shall be as outlined in the following ultimate aims:

A. To obtain a more natural and equal opportunity for each individual and family unit to share in the return of every valuable service he or it renders society:

B. Endeavoring to attain A by bringing, eventually, all occupations of man under the business management of those regularly engaged in them, and by trying to find a reasonable, natural maximum which, without retarding

[b] In the MS and the typed copy, "Answer 'Yes' or 'No'" is placed after each question.

[c] Margin of MS: (These questions were written before the war, & so do not take into consideration the present inter-nation difficulties).

human progress, should be placed on the periodical and aggregate return of each group or individual, whether this return be termed profit, wages, dividends, government bonuses, etc. It is assumed that this return [will] accrue from the activity of every individual in every occupation or group of occupations.

C. In this connection, B, by considering ways and means which shall presumably (with the least hardship as to working conditions and economic stability, and with the least depression to the initiative, enterprise, etc., of human nature) ultimately give the right to every individual or family group to own enough, but *only* enough, property to furnish each family group with the natural and reasonable present living, together with a fair margin for reasonable future contingencies. And further, in this connection, considering the advisability of reducing present surplus individual property to a corresponding maximum. Suggest here the amounts you think fair for a yearly return, an aggregate return, and a property maximum.

D. In this connection, B, considering how far losses must be shared by those engaged in each occupation, and how far and for what reasons the public fund (the Majority, the People's [fund]) shall share in the loss.

E. In this connection, B, considering a plan of conducting the public fund which is established from the excess part of the group and individual return over the maximum return and maximum personal property, and conducting it so that those in the employ of the clerical organization (the government) can have no individual opportunity, financial or otherwise, not common to all.

F. In this connection, B, considering how the Public Fund shall be used—as, for example, in the matter of old age incomes, educational systems, disability, health provisions, and general up-keep in cost of conducting the public business, for recompensing or partially helping groups or individuals from losses resulting from natural causes, etc.

G. In this connection, B, considering that, after a plan has been seriously and thoroughly considered by all and agreed upon, a reasonable time (stating the number of years) shall be given for the plan to be tried out, during which period the Majority agree to submit to the consequences, good or bad.

H. Optional questions in connection with Question IV:

1. What amount would you suggest as a maximum yearly return for each individual as a just payment for his services in group or individual occupations?

2. If a total maximum aggregate return and a maximum property amount is established, do you think a yearly maximum necessary?

3. What amount would you suggest as a maximum aggregate business return?

4. What amount would you suggest as a maximum personal property limit? (Answers to 3 and 4 should approximate each other.)

5. If you think that all should have the same return for occupational service regardless of value to society of this service, or that a man who is physically, mentally, and morally lazier than another man should receive the same pay, what would you substitute to give the better man a better future hope of return for his better services? And if you can suggest nothing to offset this survival of the worst, what hope do you think there would be of keeping humanity from degenerating into animalism?

6. If you don't approve of the above plan under Question IV, what plan do you suggest in this connection? Don't make a wild prejudicial general statement; any soap-box orator can do that. Don't get excited and make an extravagant sweeping outburst; an hyperbole suggests a losing cause. If you don't want to think any plan out comprehensively, don't suggest anything. Just answer the questions as best you can.

(Note: In filling in the suggested amounts, don't be influenced by your personal case, by what you are, or what you are not making now, or by how much or how little you have. Put down what you think, if you are able to, from a broad universal standpoint.)

V. Do you or do you not think it best for society at large that any group of people (provided the total population of this particular community group, say, is not less than five million) shall have the right by a majority vote to become a "people-unit" (a nation, a country, a state, etc., as the case may be)? Do you or do you not think that the above question is unnecessary provided the other plans submitted in the preceding questions can be satisfactorily worked out? This question is based on the assumption that the opportunities for better development of the fundamental life values in every community will be so equally open to all (because of the more uniform economic conditions under more direct government procedure) that it will make little difference to a man, as far as his living conditions and opportunities are concerned, what group he is associated with— the difference, if any, being from the viewpoint of personal affection, sentiment or preference for climate and similar conditions.

VI. Do you or do you not think it advisable that a United or World Police be established until the fuller development of the world social consciousness makes it unnecessary to enforce the will of the Majority in each people-unit (country or nation), and that the function of this police shall be to suppress with force those who oppose with force the will of the Majority?

VII. Do you agree that your answers to the foregoing questions shall constitute your conviction, will, and expressed desire that your government organize its machinery so that it (the government) in co-operation with the other governments or bodies directly expressing the Majority Will of the other countries (people-units) throughout the world can effectively (if only gradually) develop its ability to carry out in full the fundamental principles of the directly expressed will of the Majority?

If some such questions as these could penetrate at the same moment in the minds of all men and women in the world today—if this miracle could take place—do you think nothing would be gained?

The hard-headed business man (so-called) shakes his head and says, "Why discuss miracles?" The over-cultured professor of sociology says: "If all men and women could write and read, not ten per cent would read your questions, not ten per cent would understand them, and not one-tenth of one per cent would send in answers."

We will admit that the questions could be much more ably drawn, could be made simpler and shorter, but we will not admit that even as they stand only one per cent of 1,500,000,000 people would be interested. We have a premonition based on no adequate proof or experience, based on nothing more than a meagre personal impression, based on nothing more than intuitive conviction (whatever its source) that if this or similar questions could in some way penetrate the mind of every man and woman alive today, a majority far over fifty-one per cent would return answers—intelligent answers, answers that would contradict a common impression (far too prevalent) that only a few can think, answers that would help to pull the world towards rather than away from whatever divine standard the Infinite has conceived for humanity.

If thirty days from tomorrow afternoon at six o'clock a universal voice from every part of the world could flash its way into the total world mentality, do you think nothing would be gained? If at that instant a universal message could resound around the world "like the voice of a great Amen" do you think nothing would be gained? Could even the most abject Schopenhaueric cynic of the most effectively organized kind of pessimism answer, "Nothing!" and not lie?

A giant has been strolling down through the ages, occasionally walking erect, occasionally crawling on all fours, but ever steadily advancing—now painfully, now easily, now almost hopelessly—but ever slowly learning, though at times discouraged by his experiences, at times encouraged by them. Day after day, age after age, he has been witness to multitudes of sacrifices for his cause; he has stood by and seen many slain for his cause. He has seen Christ slain for his

cause. He has seen Ferro and Moore[d] and Lincoln slain for his
cause. He has seen martyr after martyr slain for his cause until his
eyes have become dim. And he now proposes to stop the slaughter,
for he is approaching a poise of mind, a strength of heart, that
begin to come somewhere near the expression of his soul. How long
before the few, the group, the hog-mind, the lower value, the Minority, will see the stupidity, the futility, of opposing this God-given
power, and learn in accepting it to do a man's share in bringing the
world, the Majority, the People, nearer a truer inheritance?!

II

The world's greater minds have always been of the Majority—not
in the Majority, but always *of* it. The underlying relation we have
in mind between the Majority and the Minority is one of procedure,
rather than of the right or wrong (which in themselves can never be
perfectly determined) of the definite aims or ideals [of the Majority
or the Minority], all or any of which may or may not be a part of this
basic and perpetual procedure. The procedure is interested in the
absolute—or better, in perfect or total expression, in the reaching out
for the future rather than arranging the present. The multitude of
the definite aims either are of the Majority, hence of progress, or of
the Minority, and hence of decay—insofar as they are willing or
unwilling to be a part of "the procedure." The Majority is born in
total expression, as far as such a thing can be total. The Minority
is born in "present commodity" or "self-will," regardless of the value
of its various definite aims or ideals. As soon as a man reaches that
weak mental state akin to the Byronic fallacy, in which he sympathizes
exclusively and completely with his own ideas, he then does not
know, and hence will not admit, that his idea or theory in particular,
and that any idea or theory, cannot under any law of nature or
human nature be with absolute certainty the best from all, or from
the same, standpoints for society—he becomes of the Minority and
valueless to society. But the moment his idea, by virtue of his own
tolerant and universal attitude, is accepted, experienced, and approved voluntarily by the people—he becomes of the Majority and

[d] The MS reads: "he has seen Ferro and [blank] slain for his cause. The
name "Moore" was inserted at the time of typing. But the reference must
be to Ferrer and Morral. See Note 67.

valuable to society. The old Prussian conception of the State illus-
trates in a way what we mean by "Minority"; and if it can be imagined that this State, as it was in every form and process, had been
accepted, experienced and approved *voluntarily* by the Majority,
then this situation would illustrate what we mean by "Majority."
The idea itself in the first case is valueless to society; in the latter
case the identical idea is valuable. And whether this idea [conception
of the State] benefits society in comparison with other ideas has
little bearing here, for a certain idea, even after being majoritily
and voluntarily approved, may benefit society only in demonstrating
that it has no benefit for society—at least in any particular stage of
social development. From Emerson to Isaiah and beyond, down
through the page-vistas of Carlyle, Voltaire, Goethe, Aurelius, Paul
and Plutarch, there is no tenet, thought, or vision without an ever-
present faith in the divine source of the "many," of all Nature—a
faith which recognizes *all* life values in their various attributes and
in their reality. These records of our greatest minds indicate that
their masters saw the truth of life-values, not by reason of their closeness or remoteness, but because they sympathized with men who live
them—and the Majority do. All religions other than those founded
upon the absolute authority of the most primitive superstitions
reveal this fundamental sympathy for spirit over form. Confucius
and Buddha to a certain extent wanted their followers to think in
terms of reason rather than form. "The private store of reason is
not great. Would that there were a public store for man," cries Pascal.
"But there is," says Emerson. "It is the Common Heart, the Over-
soul and the Universal Mind," an institution congenital with Man's
mind. Pascal is discouraged because he permits himself to become
influenced by political and religious history and not by the religious
spirit of each [history].[e] Prophecy calculated from various literal
phenomena of history seems more discouraging than [is] necessary.
In his chapter, "The National View of Civilization," Professor
Petrie[f] says, in part: ". . . government is of great concern, but of
little import. . . . What man *does* is the essential in each civilization, . . . the relations between the different classes of a country, are

e The passage beginning with "The private store . . ." occurs in a slightly
different form in *Essays Before A Sonata*, p. 34.

f Sir (William Matthew) Hinders Petrie (1853–1942), English Egyptologist.

merely subsidiary. England, France and Russia will be remembered
by Newton, Pasteur, and Mendelieff, when all their forms of government are forgotten."[g] But, possibly, if there had been a growth in the
science of government analogous to that of the other sciences—or,
better, if more care had been taken by society in general to make the
science of government keep pace with social evolution—there might
have been more Newtons, Pasteurs, and Mendelieffs to be remembered. In his formula of civilization periods, the same authority,
Petrie, places at the start an autocracy of greater or lesser scope, then
an oligarchy in which

> the unity of the country can be maintained by law instead of by au-
> tocracy. This stage varies in length; in Greece and Rome it was about
> four centuries, in Mediaeval Europe about five or six centuries.
>   Then gradually the transformation to a democracy takes place. . . .
> During this time . . . wealth—that is, accumulated capital of facilities—
> continues to increase. When democracy has attained full power, the ma-
> jority without capital necessarily eat up the capital of the minority, and
> the civilization steadily decays, until the inferior population is swept away
> to make room for a fitter people.[h]

But an over-rigid analogy suggests an over-truth and reminds us of
what Thoreau said about going to old men for advice and thus learning that anything that can be done, but hasn't been done, can't be
done. Perhaps "Old Man History's" picture of the ebb and flow in
the oceans of previous civilizations may not furnish a perennial background for illustrating the limit or quality of ours or of all future
civilizations. The democracies of former periods were not underwritten, so to speak, by the quality or quantity of present-day assets
in social consciousness. The rank and file, until comparatively recently, had little opportunity for mental development—in fact, little
opportunity for anything except the right to stupidity, which was
used either for no expression or mob-expression. That mob action is
not uncommon today does not invalidate any of the above theories
or expressions or take aught from our hope. It is but a relic of fetish
worship, or of the old-fashioned idea of trusting all to a leader—to
one instead of the *many*—a spasm caused by the old tendency to
personal and impulsive, against [as opposed to] collective, thought.

[g] In *The Revolutions of Civilisation* (London and New York, 1911), p. 123.
[h] *Revolutions*, pp. 123–124.

The action of a mob is often a miscarriage of a true expression because of the underdevelopment in the machinery of true expression. The action of a mob does not necessarily mean that a majority of its members are stupid, immoral or brutal. If they had been trained or more accustomed to direct and definite processes of collective consideration and expression, of turning to themselves instead of turning to leaders, their righteous indignation would not so easily turn to crime, and their unjust indignation would be more easily dissolved. The first impulse, whether of high moral import or of low animal instinct, would function or not function, as the case may be. What we are trying to say is that, in our opinion, if the Majority Mind had been trained in some more direct method in expressing and taking responsibility for its impulses, there would be fewer mobs. The average mean [middle] mentality of our democracy is probably equal in quality to that of the aristocracy of the Grecian civilization in the time of Lycurgus.[1] Possibly the average mind in the United States today could, after a short period of specialized concentration, equal in quality of thought-substance [the average mind assumed in] Plato's *Republic;* that is, an absolute, not a relative, comparison would show that the Majority Mind of today has gained much of the power that only over-average minds had in Plato's time. And so, Pascal stares at the distinct struggle of the group led by the individual rather than [at] the imperceptible progress of the individual led by himself. This struggle is as much privately caused as privately led. For ages, [for] physical reasons (or perhaps more strictly, cosmic influences) the group has had to depend upon the individual as leader. And the leaders, with few exceptions, have restrained the Universal Mind and trusted to the private store.

The term "leader" is used here more in the sense of the opportunist who sees, no matter what the cause, a chance for speculation in self-profit (in wealth, power, glory, etc.), usually in the common and many situations current in the running of a community's military or political machinery. Whatever quality for success was given him in this way, he planks down, regardless of all else. Napoleon is a good example of that kind of leader. But the possessors of the higher and greater influences which reach even beyond the human

[1] 396—325 B.C. Attic orator who managed Athens' finances for twelve years.

and moral to deep spiritual values, though essentially leaders, are not usually catalogued as such. Ruskin is a good example of this kind of guiding influence. However, thanks to the lessons in evolution which Nature has been teaching since and before the first page of the *Vedas*, the public store of reason is gradually taking the place of the once-needed leader. From the Chaldean tablet to the wireless message, the public store has been wonderfully opened. The results of these lessons, the possibilities they are offering for ever coordinating the mind of humanity, the culmination of this age-instruction, are seen today in many manifestations. But in their working-out, probably by reason of tradition, the hog-mind of the few, the Minority, comes too easily into play. The owners of this article have too easily had first say, and so they (for want of a better or worse name) have been called "leaders." But now even these thick-skins are beginning to see that the movement is the leader, and that they are only clerks. Broadly speaking, the effects evidenced in the political side of history have been so much of the physical because the causes have been so much of the physical. As a result, the leaders, for the most part, have been under-average men with skins-thick, hands-slick, and wits-quick with under-values—for no one but the Infinite can be quick with over-values, and these men quite probably if differently constituted would not have become leaders. And so the day of leaders, as such, is gradually closing—the people are beginning to lead themselves— the public store is being opened; the Common Heart, the Over-soul and the Universal Mind are coming into their own. "Let us believe in God, and not in names and places and persons." Thus speaks America's greatest statesman, and one who never held public office.ʲ It is discouraging for thinking persons nowadays—and the Majority today are thinking—to go to the polls and find nothing on the ballots but a mass of names and party emblems staring dumbly up at them. Election day seems less and less to measure up to the need for expression. On every hand, we see and feel the pent-up desire for self-expression—a desire of the Majority to register their convictions. It cannot be permanently satisfied or adequately registered in terms of any few, any group or any minority, for prejudice has no part in

ʲ Emerson. For the quotation (which is also in *Essays Before A Sonata*), see Note 18.

social progress (no more than it has in the evolution of nature), or in the advance of morality, or in the spiritual life.

III

If a security of outline in all aspects of life is better reflected by remote cosmic laws than by personal speculation towards the immediate, we are perhaps more justified in talking primarily on world terms; besides, it is just as easy to *talk* in world terms as it is in terms of the back yard. And it is a fairly safe way of avoiding troublesome details of the concrete. It is easy for us in the United States to criticize what we do not like in Turkey, Russia or the South Pole. It is not quite so easy to always remember and put into practice a suggestion of Thoreau, which in substance is that the sincere *example* of one good man will do all mankind more good than all of Man's elaborately devised admonitions.ᵏ What can we do in this country to better learn to express or visibly reproduce for the common good the better feelings of our hearts and the better thoughts of our minds? How can a truer expression of the Majority be obtained? One thing is certain: it cannot be obtained overnight—and if it could it would be a bad job. And another thing that is certain: for its eventual attainment we must keep constantly at it, and not constantly [keep] thinking or saying that it cannot be done. In the next place, the Federal Constitution furnishes the mechanism, in some ways fundamental and in some ways embryonic. If we can draft every able-bodied man to fight for us, we can draft every able-minded man and woman to think for us, and the Majority are able-minded. It seems to the writer that the men who signed the Declaration of Independence and drafted our Constitution had the hope of some such ultimate process in mind. But more direct means of popular expression were obviously impossible in 1776. To place more responsibility upon the electorate is in accordance with the general design of our government. How much it will stand without causing confusion and inefficiency is what must be learned by sane experiments. To get orders from the people on fundamental questions is an easier (or simpler) thing to suggest than to tell how it can best be done, and to know what are and what are not "fundamental questions."

ᵏ A marginal note reads: "look up exact quotation." The passage was quoted in *Essays Before A Sonata*. See p. 59.

But assuming that it all can be done, and well done, the plan that does it will tend to perfect rather than change the form of our Government, though it will gradually eliminate all political parties and tend eventually to make the government in itself but an efficient clerical organization which shall carry out in detail the basic plans that the Majority propose. The general idea seems to us to be possible, and to be as practicable today as it was impossible in 1819. Why it is not impossible now, it strikes us, can be seen for several reasons: for instance (without going into detail), by a study of the illiteracy ratios as far back as obtainable, and in the fact that today a man can sit down and talk to his brother in San Francisco, receive a co-daily message from Cape Town, and hear the voice of a dead man make a speech on modern business efficiency—and all in the same three minutes. Political parties were, of course, in their inception, but ways of natural expression concerning certain social or political principles which could not be expressed by other means at that time. What we have in mind (and we believe millions of others have) is something more than [government by] "initiative" and "referendum"—an institution about which the most surprising thing is that it was not adopted long ago under a national constitutional amendment. It is now, we understand, still before the Senate or House Judiciary Committee. It is one of the most, if not *the* most, important questions before Congress today, and it ought to be adopted immediately. The experience generally reviewed, [that] of the twenty-one states which adopted referendum constitutional amendments previous to January 1919,[1] has shown some good results, but even if this experience had proven decidedly otherwise, it would be no indication that the plan was useless or impractical. Even Mercury could not run a mile in ten seconds. That the referendum idea is taken seriously and that the non-voters do not throw the results towards Minority rule is shown by the percentages in the returns of the states using the referendum from 1904 to 1916. The important measures submitted received 84.6 per cent of the total vote, and the less important measures 68.3 per cent, making an average of 75.7 per cent. In the vote for President (1916), in fourteen States, 4,355,-062 out of the 4,785,783 votes were given to the most important

---

[1] Oregon made initiative and referendum laws a part of the state constitution in 1902. Most other states that adopted such laws followed the Oregon pattern.

measures. This shows that people are willing to take responsibility, and for our part we believe they will act wisely under it. The experience of referendum proceedings in Switzerland[m] shows more favorable results than otherwise. However, the initiative and referendum, at its best, is remedial or corrective rather than constructive; it is more an emergency expedient than a creative organic force. There are many difficulties—so many that even the most uninterested may become interested in the process of obtaining, or learning how to obtain, an accurate expression of the component-public mind—of the thought of the Majority—and of using it for the common good. The process must have to do with total expression—not group expression, not leaders' expression or mere representative expression, and not the combined expression of [certain] group or individuals. Naturally, each group will propose and vote for measures that favor its pursuits, but a total-people-consideration will tend to discover the prejudice, the self-factor, the hog-mind part in group or individual expression. The group must not function as a group, or as an individual representing any group or groups, or any few, or any individual.

Every individual will have a chance for all expression, but not primarily as a group or party man, for the expression will be approved or not approved by all individuals, and by them not primarily as group men or partisans. It must be assumed, in the final analysis and consideration of all social phenomena, that the Majority, right or wrong, are always right. If the farmers of a country happen to number fifty-one million, and all the other groups together number but forty-nine million, the farmers will be right, right or wrong—that is, socially speaking, purely—and, incidentally, more individuals will become farmers. But it is hardly possible that one group or even a few groups will constitute the Majority, though if they do it will be because they represent the greatest essentials for all, and hence the other groups will be so necessary and important to them that they, the Majority group, cannot monopolize even their own efforts—that is, not for long before they would find that this would make it so much the worse for them. Though in this connection, in deciding any measure that relates particularly to group interests and occupations, if the Majority think it best, a two-thirds plurality vote could be adopted, or some such statutory requirement as that which obtains in New Zealand.[n] A small majority decision naturally does not relieve the tension that a plurality does. A large minority is a weight sometimes against the better carrying out of a majority measure for the common good. But organically speaking, whether the majority is increased by some higher set limit in particular voting measures is a detail that the Majority can settle for themselves.

The principal difficulty in any plan of functioning mass expression will not be, we believe, because the Majority Mind will not act normally, that is, intelligently, if the premises are all before it (a difficulty which many of those who class themselves as "artistic" or "aesthetic," or who feel that theirs is an ultra-intellectually-sensitive temperament will call insurmountable). The difficulty will not be one of constitutional procedure, or of perfecting a plan under our Federal Constitution—a difficulty which to some legislators, especially of the lawyer class, and to some elderly editorial writers will be insurmountable. The greatest difficulty, it seems to us, will be in distinguishing or separating the fundamental from the secondary, the basic from the detail, and in determining when a particular aspect or tendency passes from the minor to the major—in focusing on and knowing what are the few great questions, not what are the many secondary ones. The questions in which the moral element is more predominant than the economic will not be difficult for mass disposal—for instance, those of child labor, the League of Nations, the right to strike of public officials (including policemen and firemen and any who have to do especially with the protection of women, children, invalids, etc.); universal compulsory military service, universal training, etc.; prohibition, war of conquest or intervention, etc. But in measures predominantly economic or of the business relation, the many-sided technicalities and intricate phases make them seemingly discouraging subjects for popular consideration and decision. The tariff is one of these issues, though it is not the problem it has been. In many of these economic questions there is often one

[n] New Zealand adopted the initiative and referendum procedures in 1901. The Prime Minister must have a majority.

vital point which, if clearly demonstrated, would tend to solve the total problem. For example, if it could be demonstrated to open minds (and an unprejudiced state of economics has brought practically all economists to the conviction that it is a truth that can be proved) that tariff protection does not raise wages or keep them up except in unnatural or non-indigenous occupations or industries—if the Majority could clearly be made to perceive this point, the whole tariff question° could be settled comparatively quickly, accurately, and presumably more satisfactorily to all. But in many cases the Majority will not have an easy time in doing their duty.

IV

The various suggestions which are outlined in this paper are but to illustrate what one man would feel like including in his primary or suggestive ballot. Doubtless some, perhaps all, of his plans will not be acceptable to the Majority, and in that case there are presumably good reasons that they have little value, at least for the present. To some, merely suggesting a remedy for either a national difficulty or a cold in the head, suggesting it in any but a cursory way, is an indication of a dogmatic state of mind on the part of the suggestor. If any of our paragraphs seem dogmatic, it is not because of any premeditated intention.

Considering plans or experiments for increasing the common unit of comfort—as, for instance, the federalization or nationalization (or call it socialization) of public utilities and industries—the intermediate process is where the thought must be given, rather than at the obvious beginning or end. For instance, the railroad man may say: "We want more money to live on; therefore, let us all manage the railroads and we will have more money." These are obvious starting and ending aims, but how can the men be sure that if they do manage their industry they will have more money? The writer thinks that eventually, if they can weather discouragement, they will have more, but it will be by a process in which they will have to solve [problems] and take responsibility for many things they do not now.

° Tariffs had been lowered by the Underwood Tariff Act of 1913. The question in 1920 was whether or not to raise them again to levels resembling those of the McKinley Tariff Act of 1890. They were raised by the Fordney-McCumber Tariff Act of 1922.

The Plumb[p] plan has many good working ideas; so have other plans. But suppose the public won't use the railroads enough to make them pay? Or suppose that while group management is learning, experimenting and perfecting its efficiency there are losses (or call them "disappointments," if you don't like the word "losses"), if only temporary, and that the disappointments are greater than those other groups suffer, is it the railroad workers' duty to the Majority to continue in the railroad business or to go to more prosperous occupations?

Contingencies like this will have to be planned for in advance to some extent if any group management is to come out where it expects to. Group management can only be successful by the same process as that of private management, mixed management, or of any kind of management; i.e., by the highest kind of mental and physical effort—not the longest hours, or the most arduous kind of work, but by the highest kind of intelligent effort. The writer believes, from observation and experience in his business which has brought him in contact daily with many men and of all kinds, that eventually direct majority management will be the most effective way of conducting all business, broadly speaking, from the standpoint of efficiency and satisfaction to the individuals interested and to society as a whole. Possible exceptions, at least for some time to come, will be those specialized or professional occupations—groups in which there are comparatively few workers. It has been noticed, in the writer's experience, that in the majority of instances where the officers of a business have put into practice any measure that has proved to be of benefit to the company as a whole, the fundamental parts or ideas of the measure had been sensed and approved, often silently, by the majority of those connected with the business, and that the measures which did not prove to be of benefit had the approval, usually, of only the minority. It is conceivable, and to the writer presumable, that in any business (particularly in the production of staple goods and necessities), if *all know all* the facts that can be obtained regarding *"costs,"* the majority of all vitally interested in any particular group can determine and settle the contingent ques-

[p] Glenn Edward Plumb (1866–1922) lawyer. The Plumb Plan for reorganization of the railroads called for control by a commission of which one-third was to be railroad employees. The plan also suggested that a percentage of the profits be distributed among the employees.

tions of hours, wage scale, and other basic problems of management
more efficiently and satisfactorily to all concerned, including the
public, than the majority of only the officers or directors. If in a coal-
mining difficulty, for instance, the actual yearly profits of those own-
ing the mine and the relation of these profits to the invested funds,
property valuation, services, etc., were to be a matter of public record,
the problem would be simplified, to say the least. The years of inception and experiments of this kind of management may prove disastrous to some concerns [companies], but in the final working out,
management by the majority (i.e., of all workers, mechanics, clerks,
salesmen, officers, directors, etc.) will, in the writer's opinion, be
more successful in more ways than the management of a minority
(the "Board of Directors"). For instance, in the United States Steel
Company, if its whole industrial body could know all the underlying
figures and facts of operation, all workers (from the President down
to the stokage) could decide more accurately than the officers or
directors alone whether a six- or twelve-hour work-day would be
better for the success of the business, and hence for each man's individual success. In other words, if majority management or industrial
democracy can be better developed, the true spirit of the workers
(body and mind) can be better met, and, correlatively, truer progress
can be better obtained. Human nature so constitutes man that he can
walk a mile faster with less effort if *he* decides he ought to than if,
before he has a chance to think about it, he is *ordered* to.

Among the fundamentally important questions is the one of determining when a group occupation becomes, in character and in size, a
Majority business—i.e., when it ought to be nationalized, and how.
In working out these problems, the broad underlying premises should
not be for the owners alone (if there be any) to know about and to
decide upon, or for the workers alone—or should they both have
the final say? It is a matter for all who use the product of the particular group, whether the activity be transportation, fuel-production,
making bricks, or painting pictures. It is a matter which the Majority
must decide and then support.

And the Universal Mind will have many questions asked of it,
and it must ask many questions in return. When old age annuities,
disability incomes, etc., are discussed, it (the Universal Mind) will
ask how much each citizen can contribute for these benefits through

the public (the Majority) funds; for that matter, how much the share of each shall be in paying the running expenses of the Majority business. The Universal Mind will probably be interested in the Federal budget system, so that each member of the Majority business will know where his money goes. And the Universal Mind may wonder why someone in Congress did not think about this a good many years ago.

Plans for freeing the congestion of personal surplus wealth or property may come before the Majority Mind, and it will have to listen to various plans of diffusing this coagulation. It may be asked how far a graduated marginal production could help to this end? How much of a limit can be put to the right to own personal property without lessening personal initiative and the enterprise of the country at large? Or, how can you limit a man to the amount of money he can make without killing the goose that lays everybody's eggs? In this connection, almost anyone will admit that some are overpaid and some are underpaid for the service they render society. It is doubtless true, but probably not to the extent some assert, that with the making of great personal fortunes during the last one hundred years or so came a great material advance and prosperity in this country. But, if the stimulant of this [the making of great personal fortunes] and the system, generally speaking, that was built up around it was needed once, it is not today—at least not as much so. It is felt now that personal initiative, enterprise and courage to undertake projects with great possibilities (both ways) and individual capability is overrewarded and that chance plays a too great a part in this over-reward. Some men feel that if they are willing to stake their all in promoting the plans that should benefit society they are entitled to all they can get out of it, if for no other reason than to even up for all they may have lost in private enterprises. But nowadays, why should one man have the chance to risk all if there are thousands, perhaps millions, of others who, if they have opportunity to know the premises, are willing and able to share a *part* of their all with him in the risk (assuming that this enterprise and its hazard is necessary for the progress of society; or, at least, that the Majority think it is)?

It is not so much the harm, physically speaking (in some instances it has been far from harmful) that the congestion of wealth in a few does [which concerns us]; it is, rather, the power in many departments that this congestion gives a few. And further, it is not so much this power per se that causes the trouble as it is the state of mind that it produces in the many. There is an intuitive, often unexpressed feeling, almost universal (i.e., of the Majority), of amazement that such a congestion of property and power can exist in a democracy, and further that it apparently exists as a natural phenomenon. This feeling tends to produce hopelessness, or at least a careless spirit, that handicaps the latent initiative of the many. How can it be worked out so that many, many more, even the Majority, can feel better about it [that such a congestion of property and power can exist in a democracy] and be better for it?

One hears more good objections in this connection than good constructive suggestions. Possibly the principal objection to a plan of individual maximums affecting property ownership or yearly returns of income from all occupations (profits, shares, dividends, wages—call them what you will) and for any individual compensation received for any service to society—to all this the usual and first objection will be that such a plan is (*a*) an unnatural, arbitrary, rigid and inelastic process, and hence (*b*) that it will stifle, at least retard, personal initiative, enterprise, enthusiasm, and even genius. If there can be found in natural history, inanimate or animate, any law that indicates that nature favors permanent congestion—that the largest part of the land is sterile, and a very small part fertile—that a few stomachs only need most of the food supply—that a few stomachs only can digest a regular dinner—then there may be found in the system of property congestion an analogy with the way nature works, and if so the objection (*a*) will be more convincing. Again, as to (*b*), the germ of human creative endeavor has its birth in a place nearer to the soul and inner consciousness than to any external stimulant. No genius ever stopped creating because he knew he never could make a million dollars. No genius was ever a pure pragmatist. If a pathologist will quit his laboratory because he knows that he can't own more property than will furnish his family with reasonable present and future needs, it is certain that if he should continue his research for a thousand years *he* would never run down the tubercular bacilli. Society would lose nothing by the loss of *his* labor. A man who will not work because he cannot share in an eventual monopoly furnishes prima facie evidence that he is not a part of the "survival of the fittest." Nature will always furnish a normal number of those individuals who will render better service for reasonable and natural returns than the above minority species.

What is the difference between an art inspiration and a business inspiration? Is it a difference of quality or reward only? Reward has to play an important part in a business effort, and by nature the reward has to be material in quality, to a great extent. But the reward in an art effort has little to do with its cause, and therefore the less material it is, the more natural the effort. The difference is then, it seems, a matter between quality with little or no reward and quality with strongly related reward.[q] If Edison had known in advance that he could be worth in property no more than Beethoven, would he have stopped inventing any more than Beethoven would have stopped composing? If there is any fear that as soon as a man obtains his maximum he will start in loafing, it would be an easy matter to enforce a constitutional provision requiring every citizen (at least until he reaches a certain age) to certify to a certain amount of daily work, whether it be hoeing corn or painting landscapes. For our own part, we hope some day to obtain our maximum and retire *to* business on ten acres and dig potatoes and write symphonies. Ninety-eight men out of a hundred who have been industrious enough to reach their maximum will find no pleasure in doing nothing, unless senility or bad health opposes them. At the inception of a future maximum plan there might be some despondency, and there might be some falling off in initiative, but things would eventually respond normally. It appears to us that the most valid reason against the plan might be one which is less valid today than it might have been fifty or a hundred years ago: the value of concentrated material support [from individual patrons] in the encouragement and advancement in scientific and medical research [such support] is appreciated today; would it have reached this stage had it not been for its individual patrons?[r]

For argument's sake, suppose that the amount of money that Mr.

[q] The two preceding sentences were put together (by the typist or by Ives in dictating?) from a scribbled insert which reads: "it is a matter of the quality of reward—the reward of the 1st *should* never be material, of the 2nd has to be material for the most part."

[r] This sentence, which softens the idea expressed in the preceding one, is not in the MS, apparently having been added at the time of typing.

Rockefeller now owns had been divided up equally among the
population in the states, say, in which the oil was produced: perhaps
a hundred and fifty million divided by twenty-five million—or sixty
dollars. Would this sixty dollars apiece have gone into a few more
cigars, a few more automobile tires, or would each recipient of this
sixty dollars simultaneously have turned part of this, or even fifty
cents of it, to establish a foundation to discover the cause of cancer,
or to study a way to reduce infant mortality? The recipients probably would have contributed generously if they had been so organized and [made] conscious of the duty of doing so. If some such
maximum property plan should go into effect today, would the
Majority continue from the public fund this kind of humanitarian
work?[s] In our opinion they would. The prejudices inferred, we admit,
against some of the present foundations for general betterment would
be removed. Society would be receiving benefits from itself rather
than from an individual (no matter how sincerely altruistic), and
society, we believe, would feel better for it, and as a result would
probably encourage activity along these lines. And some may say,
in this connection, that any great movement in enthusiasm of one
man is more potent than the diffused or semi-enthusiasm so common to members of commissions, clerks or executives. To this, it
seems to us, the answer will hold that was given above when the
cause of individual creative impulse was brought up.

"Well," says an open mind, "suppose that the plan will not in-
terrupt personal incentive to work and create; how would you work
the plan out in detail?"

Only the outline, not the minutiae of details can be given here.[t]
A great deal would depend upon the sincerity of the Majority in
giving this, or any plan for that matter, a fair trial. The premises
and technical information that the clerical force of the Majority

[s] A five-page MS in the Collection is marked for possible insertion here
("Insert—p. 45 line 8 or later?"). The insert begins, "Suppose a man is
worth $500,000, . . ." It then illustrates in detail how the man's property
would be limited in accordance with the plan. Ives apparently decided the long
illustration was not necessary, as these pages were not together with those
given to the typist.

[t] The MS reading is given for this sentence. The typescript reads: "We can
do little more here than to outline in a minousher of detail." This is a variant
which may have resulted from dictation. The next sentence may have been
inserted in dictation, as nothing in the MS corresponds to it.

would need for a starting basis would practically be little more than what is now required from each in the income tax questionnaire. The two chief problems might be: (*a*) to determine what a natural maximum was, and (*b*) to determine a method of fairly arriving at appraisal valuations, which would be made periodically, and would be both mean and terminal in nature. The first problem would be less difficult than the second, we believe. Under the present measure of living costs by money valuation, the maximum would probably run from $50.00 to $100 or $150 per week, or, measured by property, say, between $50,000 or $75,000 to $125,000 or $150,000. (Personally, the writer feels that it should be under $100,000, and possibly under $50,000, later.) It would probably be found simpler and more natural to have the maximum property equal in amount to the maximum return (share, profit, wage, dividend, etc.) to the individual or individual share in any group occupation. The excess, or surplus property, or yearly return surplus from occupational service, would, in a general way, constitute the public fund of the Majority. The general or public fund belonging to the Majority would automatically absorb the excess from the maximum, but presumably a marginal process could be devised so that the periodical appraisals would not be too severe in effect, and so that uneven business conditions and fluctuating values would have some natural leeway. For example: Suppose $50,000 is the maximum at the beginning of the year. A man likes to retain $25,000 in the business he is actively engaged in at the end of the year. Suppose this share has grown to $70,000 in value. Suppose the marginal leeway is 25%. Thus, this man will retain $62,500—$7,500 going to the general fund. A certain amount of the excess might be allowed to go back to others in the group who have not obtained their maximum. Or, perhaps the marginal excess, in this case $12,500 only, might go to the other business workers. Or again, this man who has reached his maximum might be given the option of returning the margin to the group or public fund. Naturally, he would be inclined to turn it back to the business, either in the form of group assets or group profits. That is, any excess in the yearly share of any individual or individuals could, at the option of each individual, be turned over to others in the group to count toward their maximum yearly share or aggregate property maximum, or else it could be converted to the public fund.

Naturally, the ordinary business common-interest of the group will tend to reward those who are found to do the most for the success of that particular occupational group.[u] This tendency may not be in the ascendency today, but in normal times the inevitable laws of nature and of all progress will tend to reward the Majority who render more efficient mental and physical service than the Minority who render inefficient service. Those who value ideals will, in the general course of things, be recognized and better paid than the ones who render difficult routine physical service without furnishing creative thought. This is hardly in accordance with the tendency of today, in which an uneducated, inefficient house servant may be better paid than a school teacher or a technical expert who has spent considerable time and money in his training and apprenticeship. Naturally this [plan] will tend to set right the injustice of these inequalities. When it is much easier than it is today for all group workers to know all the vital facts in their business, greater ability and greater service will be rewarded over inferior ability and inefficient, lazy service. In a successful group, all of the workers would have a chance of obtaining their maximum before there would be a total excess for the public fund. Group workers would solve their own problems. The Majority management, if they decide to have one, would see, for their own interest, that the industrious and capable ones have better chances for reaching their maximum than the lazy, less competent, immoral and, so, less valuable members. And the total groups (for everyone would belong to some occupation) would see and could see more readily and effectively than they do now, that any one group could not, at least for long, have a decided economic advantage over the others. The plan, we believe, would tend to reduce personal speculation—the chief source of wealth from monopoly. The possibility for group speculation would be limited, as it would have to be done on such a wide scale—that is, in such an open way for reason of the large number of participants—that it would be harmless to the community in general, in most cases. The Majority would soon learn to take care of such group greed. Furthermore, the risk would be much greater than the return, and

[u] The following section beginning, "This tendency," down to "In a successful group," was dictated. A marginal note reads: "insert while dictating to Miss [name illegible]."

in this connection a public record could be required, perhaps monthly, of all individual and group profits, incomes, etc., or any valuable figures or statistics that the Majority may desire. Maximums would not be quickly made, and a thoroughness of technique would be more attractive than it is now. We believe that this plan would also tend to minimize and stabilize the retail prices of essentials, making sudden maximum attainments not common except in cases where the individual or group renders some unusual service to society, such as an invention, or particularly efficient production. A different adjustment in all lines of business would be required in developing this maximum plan, and [this adjustment] would offer many intricate and delicate problems, but perhaps no more than exist today. Eventually, we believe, it [the plan] would simplify all business relations and all life. It might be found advisable from many viewpoints to come down to a final maximum gradually, perhaps over a period, say, from five to fifteen years. The effeminate members of the Majority among the men may not have the patience to work out this plan, or any plan, and the masculine members among the women will have the same trouble. But both of these elements (called today extremists or ultra-radicals), though they make a noise, are in the Minority, and they are learning that throwing saucers is not the quickest way of getting soup. The only way to try a plan out is to *try* it out—not "fuss over it." However, this is a detail; most men and women have latent patience. A little compulsory (excuse the word) hard-thinking will bring it out.

Now, the last objection that we will raise to our plan is this: Can the great surplus that will go to the Majority be managed honestly and efficiently and for the good of all? How can you keep trouble, graft, personal animosity, and jealousies from clogging up this big auditing and semi-executive machine?

The difficulty, it seems to us, will not be in finding the right kind of men, but in finding the right kind of system; but that will be no bigger a problem than many others that have been worked out, even during the last ten years. In the first place, if no one can own enough to take desperate chances for, there won't be many "huge steals" to worry about. Sudden individual accumulations would show periodically on the public records, and their presence [could be] easily or not easily explained; and in the latter case the bottom of the trouble may be easier to trace than it is today. Crooks usually start by taking easy chances, and if the chances are against them to start with, the problem will be one of congenital criminal tendencies, a comparatively insignificant class [of criminals] in proportion to the whole. If the government becomes a big business plant rather than a big political plant, the grafting official will be in about the same boat as the absconding bank cashier is now. A check system of open accounts is not a difficult thing to make work. Besides, there would be, presumably, a national budget. The grafting, whatever there is, would be along petty lines. The government would deal in credit accounts and some physical property, rather than in bulk chances.ᵛ It would be as difficult to get away with anything as it is now in the Federal Reserve Bank, or any large insurance company. Having a friend on the inside won't do you much good if about all he can do is to check up figures. There might be a chance for irregularities or small bribes in the appraisal department or in the clerical committees that consider the compensation from the public fund for certain group losses, but certain forms of recording devices would reduce this temptation to the minimum. The government, it is assumed, by this time would be a law-enforcing body rather than a law-making body. If the Majority should consider it best that the surplus of the public fund be used to underwrite or encourage the extension of group occupation projects, the clerical officers in this department might try to be influenced—but even then, definite requirements would take the place of personal snap judgment, which is so common in new business ventures now. The government department heads would have but a small margin of influence within their power, and, furthermore, the capital would be given to certified groups and not to individuals, and all in the group would know the exact amount and purpose of the money received, and all would be responsible to the Majority. The use of the public fund, primarily, would be for routine government running expenses—the cost of appraisals, taking care of property converted to the Majority, health, disability indemnities, old age pensions, etc.

If any such plan should go into effect before the veterans of the last war are all dead, the writer believes that one of the first uses

---

ᵛ The MS reads: "securities." In the margin of the MS there is a note, "find better word."

of this majority property should be to compensate to the fullest possible extent the two great divisions of human beings who through no
direct fault of their own were the worst sufferers from the latest
tragedy of Minority rule, and the traditional processes of the hog-
mind: (1) The soldiers who still suffer any impairment from the
slightest wound to the most horrible mutilation, such as may keep
them from living their lives as they could have lived them if there
had been no war. If we should give our all, how little this return
would be to a boy who has lost his eyesight? There are instances in
this country where wounded boys, who, if they had had money
enough for special treatment and operations before it was too late
(in many cases it is not too late), could have regained their normal
condition—or a condition at least very much better than the one they
are in. (2) The second great class of sufferers, the children, especially in the devastated districts, whose health, and perhaps souls,
have been mutilated by the hell they have gone through.

In the plan we have under discussion there probably would be
less, possibly no need, for taxation in its present sense; if any, perhaps only in relation to the largest annual individual incomes. Another function of the majority fund would be to liquidate government bonds.

The above suggestion of a maximum property right doesn't mean
that the writer is convinced it is a practicable way of solving some
of our difficulties. It is simply to illustrate what one man might wish
to include in his preliminary ballot or recommendation for majority
consideration. In fact, to some, such a suggestion would be a conclusive reason why direct legislation should never be tried out, but
in our opinion if the Majority were to decide, after thorough consideration and a wholesome digestion of the facts in the case, on no
change, or were to decide to try any new plan from a single tax to
socialism in its essence or any other "ism," it would be the attitude
of all, even at great cost and possibly suffering, to accept the bad
with the good, and, with open minds, to give the idea a fair trial,
trusting that by natural processes the good would take its orderly
place and the bad would be discarded. If the people (the Majority)
make fools of themselves, they *make* fools of themselves, and we all
will have to stand for it. But, it is certain that they won't do it for
long. If the Majority has the right to make its own mistakes, it will

be courageous enough to admit them; a mistake admitted is half corrected. We see many shake their heads at this (and other things we have said), but that is a natural exercise and one we wouldn't stop if we could.

And before long the Universal Mind, the Majority (the People) will come against the interest problem (that great eyesore to all of the halfway, even perhaps the three-quarter-way, thinkers), the mortgage, the bonded indebtedness—the result of man's accumulative effort, of his pathetic straining upward and sloughing backward in the process. The question primarily is one of honor or dishonor, of going ahead in the future or of just living along—of sudden immediate relief, perhaps only for ten days and then stagnation—or a steady, difficult, and slowly realized process, but with a greater ultimate gain. As an absolute value, interest is an evil; or, at least, it is unnecessary, theoretically. As a relative one, it is an essential. But to refuse to recognize this truth is like forsaking absolute law. Interest from a purely social standpoint ought to be unnecessary, and it will be when every man shall live out his life expectancy, when men are equally and perfectly healthy, when men are equal and perfect in mental power and industrial efficiency, and when all possess fundamentally equal moral perfection. When the first man forgot something that other men remembered, interest started. He then needed leverage to get going again. Interest is a crowbar which helps two men to move a stone which without the crowbar could not be moved by ten. Two men ought, perhaps, to be able to do the work of ten men without the crowbar, and when society gets further along on its road to perfection the crowbar of interest may then be discarded.[w] Unfortunately, without this interest leverage, without this collective concentrated primal strength, the pyramids, the railroads, and a good part of the world would not have been built. Bonds now in the savings banks are there because they paid for our grandfathers' labor. We could burn them up, but will our grandchildren labor without being paid? If one generation lies down and repudiates [its responsibilities], will the next generation not put all men down as liars? Evidence of death may be an evidence of labor paid for, of an inven-

[w] The two preceding sentences replace one shorter one in the MS, which reads: "It is the crowbar that will move a stone that takes five without, but shouldn't take two to move."

tion paid for, of a desperate chance paid for, of a sublime sacrifice paid for, or of a colossal fraud paid for; how does one man or all men know which? And if all did know, would they punish the skunk or the genius by burning up the evidence, the scrap of paper, the bond of honor or dishonor? Interest is an unfortunate thing that gives the unfortunate a chance—sometimes, a fortune. It helps even up the unevenness that should not be but is. Capital is a part of nature, or as Huxley says, "the mother of labor,"ˣ but interest is *not*—not inherently. However, the same cause that has made capital such a social disturber of the peace makes interest one—the over-ownership of it by a few (the Minority). Now suppose the Majority, after careful and thoughtful deliberation, develops a conviction—not a ladylike, saucer-throwing extremist kind of enthusiasm, but a *conviction* —that a certain freeing of personally congested wealth is a part of natural progress, and measures the maximum by something that will furnish a normal living and a normal future, and arranges that the excess surplus remainder shall go into a general Majority fund. Suppose that as a result a million dollars in four per cent first mortgage railroad bonds finds its way back to the Majority fund. Then there will be two things that can be done with these bonds: the interest, as it is paid to the public account, may go towards the general expenditures for sustaining the common benefits (as outlined in other parts of this paper), or the Majority government may cancel the particular debt on that railroad. Therefore, those in that particular group will have so much more group profit, share, or whatever they call it, because they won't have to pay interest any longer on this million dollars. These are the only ways of wiping out interest—the only ways that will do the present generation or future generations any good. The Majority can decide which of these two ways they will adopt. As a matter of fact, both are just; it will make little difference to the community at large which is selected.

The Majority Mind will have to listen to many discussions running from the specious to the relevant, from the personal, partisan, and prejudiced to the abstract and visionary. The owners of the Majority Mind will have to learn how to use this inherent possession more and more effectively as years go by. They will develop their

---

ˣ Ives probably means Ricardo or J. S. Mill, not Thomas Huxley.

power of selection. They will learn what efficient eclecticism is, and
how to separate the inventive[y] from the constructive, how to segre-
gate the isolated party, or group-hog of the Minority, from the isolated group-unit of the Majority. The Majority Mind will have
before it, especially during the first few years of our experiment, a
heterogeneous mass of conclusive reasons for doing and for not doing
the same thing. Suppose the question of nationalization or socialization of some fundamental occupation is up for discussion—say, the
railroads. One side may furiously rush in and shout that the privately-
owned railroads are over-capitalized, and the other side may say just
as furiously that they are under-capitalized. The Majority Mind,
sooner or later, will say quietly: "You're both prejudiced. Show me
the premises, give me the facts and your authority for them." Then
one side may suggest that in Germany, France, Italy and Austria,
where the railroads are socialized, the capitalization per mile runs
from $120,355 to $158,185 as against the railroads in the United
States under private ownership, where the capitalization is $66,000
per mile. The same side may say that the Austrian railroads under
public ownership lose $50,000,000 annually, or quote as evidence in
their favor the following freight rates: $1.37 in Germany, $1.31 in
France, $1.51 in Austria, per ton mile, and but 72¢ in the United
States. The other side may plead that these figures are facts before
the cause, and produce exhibits showing the relative capitalization
during the various periods under the different kinds of management.
They may be able to prove quite logically that the higher freight
rates are, to a great extent, due to the inefficiency of low wages—too
low to sustain relative living conditions, and too low to encourage an
increase in the average mentality and initiative among the workers.
It won't take as many years as many think before the public mind
will be able to assimilate evidence in questions even as puzzling as
that of transportation, and to decide so that wholesome progress can
be made. The writer is willing to go so far as to believe that, if the
various railroad bills before Congress now[z] could be submitted to the

[y] The MS clearly reads: invective.
[z] The bills under discussion would have preceded the Transportation Act
(Esch-Cummins Act) of February 28, 1920, which returned the railroads to
private ownership (the government had assumed control on December 26, 1917,
as a war measure).

consideration of the people and the opinion of the Majority taken, the result would be astonishingly acceptable in point of efficiency, fairness and level-headedness. The final disposition of almost any big question should rest with the Majority, and not alone with the private owners of the roads and securities, with the officers, with the workers, or with the few hundred minds in Congress (granting that these Congressional minds are above the average). And the writer believes a very overwhelming majority [of those in Congress] do sincerely strive to represent public opinion in so far as this can be known through the present obsolete and extremely ineffective, almost stupid way of ascertaining public opinion. The one hundred millions of people who use or will in the future have to use the railroads, the millions who have their savings in banks, insurance companies, benefit organizations, etc., should have no necessity to ask the same old question: "Where do we come in? Are we going to be "hans schwagelled"[a] again by this or that minority group?"

The farmer who takes a railroad ride but once every ten years has just as much right, and more right for that matter, and has just as much ability, if he can read English, to pass intelligent opinion on transportation questions as the most efficient railroad brakeman or railroad president. For about the same reason, Senator Fall is the last man in the country who ought to have much to say about our relations with Mexico, for, having the facts he cannot see them because of his inherent ideas in relation to *his* property in Mexico—ideas we admit that almost anyone in his position would have. Because of this, his position and attitude is normal and natural, but it is that of the Minority, not the Universal Mind. The power of visualization is in the inverse ratio to the training his mind has had in the development and care of his own personal business property.[b] It would take an abnormally strong mind for a man in Senator Fall's place to give judgment of any value in the above instance.[c] But the judgment of the Majority, with all the facts before them that Senator Fall has before him, would be, by all laws of Nature and human nature, of great value.

One of the big problems of the plan of developing correct legisla-

[a] A germanized corruption of the English slang, "hornswoggled," cheated.
[b] This sentence added at the time of typing.

[c] Ives was correct in assuming that Fall did not have an abnormally strong mind. For later events in Fall's career, see Note 66.

tion is that of assimilating the underlying and important facts and coordinating them in a comprehensive digest—no easy job, but one that Congress (the clerical machine of the people) *can* learn and must learn. And if the Majority, as they doubtless will, occasionally decide on plans that won't work out, the Majority will at least have the satisfaction of suffering from their own mistakes. They can't side-step the responsibility, a thing which in itself will tend to produce more accurate thinking and greater efficiency in Majority government.

V

A very important part of the government machinery will have to do with the departments co-ordinating the ideas received in the suggestive ballots, so that the important and fundamental questions for pre-election consideration and study can be presented with arguments from all viewpoints, and [with] all the facts that can be gathered on the premises.[d]

How can an extension of Majority expression and decision be obtained and made more practicable? How can the plan be worked out? As suggested before, as far as this country is concerned, the Federal Constitution first offers a way, and secondly, the plan can be worked out by faith in the powers that God has given man. Certainly nothing can be accomplished by throwing up our hands and saying, "It can't be done." The greater the problem, the easier the solution. This is often more a paradox than a contradiction. A constitutional amendment covering the complete procedure would, it strikes us, be a more effective way than a series of qualifying clauses to the original articles, if such a process were possible, which apparently is not [the case]. An amendment relating to the ways and means of functioning the action of the Government on direct popular expression would qualify presumably to Section 1 of the first article (Legislative Department) and include and extend the legislative powers enumerated in the eighteen items under Section 8 of Article I. Presumably, then, the legislative power of a direct electorate would relate specifically to Section 5 [Article I], Article XI-5-14, Article III (Judicial Department), and, broadly speaking, the other articles need not, and in the writer's opinion should not, be affected—

d This opening paragraph is not in the MS.

at least until a practical application and procedure of direct legislation be perfected by experience. States' rights would presumably
have to be reduced to the minimum, except in essentially local
matters.[e]

Doubtless, elderly lawyers of great national and corporation fame,
and many famous old Senators of fine legal mind, will find an
incredible number of obstacles against carrying out the plan—even
to the idea in its inception. Months, perhaps years, of committee con-
ferences of these great men will bring out grave legal impossibilities.
But quite probably a young law clerk of average mentality, or a
staff of our many underpaid professors in our many law schools or
colleges, could draft in a comparatively short time a provision that
would do as a beginning—an amendment that would be something
that the Majority would accept. In fact, drafts have been made and
we would be pleased to submit them to anyone who is interested,
even if that should happen to include a Congressman.[f]

Assume that Congress approves (an assumption very easy to write
down) the plan in principle. There could be, until better ways
offered themselves in practice, a suggestive or formative ballot, in
the nature of a general survey, taken, say, six or eight months before
a general or yearly election. This would relate to general economic
business, internal and international questions, except those that come
from emergencies, war, intervention, etc. It would not be difficult to
arrange for emergency ballots. There is no reason why, in two weeks'
time, the machinery for registering the will of the people in any crisis
could not be worked out. Twenty million men were registered for
military service—registered efficiently, and all in a day—without a
great deal of time spent in preliminaries.

The League of Nations today is an instance of what an emergency
question would be. It may be remarked, in this connection, that the

[e] The three preceding sentences, including the references to the Constitution,
were inserted after Ives followed a marginal note to himself: "check this up,
get copy of constit." It is possible that the sentences were dictated, the typist
not knowing whether to use Roman or Arabic numerals. The usage has been
corrected except for "Article XI-5-14." Article XI, in the "Bill of Rights,"
an amendment affecting Article III (The Judicial Department), consists
of one sentence, without sections.

For the passage in the MS which these sentences replaced, and which contains the germ of Ives' later "20th Amendment" scheme, see Note 68.

[f] See the following chapter, "The Twentieth Amendment."

people would clear this matter up in as short a time as the Senate took to muddle it up.

Congress, as it were, would receive the raw material from the people and learn how to refine it.[g] The suggestions in the various ballots would be classified broadly as economic, moral, educational, industrial, financial, foreign, etc. Matters coming under the moral caption, for instance, would presumably have to do with problems of child labor, the evils of race prejudice, liquor, prohibition, etc.

Probably no question is predominately this or that. All economic questions have a moral side. If we were asked to classify the League of Nations under one of the above headings, we would be inclined to put it under that of "moral," though it is at the same time fundamentally a question of foreign and economic relations. But the moral part looms so big—the question of whether one group of people is going to do as little as they can or as much as they can to help humanity—that it seems to us its significance is predominantly moral.

Under the heading of "education," it will be learned to what extent the people feel that schooling should be compulsory. Should a high school education be offered to all, and if so, should not the government contribute to this end? For instance, in cases of families without fathers, or where the father is disabled, shall the majority fund sustain the family while the children are completing their education? Universal compulsory high school education for all, say up to 18 years of age, would thus be possible, and the results of this plan to the country at large would be inestimable.[h] Incidentally, we believe that if the salaries of the teachers throughout the country were a matter for public approval, the disgracefully low salaries of the school teachers of today would be a thing of the past. The public would soon learn that if there is one kind of work which ought to have the highest kind of pay it is that of those who are responsible for training the minds of youth.

[g] The six preceding sentences were constructed from a marginal note in the MS which reads: "Today—the 'League of Nations' would be an emergency question for which an emergency consideration vote could be arranged for (the people could clear the matter up in 3 hours—this Senate has been at it a year)."

[h] Although the Kalamazoo case in 1874 established the right of school boards to maintain high schools on general tax funds, it was not until 1950 that all states required attendance at least to the age of sixteen.

Under the caption "economic," opinions about free trade, high tariff, low tariff, a graduated scale or a gradually reducing scale could be learned, as could also the length of time during which any certain plan might be tried out. Under the same heading could be suggestions regarding living costs, taxes, budget systems, and plans for open public ledgers, showing where the money is going. In this connection, it might be suggested that if a ledger giving all personal profits, incomes, etc., were a matter of public record, many sore points might be cleared up (and perhaps a few others made).

Ideas in relations to Capital and Labor, which of course are interwoven with many internal questions (wage or minimum incomes, problems of distribution, the value of the middleman, the problem of strikes, group management, trying out arbitrary regulations of retail necessities) might come under the head of the industrial subdivision of the economic caption. Thus it is reasonable to assume that opinions of value, perhaps of great value, would be gathered.

Congress, the clerical machine of the people, would prepare the questions from the opinions and decisions in the suggestive ballot and arrange them for the final election. Then, perhaps, three months could be given for assimilating and classifying the results of the preliminary ballots. Selections from the ideas occurring in the greatest number would have a preference for place in the final ballot. Perhaps at first the issues should be limited to, say, the first ten or fifteen questions in popular interest. These, or a great part of them, would probably be questions that had been prominently before the nation for a considerable period. After the ballots for the final elections were completed, they could be distributed to the people, together with the fundamental argument for and against each issue, reduced to as clear, comprehensive and concise a form as possible. Each voter would have to be made to understand definitely that any issue which is approved must be given a long enough time to be thoroughly tried out. If its results are so obviously disastrous that a repeal seems a matter of overwhelming popular opinion, such a repeal, of course, would logically have to be made by the same direct expression that passed the original measure.

During the three or four months of consideration before the final election, bureaus of information could be opened with a view of answering peoples' questions and giving all the facts that could be

obtained along any line [on which] the voters may want enlightenment. (I wouldn't want the job of running one of these bureaus.)
Government bulletins could be issued in connection with these
bureaus. The mis-statements, ambiguities, and personal animosities
of stump politicians would be obviated to some extent, at least—the
writer thinks, to a great extent—for where would the politician in the
personal sense come in? The various parties could still elect their
representatives if they wanted to, but politicians would be powerless,
in the old sense, to do much except to carry out or learn to carry
out any detail the mandate found in the fundamental principles
which the Majority may have laid down.

The other functions of Congress would be to enact secondary
and technical legislation, though to draw an arbitrary line between
and to know what is purely secondary and what is purely primary
legislation will be a problem for a good many years to come, perhaps
one that will never be perfectly solved. Doubtless, though, years of
practice in direct majority government will make this problem less
perplexing. Generally speaking, Congress will have to attend to whatever matters the primary issues (determined by the Majority suggestive ballot) do not treat with. Obviously, as years go by and the
Majority is gradually straightening things out for itself, the work of
pure congressional legislation will be less and less. Congress will
probably find it expedient to furnish reports to the people—State
bulletins giving exhibits or digests of results obtained or not obtained, especially in the more intricate matters of economics, finances,
etc., where the results cannot be easily seen for themselves. It would
also be the work of Congress to keep an accurate record of how
various laws, especially the technical ones, worked out, and to know
when repeals of obsolete or impractical laws should be suggested.
Today, under secondary or technical legislation, would come probably such matters as forest conservation, sanitary codes, auditing the
public fund, etc., which the people would naturally want to entrust
to commissions of technical authorities, and Congress should be in a
position to furnish these technical commissions from their members.
In fact, quite probably Congress would become but a body of technical experts or specialists in economic, social, industrial, agricultural
and scientific matters; transportation, distribution, and all basic occupational subjects and conditions. It would probably be found that

more efficiency could be obtained by making membership subject to Civil Service examinations rather than by territorial elections—the tenure of office depending upon the results shown by each member rather than upon arbitrary terms. The President (or executive head clerk) would supervise and do what he could to help Congress carry out the peoples' ideas. He would quite probably be head of the Foreign Department.

To make this majority process of greater value, all normal-minded men and women over twenty-one (though lowering the age to eighteen might be advisable, as then the benefit of discussions in schools and colleges could be a factor), all citizens should be *required* to give consideration to the issues as they appear, and to vote at both primary and final elections. Perhaps it might be practicable to have each voter pass some kind of an examination on the questions at issue, but not too severe a test. The humiliation of not qualifying might spur the laziest minds to think, until all are literate. Possibly a plan of oral presentation and testing might be worked out, but if the Majority provide education for all, the illiterate will have only themselves to blame for their lack of opportunity. The very fact that certain questions must be answered at a certain time may in itself stimulate an interest in the subject matter and a reasonable amount of time in the study of it—time that otherwise would be expended in too much motoring, poker, or loafing. A thirty-minute daily discussion of our vital problems around the dinner tables of our thirty million families might save or help to save the world.

There will be many, probably too many, to whom any idea of direct government is revolting. They will call it all a colossal impossibility, a hopelessly impractical vision, a scheme that will kill civilization. [They will say] that it is absurd to assume that the people are competent to govern themselves, that the people must have leaders to think for them, etc.; that all business and successful men will be ruined, that the unsuccessful will be more unsuccessful, and that the poor will be poorer, etc.; that there will come as a result of this freedom of expression a heterogeneous mass of wild suggestions from the cranks and cracked brains who will be the only ones to take any interest in the scheme, and, incidentally, [take an interest] for the money they think they can grab out of the chaos; that things will go on from bad to worse until all of mankind will be floating—dead and dishonored on the stygian waves. And those who don't see quite so much tragedy say that the plan requires too much of the people; that they won't have time to study the questions; that it would require every citizen to qualify as a professor of economics or sociology; that the idea of mass expression runs counter to all primal laws of nature, human nature or evolution, and of all phenomena seen in the history of social progress.

Well, perhaps; but with the mess the world is in today, it might be well for something to run counter to some of these laws—the ignoble part of them. Perhaps all these voices are right, but we doubt it. We doubt that anything, fundamentally, in the plan runs counter to Nature, organic or functional. We doubt that the plan will be a colossal impossibility, except to the timid or a hopelessly impractical vision, except to a fearful and lazy mental muscle. We doubt that it will require more time for study than millions of men are giving today to similar problems, perhaps some of these same problems. Because a man doesn't express an opinion, don't assume that he has none. Ask him, and find out that all mankind is thinking seriously today, and is interested in its thought, and it is not likely to carry us towards the Styx. The loudest shouters (always of the Minority) may be pointed that way, for most minorities end there.

And the quality of the thinking won't be as inferior as some of the timid voices think. Any village idiot (that is, any ordinarily bright village idiot) will probably see that if he gets thirty dollars a day for digging potatoes, his wife won't be able to buy them for a dollar per bushel. He probably will be able to see that the farmer can't send the potatoes to market if the truck drivers' charge plus the cost of digging is more than what he can sell potatoes for. He, the idiot, probably will not be able to see, at least at first, that if the personal wealth of the world could be divided up tomorrow among everybody, his share might not be much more than a week's pay (although it might partly be as high as a 1920 pair of shoes) and that the money he is paid in after this portion might be good for nothing; though in this connection he probably might be able to see that if he should be put in a balloon with another man and they both agreed to let the gas out in order to divide it up evenly so that each could take his share home in his pocket, they might reach some other place besides "Home." He probably, after a little patience on the part of his teacher, could be made to see that property and wealth are not always the same thing, but it probably would not be fair to expect him to see as clearly as normal minds why the abolition of all personal property is a physical impossibility, or, in other words, that it is only possible when civilization is abolished. It is a problem of degree, and one in which Nature acts as adviser. The theory of total abolition [of personal property] is anomalous. There must be a point where abolition must stop before the world dies. Will it be a point just before [the abolition of] a man's farm, or his house, or his collar button, or his teeth or hair, or the very "breath of his nostril"? Nature clearly states no definite point, but says there must be such a point. The Majority, after reflection, testing out, and practical experience, will find about how much a man must own as a maximum to develop his natural composite personality, or to satisfy his ideals and to help himself measure up to each natural human value, and satisfy normally his instinctive desires. They will reach eventually that definite point in Nature's measure which will give each man enough freedom without encroaching on the same freedom of others, and [the freedom] under which he, as a rational human being, can provide himself and his family with the requisite material, moral, even artistic and spiritual essentials for the present and the future. (The clumsy phraseology of the foregoing sounds as if the finding of this definite point was a formidable problem, but it is the writer's belief that if Nature rather than custom be the fundamental guide, it will be found, after a reasonable time, fairly readily.) There are many facts or combinations of facts that are platitudes to specialists or to those who study, experiment, and test out in their comparative value, both in point of time and practice, the general or specific effects of any sciences that have to do with the human relation—platitudes that could be readily understood by the people if there were ways for more systematic presentation and consideration of the truths underlying these platitudes. Hence, after these phenomena (call them truths) become clearer and more familiar to the Majority, they appear as platitudes because, it is reasonable to presume, many more minds are occupied with the various subject matters, and the law of average has a better chance to work. As a result more, perhaps many, valuable truths will be discovered to help the Majority man round out his life values.

The moderate man will tell us that it takes time to do research work, that one man may have to spend a lifetime in discovering but a grain of truth. But here (that is, in social evolution) we claim that the subject matter is the observer, that social evolution is an automatic research process in itself, that while the research has been going on the observers have furnished the exhibits, though they have not always observed for themselves, or at least have not had the proper opportunity for observation. But if the Majority could all become observers, then something that took one man a lifetime to discover may be discovered by a million minds in a month. Thirty minutes a day of Majority-collective-observation may unearth one missing link in our journey towards the millennium. There is no man or woman in the world today, provided that he or she is physically and mentally normal, who cannot, no matter how arduous his or her occupation, give serious study of say thirty minutes a day for three or four months to the dozen or so questions with their classified facts and digests of the arguments from all important viewpoints. And in the process, who knows but that some ideas of great benefit to the majority of the people will appear. The farmer, our most essential worker (in the final analysis, the only essential worker excepting the school teacher), and one who works long, continuously and hard, has, as some of the political history of this country shows, been able to give his share of time to public questions without in most cases losing his crops or his head. We won't try to discuss here whether this is because of his outdoor and more natural wholesome life, or, possibly, because his work does not require such continuous mental concentration as some, or because his thought is not so apt to be interrupted by the rapid, half-digested, popgun, ill-assorted, prejudiced-personal, local arguments to which the city or factory worker is subjected. We won't stop to discuss this here except to remark that it seems to be a fact that whenever there is a collection of human beings, it is observable that something in human nature causes talk, and plenty of it, to come first, and thought, and not much of it, to come last.

Perhaps city life itself is an unessential. Perhaps it is caused nowadays more by curiosity than necessity—the restless, nervous curiosity of men that Thoreau may have had in mind when he said that rubbing elbows together does not necessarily bring minds closer together.[1]

[1] The same reference is made in *Essays Before A Sonata*. See p. 56.

The man who argues it is "catch as catch can" is usually wrong, and the man who argues best with his inner consciousness is usually right. Because a man goes through a crowded city in a crowded subway to a crowded office, and spends a crowded day over a crowded desk in a job that requires crowded action (usually called "quick action") may not mean that his social consciousness is greater than the trapper. It may only mean that he has forgotten something. Big business may accomplish everything but a big life. All this is not to be taken as a suggestion that the town man must get ready to move to the farm when our "Majority-rule Band" comes down the street. It is, rather, but a passing remark to say something that everyone knows: that if a man have the premises before him, his own mind will work from them better than from the tongue hung in the middle of his friend across the table. We are inclined to feel that this moderate man's "lack of time" argument is due perhaps to an over-consideration (common to moderate) of what *has* been done, and an under-consideration of what *can* be done.

Another man who has voted all his political life the straight ticket of his father and grandfather (and of his great-grandmother, if that had been possible)[j] gets rather indignant: "Why all this talk? The party platforms do all you propose."

Now, the unfortunate part of this remark is that it is not true to fact. The party platforms do not, and it is doubtful if they ever will, do what is proposed. It is true that in the platform lay the origin of all parties, and that there was a time when platforms functioned more than they do today. There is a certain educational value in platform discussion, but it is always overshadowed by party personality, party tradition (for its own sake), party power and party self-consciousness, and deformed by election campaign hysterics. The "Free Silver" plank[k] in the Democrat platform of 1896 stimulated mental effort on the part of the electorate which may have done as much good as the defeat of that issue. The result of the election showed that when the people have an intricate question put up to them, even on short

[j] The 19th Amendment, providing woman suffrage, was ratified on August 26, 1920.
[k] Free and unlimited coinage of silver, with the ratio to gold set at 16 to 1. The Democratic candidate, William Jennings Bryan, was defeated by William McKinley, whose platform upheld the single gold standard.

notice, they have power to sense its virtue, dig out its fallacies, and act normally and wisely. In 1896 many Democrats voted against their party; but, on the other hand, there were Democrats, who, though they did not believe in bimetallism,[1] voted with their party. They preferred to place party ahead of principle. There lie some of the perplexities, mental and moral, in the party system. Party platform without party might come as a relief to many; in fact, our plan might be called a selective-majority-composite party platform, with all parties eliminated. If an interest in the party dominates the interest in the platform, as is usually the case after the campaigning is over, the acts of the party in office begin to assume a professional color, and then representative processes become more second-handed and loose-jointed than ever. It may be that a voter makes his choice at election by reason of a particular platform issue, and his ticket is elected. But, before much is accomplished in relation to this particular issue, another congressional election comes along. In this election, perhaps the interest has been primarily local and personal, and as a result there is political change in Congress. As a result of this, the measure that our voter originally voted for is defeated. And so, this voter is inclined to feel that representative government sometimes functions very inaccurately, to say the least. Again, if there be only two or three parties which have any chance of being elected, and in the platform of each there is an important measure which this voter favors, and also, in each platform there is an important measure that he opposes, he may feel that representative government underwritten by parties does not give him much chance to express his convictions.

Another aspect of platform and purely representative government is illustrated in the case of a man who runs on a platform in which a certain predominant plank carries him into office. He sincerely believes in the virtue of this particular principle while advocating it before the voters, but after election, in the soberness of reflection or in a period of serious thought which he might have been perfectly free from during his successful campaign, it comes over him that the plank is fundamentally wrong. To make a long story short, he decides that he cannot conscientiously vote for this measure. Assume that the mind of his constituency has not changed; where does his

[1] That is, the use of both gold and silver to set the monetary standard.

duty lie? Should he, if he can, refrain from voting on this measure, or should he vote for his constituency against his conscience, or for his conscience against his constituency; or should he resign? The last way might be the way nearest right, but at its best, the solution is something of a dilemma. There may be many other questions as important as the one in point in which, by reason of his experience, he can render valuable service to the government—service which he cannot render if he resigns.

Any hypothesis, if we may digress for a moment, with as tenuous a shaft as the foregoing cannot be suggested as an argument, much less as a valid reason for anything good or bad, without arousing a type of man found apparently in every land and in every age. He is the most insidious incubus of representative democracies. Even in the most perfect kind of a direct democracy, he could probably subsist, but the food, presumably, would not be as tempting as it is now. The man of this type is usually found among the chronic backward-looking traditionalists. His one great war-horse is his power of suspicion. His every fiber reeks with suspicion—suspicion in its hundred forms, perfect and imperfect in its highest passionate efficiency, a suspicion of everything and everybody but himself. One of his deepest pleasures is any evidence, no matter how indirect, that will even partially seem to confirm his suspicion. His greatest sorrow comes whenever the facts which prove his suspicion groundless and heavenless are stuck so forcibly under his nose that he *cannot* blink them off. His deepest pain lies in the fact that everybody is not as rotten as he says. He can hardly be called a pessimist, for he always has hope in his power to pull the world back into his slough. It is a platitude to say that suspicion is the river of cowardice. Its one favorable value may be as an antidote to over-enthusiasms. However, the value of this quality probably is quite negligible when it is remembered that a man who tries to hitch his wagon to a star and falls over a precipice, wagon and all, and dies, leaves a greater experience for the world than the wagon took out, and perhaps simultaneously he finds a greater world for his own soul. He finds something greater than the man who hitches his gilded star to a mule, and is kicked back into a stagnant pool, where he lives forever, safe and sound in his swamp, and in his ecstasy of splashing mud on mankind. Every time this man hears or overhears the word "conscience," he pricks up his prejudiced ears, and lifts up his raucous swill-pail of sarcasm, and pours out the same hopeless stuff that has been encouraging all decay from the time Cain killed Abel. "It is too bad," he says, "about this moral legislator of yours. Not one in a million is troubled with a conscience." Of the world's greatest lies, this is one of the greatest, and this man is constantly telling it. If what he says were true, if his state of mind (and it is by no means an uncommon state of mind, though it is decidedly a Minority state) were caused by a true translation of the rule rather than the exception, it would take away all intelligible reason for the cause of all human existence. It would mean that there could be small claim for any distinction between human life and life in the most luxurious pig-sty. It would mean that Man has grown so bitter morally that the growth can hardly be measured. It would not quite mean that death was Man's only hope —and death without a God, or even a poor substitute for one. It would not quite mean that—at least until the last man in the last billion who possessed the last ray of moral consciousness has died.

The mind of chronic suspicion is the greatest enemy human progress in any form has. If there is one ideal value which social evolution must have as its cornerstone, it is the belief in the innate goodness of mankind. We must not confuse the belief of this with the manner of its perception. If its manifestation is not always within one's vision it may be our fault. On the other hand, if it is over-evident we may undervalue it. A faith in it is a faith in God in Man. Unfortunately, science, or its by-product, "efficiency," has not yet rigged up a stethoscope for piling up statistics relating to the nature of the soul and its disclosures to the inner consciousness. When that recorder is perfected, it will show that there is not one legislator out of ten thousand (or out of a hundred thousand, if there be that many) but whose conscience plays a stronger part than any force within him. It [conscience] does not always function as it should, but it functions better than many believe. It [the recorder] will show that not one [legislator] is totally and permanently deaf to its [conscience's] voice, and it will show, the writer is morally certain, that there is not one-half—no, one-tenth or even one-hundredth part—of the graft, hypocrisy and vindictiveness in our legislative bodies that some (too many) of our timid citizens think. The amazing thing is that after all the depressing and materializing processes of back-door politics which many legislators, from the smallest city alderman to the Member of Congress, have to go through to be elected, there are present in such a large degree a willingness to stand for conscientious conviction, an intellectual grasp, a tolerance, and an inclination to listen to those who disagree and to be fair to many that are unfair in return. The exceptions to the foregoing seen in the 1919 Senate can be perhaps forgiven on the ground of "de senectute"[m] and the long dulling of the greater inherent qualities by long years of party loyalty—a picture sacrificed for its frame. But the effeminate timidity that some political leaders in the Senate have exhibited during the recent League of Nations discussions[n] (especially [the timidity of] the leaders or politicians who are opposed to a league in any form or to the idea in principle) can hardly be excused on account of "old age." Their attitude against the League of Nations (no matter how imperfect in detail the plan may be) means that they believe that the majority of Americans are physical cowards and care more for their pocketbooks than for the opportunity of taking a chance in the first big effort the world has ever made to do away with mass murder. If the Majority want to put themselves in the timid hog-mind class, all right. But a few men in the Senate should not have the exclusive right to determine the quality, the courage, and generosity of the Majority (the People). Some of these 1820-minded men may, through their obsolete mental machinery, think that a League of Nations will not do away with future wars, and it is fairly reasonable to suppose that it will not entirely. But these backward-looking men are never able to propose any better plan other than that of going back to the same old expedients that have caused war upon this planet from time immemorial. Their vision is not big enough to join in the vast attempt to pull man out of the swamp of blood that he has lain in for ages. The low mentality of such minds can be better excused by puerility than by senility.[o]

But going back to the broader viewpoint it seems certain that God

[m] "On account of old age."

[n] President Wilson presented the Treaty of Versailles (to which was attached the Covenant of the League of Nations) to the Senate for debate on July 10, 1919.

[o] The preceding four sentences are not in the manuscript, perhaps having been dictated to the typist.

wondrously inspires men to whom great responsibility is entrusted
with strength of purpose, breadth of vision, mental, moral and
spiritual powers far from perfect, but far, thank God, from the insults
of our cowardly, material-minded, chronic fault-finding, suspicion-
swill-feasters who so clog up their narrow mental lanes with the
Tweeds,[p] the Kaisers, and the Herods that the Lincolns, the Savo-
narolas, and the Christs pass unnoticed. There may be, for a while,
some organic or physiological need in the body politic for a grain
of this kind of serum or anti-toxin, but if it is ever given Man in an
overdose, if the poison becomes a habit, if suspicion in its purest form
ever gets the lead, it is all over with the world. The more the respon-
sibilities of the present law-makers are shared directly with all, the
Majority, the People, the less encouragement these personifications
of undervalues will have, and the greater the chances of the world
for benefit in the evolution of its governments—an evolution making
them governments of principles, not parties; and of perfect truths,
not perfect prejudices. "The government of the world we live in,"
said Thoreau, "is not framed by a few in after-dinner conversations.
It is a government of a few fundamental truths of Nature, not of
many political expedients."[q] We feel free to say that his government
conducted by all will be virtuous, for innate virtue will no longer
be perverted by the Minority (the Non-People) and their sub-natural
institutions. We feel free to say that Thoreau's government will not
bring the millennium, but that it may bring a practicable application
of an uncommon common sense. For is it not sense, common and
uncommon, to assume that Nature is willing to entrust the management of the earth to those to whom it belongs—that is, to those who
have to live on it? Is it not sense, common and uncommon, to assume
that Nature made the majority of the brains in this world with the
same power to act normally (that is, rightly) provided they have an
equal amount of the right kind of [brain] food to act upon, as she
made the majority of stomachs with the power to act normally if they
have an equal amount of the right kind of [actual] food to act upon?
And universal education is fast on the way with the right kind of
[brain] food. And then is it not sense, common sense raised to its

[p] William Marcy Tweed (1823–1878), notorious New York City politician,
boss of Tammany Hall.
[q] The quotation, also in *Essays Before A Sonata*, is free. See p. 62.

highest possible power, to believe that all grown men and women
(for all are necessary to work out the divine law of averages) should
have a direct, not an indirect, say about things that go on in this
world of ours?

Another man, thoughtful and quite free from unnecessary suspicion, but prudent, asks if there isn't some danger that the Majority,
even after due time for consideration, may become hypnotized by
some wild, hog-minded schemer, and so blunder into some cheap,
delusive, some half-digested lure of a panacea that will ruin the
country or ruin the world. It seems to us that there will be no more
chance of that in a government of more direct Majority expression
than there is now, for education cures stupidity, and responsibility
begets deeper and clearer thinking. Again, Americans (most of them)
have been free men for centuries—at least they have been free to
think, and usually (except when the country occasionally passes
through a neurotic low ebb) free to say what they think. And they
are not likely to give in to the more recent arrivals who in their
foreign homes have lived with the inheritance of centuries of
monarchism and absolutism hanging over them—an inheritance that
causes in them at first, when they are suddenly free from it, a
confusion of the term "freedom" with the term "self-will"—an inheritance that has so repressed a normal development in social consciousness that its possessors lose perspective, and they experience
an over-reaction. The majority of Americans appreciate this [over-
reaction of the more recent arrivals] and are more [than they] inclined to wait for a normal process of adjustment than to jump in
half-cocked to this or that vagary. All of America comes from
Missouri[r] when the wild-eyed sleight-of-hand and -head [magicians]
start conjuring. There is no more danger that the Majority will adopt
in a hurry any plan of decidedly doubtful value, unsupported by
some favorable experience, than that the great middle-class (and the
whole country is one great middle; the so-called upper and lower
classes are as transitory and elusive as the proverbial flea) will sit
down and let some hog-minded self-willed Minority agent take away
by force any of their natural rights, freedom or property (we won't

[r] For the reader not familiar with American colloquial expressions: if you
come from Missouri, you won't believe anything you can't see.

spoil the story by saying surplus property) without knocking him down with a blow which will be heard in Mars.

In this connection, it may be remarked that a Yankee is too much interested in horse-racing and active life values to let his country be turned into a monotonous national boarding house by anyone's hand except his own, and before he does that, he will want to sample a few meals. The majority of Americans own something—a few, too much; everybody knows that. But whatever they own, for the most part they have worked for it hard with hand and brain. And if some Minority bandit should sneak down the road and try to take away by force those Americans' homes, shops, farms, or whatever they have laid up for a rainy day, or for their children, a new version of the lion and the mouse would be staged and the Minority Hog would be too groggy to applaud many of the scenes.

Among the strong characteristics of the American that can be traced from 1620 to 1920 is one that makes him always ready to fight to "have his say," and this desire is so inbred that if a militant but kindly disposed minority should try to force Paradise on him, with all its modern improvements, without his consent, he would choose Hell first, with all its tortures.

And another man asks, "How about the Minority?" There will be many individuals in minority groups, and perhaps whole minority groups, who feel that their ideas still have virtue—who feel that in spite of the fact that the Majority has not yet adopted their issues, they (the Minority) are still right in their convictions. This part of the problem seems to make its own deductions. Murphy's one alternative becomes three here. The Minority man can do as all good losers do: (1) abide by the winner's terms, live up to the Majority law like a man, and at the same time be free to keep up the fight for his principles and ideals by every fair argument of mind and talent he has—and if there be virtue in his ideas, he can rest assured that they will eventually be accepted, or, at least, tried out by the Majority; or (2) the Minority man can go to some other country whose laws are more congenial to him; or (3) he can begin to shriek, to get nasty, hysterical, and begin to throw things around—and then the Majority will strangle him—and treat him like a farmer treats a skunk who loses his self-respect.

A summary, we were taught, was the only excuse for a peroration, and without inquiring what the excuse for a summary is, we might try one by suggesting in one sentence that: if all can view all, the resulting action of the greater part of all the Majority will be natural, normal, and hence right. And how can all view the total phenomena —all the premises—which vitally affect any fundamental life-activity? By keeping unceasingly at it, by learning how to use to the fullest extent the divine law of averages, by gathering all the news more accurately than it ever has been gathered before, by systems of government bulletins, by experiments, by accepting any influence that will tend to make men examine with interest and intelligence all possible premises which can be gathered and presented in an orderly way.

Though the highway of social evolution is founded on the spiritual and the religious rather than upon the intelligent and economic, these latter elements, if underdeveloped—that is, if their quality is not unceasingly improved—always tend to clog up the greater paths and stifle the greater values. An important aid in this direction is obviously universal education—not the kind smothered by vocational training, but the deeper process of assimilating, classifying, and distributing truth—so that we will know how to live in a truer way, and by reason of it to work in a better way. One of the underlying means of attaining these goals is, by nature, an economic problem: learning how to make it possible without an *abnormal* physical effort (the kind which brings so many men home at the end of the day too tired to think) to gain the unit of comfort, and simultaneously, to develop the mental, moral, and spiritual life. And before we have swung around a complete circle, let it be asked how the greater life can be gained unless all are urged to think with all the strength the foregoing things may give, and to say what is thought so that all can hear it, and then abide by what all the Majority, the People decide.

But—just to say something pleasant before closing—suppose that, after innate admonition, deep mental concentration and serious struggles, the Majority decides that for the greatest good of the greatest number, my last remaining piece of property, my shirt, must go to the commonwealth, and that I must live in the nation's boarding house. What matters it? Who knows but that I may get to like my part of the common shirt, or that I may get my old shirt back some day, and perhaps a new experience in the bargain? For, as Thoreau says, "you may have thrilling, glorious hours, even in a poor house."[8]

Why not make a start, if it is only to find out if a start is wanted. Why not ask this Majority giant, this great mass personality, if he is willing to sit for a trial portrait before the world's most critical artist—even himself?

And what will the picture be? Hideous, or transcendent? A caricature, or a Velasquez? At its birth, or in its youth? We know not. But as it approaches maturity, there will come, we believe, a radiance such as the world has never seen!

"Why! Why!" the Pilgrims turn and ask.

Man knows not the horizon of the soul—but Faith has yet its Olivet, and Love its Galilee![t]

[8] The quotation occurs also in *Essays Before A Sonata*. See p. 55.
[t] Last half of this sentence from the hymn, "Immortal Love, forever full" (Whittier, 1856).

FIVE

CONCERNING A
TWENTIETH AMENDMENT

INTRODUCTORY NOTE

IN THE first part of 1920 the
forthcoming presidential election spurred Ives into direct action on
his idea (expressed in "The Majority") that our government should
find a better way to register the will of the people. He hoped to get
a plan in the form of a constitutional amendment under public discussion by having it printed in newspapers. A mimeographed document of six and a half single-spaced pages was sent to eight leading
New York papers, but none of them printed it. On the rejection slip
from *The New York Times* he wrote: "My article may have but little
value, but whatever it has, is, I am reasonably certain a little greater,
than that of the society-column. It would take but little more space
than is given daily to these unimportant events."

When the newspapers failed to print his article, Ives launched a
campaign directed at leading political figures. He was not timid in
his choice of targets. There are twelve responses to his proposal in the
Collection, including letters from the offices of President Wilson,
Calvin Coolidge (then Governor of Massachusetts), Herbert Hoover

(by his secretary, Christian Herter), and William Jennings Bryan. The only real response (and the last one to arrive) was from William Howard Taft, who at that time was Kent Professor of Law at Yale.

At the time noncommittal letters began to arrive from the politicians, Ives made an attempt to get the *Atlantic Monthly* to publish his article, saying (according to a carbon of a letter of May 26): "You are at liberty to shorten it, revise it, correct its literary defects [written above the line, 'if it is good enough to have any'] etc., it matters little to me as long as the general plan can be presented to as many readers and as soon as possible."

In the meantime, Ives had had a shortened form of the article printed as a circular. On May 29, he wrote to Mutual of New York's Chicago manager, Darby Day, asking him to get five thousand of these circulars distributed at the door of the Coliseum, where the Republican Convention was to be held on June 8, saying: "The important thing is to have them [the circulars] go to the gutter *after* they go to the delegates, et al." But on June 9, a telegram from Day reported that the circulars had not arrived. Ives replied by telegram that the circulars had been sent, and on June 14 he wrote a letter to Day regretting that they had not arrived on time, and asking that they be handed out anyway by a distributing company. He added: "I intended originally to have some of them handed out indiscriminately in the streets or terminals, taking the chance that they will reach somebody somewhere who will be interested."

A cable to Ives on June 8 from L. H. Goldberg in San Francisco gives the name of a distributing company and the price for distributing five thousand circulars at the Democratic Convention, which was to take place there on June 28. There are no further documents in the Collection to indicate whether Ives managed to get the circulars distributed at that convention, or whether, having failed to get them into the hands of the Republicans, he did not bother to give them to the Democrats.

After the *Atlantic Monthly* rejected his article, Ives sent it to *The Outlook*, which also rejected it. On their letter of June 15, Ives scrawled furiously in large capital letters, "YOU WEAK SISTERS!"

A few days later, a short personal letter from William Howard Taft (dated June 19) gave Ives fresh stimulation, even though Taft's reaction to his plan was negative. He immediately began to compose a reply, although there was no indication in Taft's letter that he expected to consider the matter any further. After an ink draft, and several retypings, the letter was sent to Taft, sometime after June 22.

The last document in this phase of Ives' "Twentieth Amendment" campaign was a letter sent to New York and Brooklyn newspapers in September-October, 1920. Two versions were prepared, and in Ives' letter to the papers he said: "If you cannot print the longer, perhaps you will the shorter," thinking no doubt of the refusal of all the papers five months earlier to print his long "Twentieth Amendment" proposal. For good measure, he clipped copies of the "Twentieth Amendment" circular to the letters. But the papers did not print the letter—neither the long one nor the short one. On the rejection letter from the *New York Evening Post,* which pled lack of space because so much material on the League of Nations was being sent to them, he wrote: "The letter is not about the League of Nations—primarily—it is used as an illustration, to show the inadequacy of political parties to register public opinion."

The document on the "Twentieth Amendment" which Ives sent to newspaper editors and politicians in May, 1920 contains, besides the proposed amendment, a considerable amount of material quoted directly from "The Majority." The circular, printed later, has a slightly improved text throughout, and contains less material duplicating that in "The Majority." For that reason, the circular rather than the longer letter is the text for the version given here. It is reproduced in full except for a blank at the end to be filled out and sent to "your Senator, your Congressman, or to the President," with space to write "any suggestions or changes you think advisable."

Materials in the Collection for the letter to Taft are an ink first draft, a first typing of June 21, and a second typing of June 22, 1920, for which there are also two carbons. A note on the face copy reads: "This was written over & somewhat shortened but P. S. put in: The plan changes our Gov. if it does change it from Gov. of, by, for the Politicians to Gov. of the People, by the People & for the PEOPLE!" Since there is no carbon for the final version mentioned in the above note, the second typing is followed here.

For the letter on Harding's election, the Collection contains the following materials:

1. First and second typings.

2. Two carbons of the third and final typing, with headings added, "To the Editor of the Post." One of these carbons has the letter of rejection from the *New York Post* attached to it.

3. The whole material sent to the *World* (New York). which was returned with a rejection slip. The material includes a "Twentieth Amendment" circular.

The version given here follows the carbon copies returned by the *Post* and the *World*.

CONCERNING A
TWENTIETH AMENDMENT

I

A SUGGESTION FOR A 20TH AMENDMENT

THE following letter was sent to eight leading New York newspapers a few months ago.* To date none of them have printed it. Some of the papers returned the copy saying that space prevented their using it. The letter is long, but requires little more space than that which most of the papers give daily to the society columns. It should not be assumed that because these papers did not see fit to publish this letter that they were opposed to it; they may have thought, probably with good reason, that the plan was not well expressed or presented. However, whatever the reason, the fact that it was not printed would indicate that the editors are not especially interested in the idea. Hence this means of presentation by a circular is tried.

If you won't read all of this, read that part in **large print—at least**

* The letter sent to the newspapers was signed by the writer, but as the general purpose of its subject matter is to eliminate personalities and encourage the people to get down to principles instead of individuals, and as many would naturally think that the writer was looking for personal publicity, it is thought advisable that this circular bear no name. The printers, Peck & Durham, 165 William Street, New York City, will give the writer's name and address to any one who wants to criticize him. But if you think the plan will be of value in further perfecting our form of government and that something along these lines should be at least discussed seriously by as many people as possible in order to find a practical working out, do not send letters of approval to the writer, but go ahead and present your ideas in any way that your best judgment and common sense suggest. Any one is at liberty to reprint or use any part of this letter if he so desires.

read the proposed 20th amendment. If you do not believe in the idea fundamentally—tear this up; or better, sit down and think out your objections and then present them in any open and fair way you can.

If you believe in the plan show it to others, then sign your name on the opposite side as indicated and mail it to one of your representatives in Congress, or to the President.

The following contains an attempt to suggest a "20TH AMENDMENT" to the Federal Constitution—AN ATTEMPT clumsy and far from adequate, we admit, either in form or in substance, but as its general purpose is TO REDUCE to a minimum, or possibly to eliminate, something which all our great political leaders talk about but never eliminate, to wit: THE EFFECT OF TOO MUCH POLITICS IN OUR representative DEMOCRACY—we submit this for what it is worth.

As our political parties today, together with a great chorus of candidates, are by their own declarations out for "the common good"—that is—"for the people," and as the people believe that politics are to blame for many of their ills and as political parties generate "politics," is it not inevitable and logical that all parties will jump at the chance of embodying in their platforms any plan which will eventually eliminate the cause of these troubles—in other words, all political parties?

We hope the Republican party will not become so over-enthusiastic about this proposed amendment that it will claim a prior right to it—even a monopoly!

But seriously—if it is so, and it apparently is, that a dispassionate examination of social phenomena in this and other civilizations indicates that THE INTUITIVE REASONING OF THE MASSES IS MORE SCIENTIFICALLY TRUE AND so OF GREATER VALUE TO the wholesome PROGRESS of social evolution THAN the PERSONAL ADMONITIONS of the intellectual only—that is, in the ever-flowing undercurrent of the man relation, the ethical and religious impulse predominates—the intellect being a stabilizing rather than a primal organic force—if this is so, is it not only natural but essential, that mankind do more towards registering the results of this intuitive reasoning, and its deeper impulses and to formulate more direct means for their expression? And if this mass intuition and deeper consciousness has been valuable, even in the crude way it has had to function, of how much greater value will it be to society if

THE VARIOUS PREMISES WHICH IT NEEDS TO ACT UPON
more accurately can be more clearly and universally presented. If one
will admit that God made man's brain as well as his stomach, one
must then admit that the brain (the majority brain) if it has the
normal amount of wholesome food—truth (in its outward manifestations, specific knowledge, facts, premises, etc.—which UNIVERSAL
EDUCATION IS FAST BRINGING) will digest—and will function,
as normally as the stomach, when it has the right kind of food. If one
won't admit that, he comes pretty near admitting that God is incapable. The writer believes that THE AMERICAN PEOPLE are
willing to make or try to make a greater contribution to social
progress; that they have faith in themselves and ARE WILLING TO
TAKE RESPONSIBILITY AND if occasion requires willing to take
TIME TO THINK ACCURATELY and SERIOUSLY—AND further
that they, WITH THE PREMISES BEFORE THEM WILL BE
more INSPIRED BY THE SENSE OF JUSTICE, not only social
justice, or any relative justice—but justice in the absolute—than are
many self or party-appointed leaders. THE NEED OF LEADERS
in the old sense IS FAST GOING—BUT THE NEED OF FREER
ACCESS TO GREATER TRUTHS AND FREER EXPRESSION IS
WITH US, and with this greater and deeper freedom, the sum of all
consciousness—the people are finding their one true leader—they are
beginning to lead themselves. Utilizing public opinion in any but a
general way may seem hopelessly impractical to the hard-headed business man (so termed) and to the practical politician, altogether too
practical. To photograph with good results, the universal mind and
heart will be a big job—a tremendous job—but one that was successfully started in 1776—and the bigger the job the more reason why
the American people will tackle it with courage and equanimity.
TO BE AFRAID TO TRUST THE MIND AND SOUL OF THE
PEOPLE IS A COMMON ATTRIBUTE OF THE TIMID. There is
every reason to hold with John Bright[u] that the first 500 men who
pass in the Strand would make as good a parliament as that which
sits at St. Stephen's. Wendell Phillips, a student of history and a
close observer of men, as George Williams Curtis says, rejected the
fear of the multitude which springs from the timid feeling that the
many are ignorant and the few are wise; he believed the saying, too

[u] 1811–1889. British statesman, agitator for reform bills.

profound for Talleyrand, that **EVERYBODY KNOWS MORE THAN ANYBODY.**ᵛ Because a man does not express an opinion, do not assume that he has none. Ask him and find out that mankind is thinking—and thinking seriously and is interested in its thought. And we doubt that the quality of the thinking of the masses will be as inferior as some of the practical voices think. In working out a system of universal expression there will be severe disappointments, disastrous sloughing offs, dark days, trials and discouragements, but no greater problems than we have survived. It is the belief of the writer that **THE MAKERS OF OUR FEDERAL CONSTITUTION HAD** in mind **THE HOPE OF A BROADER DEVELOPMENT OF** direct **POPULAR EXPRESSION.** Obviously, more **DIRECT EXPRESSION** was as **IMPOSSIBLE IN 1780** as it is **POSSIBLE IN 1920.** The process does not change the form of our government. It tends to protect and perfect it. We respectfully submit the following:

SECTION 1.

Article XX. (20th Amendment.) On a day, nine* months previous to the day on which the people shall meet in their respective states to vote by ballot for electors (Article XII) for President and Vice-President, the said people of the United States shall submit to Congress all and whatever plans, opinions and suggestions which each and all desire to offer in relation to future Federal legislation; and in this connection and upon the same ballot there shall be contained not over twenty questions, the subject matter of which shall relate to whatever Congress considers, does most fundamentally and vitally affect the public welfare. Such questions shall be presented as clearly as is possible so that the answers may readily indicate the opinion of the public. All citizens of the United States, male and female (and over the age of 21, possibly 18), shall be required to return answers or opinions to these specific matters and questions which

* This was drafted some years ago but revised recently in the hope that it could be put before Congress so that it might be a definite help in the coming election. This is hardly possible now, but the "plan in principle" should be publicly and seriously discussed. The sooner some such amendment is enacted the sooner will the duties of Congress be made more manifest.

There will be no plank in any party platform more important!

ᵛ The two preceding sentences are adapted from the "Eulogy" by George William Curtis (1824–1892) in *A Memorial of Wendell Phillips from the City of Boston* (printed in Boston by order of the City Council, 1884), pp. 53–54. The passage begins, "Wendell Phillips held, with John Bright, . . ." This same document (pp. 41–47) may be Ives' source for the Faneuil Hall incident mentioned in *Essays Before A Sonata,* p. 79.

shall be returned to the Government in addition to the other suggestions, opinions, etc., that the people may wish to submit (as suggested above). The result of these suggestive ballots shall be made known to Congress who shall analyze, classify and orderly arrange these plans, suggestions and answers into subdivisions and make the complete findings public. Whichever ten of the foregoing plans and suggestions as a result of these ballots shall have been the most numerous, shall then be suitably assimilated, condensed and presented to the people in the form of proposed laws (together with an essential digest of each) five months before the final election for the above electors. Any of these ten submitted plans which shall receive a majority vote at this final election shall become by this procedure a law of the United States. Any or all laws resulting from the above election which are found to be in conflict with the laws already in force shall be interpreted in favor of the majority made law. This provision shall not affect the other legislative powers of Congress (as contained in Sections 1, 2, etc., under Article I), except in that Congress in all matters of legislation shall refer to and be guided, as far as it is possible, by the will of the people as shown in the result of the said suggestive ballots and by the order of prominence after classification in which the various opinions, etc., are found to come.

SECTION 2.

It shall be the duty of Congress to gradually liberalize and perfect the means for majority-expression and to enforce by appropriate legislation the provisions of this article.

SECTION 3.

This (proposed) amendment shall not become a part of the constitution, until after being ratified by the procedure now required, it shall also be ratified by the direct majority decision of the people; and all amendments proposed subsequently (to the time this amendment is ratified), shall be ratified by the direct majority decision of the people; and that this mode of ratification shall take precedence over the modes of ratification under Article V.

ᵂThe suggestive ballots could probably be so printed and presented that the reading of them would arrange the voter's mind in some kind of constructive order. One side of the ballot form would be left blank for any proposed suggestion or plan that may suggest itself to the voter and which is not found upon reading the classified questions under the various captions. Perhaps a longer period for the

ᵂ The remainder of this circular was extracted from "The Majority," sections III and V.

whole process than nine months would be advisable; but during the months for consideration, before the final election, Bureaus of Information could be opened for the purpose of answering the people's questions and giving all facts that could be obtained along the lines in which the voters want enlightenment (I would not want the job of running one of these bureaus). Government bulletins could be issued, courses of lectures (spoken and printed), etc., could be instituted in this connection. THE AMBIGUITIES, PERSONAL ANIMOSITIES, ELOQUENT PLATITUDES, MIS-STATEMENTS DUE TO PARTY POLITICS AND ELECTION CAMPAIGN HYSTERICS WOULD BE OBVIATED TO SOME EXTENT (to a great extent, the writer thinks)— for where, except in a secondary way, would the politician come in?

IT IS DISCOURAGING FOR THINKING PERSONS and the majority (the people) are thinking nowadays—TO GO TO THE POLLS AND FIND NOTHING ON THE BALLOTS BUT A MASS OF NAMES AND PARTY EMBLEMS staring dumbly up at them. Election day seems less and less to measure up to the need for expression. ON EVERY HAND WE SEE AND FEEL THE PENT-UP DESIRE FOR SELF-EXPRESSION—a desire of the majority (the people) to register their convictions. THIS CANNOT BE PROPERLY SATISFIED OR ADEQUATELY REGISTERED IN TERMS OF ANY FEW, ANY GROUP, OR ANY PARTY, for prejudice has no part in social progress. What we have in mind and what we believe millions of others have in mind, is something more than the initiative and referendum—an institution the most surprising thing about which is that it was not adopted long ago under a National Constitutional Amendment. However, the referendum at its best is remedial or corrective rather than constructive. It is more an emergency expedient than a creative organic force.

The greater life values may not reach maturity until the direct expression of the mind and soul of the majority, the divine right of all consciousness, social, moral and spiritual, discloses the one true leader, even itself; then no leaders, no politicians and no parties will hold sway—and perhaps no more letters will be written to the newspapers "to bore the man at dinner."

II
CORRESPONDENCE WITH WILLIAM H. TAFT

WILLIAM H. TAFT
NEW HAVEN, CONNECTICUT

June 19, 1920.

Mr. Chas. E. Ives,
38 Nassau Street,
New York, N. Y.

My dear Mr. Ives:

I have your letter of May 26th. I am very much opposed to approve
such an amendment as that which you suggest. It is impracticable,
and would much change the form of our Government. It would be
introducing a principle of the referendum, which I think has already
been demonstrated to be a failure in securing the real opinion of
the people.

Sincerely yours,
Wm. H. Taft

IVES & MYRICK
38 NASSAU STREET
NEW YORK

June 22nd, 1920.

Hon. William H. Taft,
New Haven,
Connecticut.

My dear Mr. Taft:—

Thank you very much for your letter of the 19th. You are the only
one of the many I have written, who has answered by coming out
and saying exactly what he thought. If I might be persuaded that you
are right and I am wrong, it would save me time and energy, which

I cannot well spare now. But as long as my convictions in the premises stand as they do, I feel it a duty to do what little I can to see that some such plan (not necessarily mine) for more accurately registering public opinion is discussed in as comprehensive a way as possible. I *feel* strongly that I am right, which is not the same as saying that I *know* that you are wrong.

How can any process be said to be "impracticable" until it has been tried? How can any principle be said to have been a failure in securing the real opinion of the people, when nothing has ever been tried or at least, when there has been no adequate or systematic way tested out with some degree of thoroughness to secure the real opinion of the people?

An examination of the results of the referendum, in the various states where it has been tried, is not encouraging nor conclusively discouraging,—in fact to judge accurately the virtue or faults of this or any social or political phenomena, by evidence furnished only in the experimental or formative period, is in my opinion, almost impossible; an attitude either for or against has to be a matter more to do with "faith than facts". However, the initiative and referendum is hardly more than a remedial measure. It is hardly broad enough in scope or purpose, as far as I can learn, to encourage constructive popular thinking.

A vote by the people after six months of serious consideration to ten fundamental national questions *will not* change the form of our government any more than my going to the store instead of sending a messenger will necessarily change the form of the goods bought. Representative government, as I see it, is not an organic state or institution in itself. It is a practical and expedient part of a process, which has given popular government a start. If it can be learned by reasonable tests how far for the common good direct processes can be evolved from the representative ones—these tests, it seems to me, do not change our form of government, but rather help to perfect it.

Registering majority-opinion in a more careful and accurate way than it has been registered will bring to the aid of the government a force making for wholesome, just and conservative progress in the affairs of this country—for the great body of our people are neither unreasonable extremists nor hopeless reactionaries. It is possible that the time has not come when the plan proposed in the amendment should be tried out. Perhaps the people do not want to try it—but why not find out whether they do or not?

I hope you will pardon the length of this letter. I did not intend to bother you to such an extent. Some day I may feel as you do about this question, but today I decidedly *do not* agree with you. Let me thank you again for your letter; I am grateful to have the expression of opinion of one for whom I have great respect and admiration.

Sincerely yours,
Charles E. Ives

III

LETTER TO EDITORS

October 19, 1920.

To the Editor of ——,

Dear Sir:

If Mr. Harding is elected will it mean that the majority of our voters have familiarized themselves with the covenant of the "League of Nations" and that after serious reflection they have decided against it—that they have decided to declare themselves timid and ungenerous? No, not necessarily!

If Mr. Cox is elected will it mean that they, after the same careful consideration, have decided to show the opposite qualities? Not necessarily! Though doubtless a decisive Democratic victory would indicate that the pro-League sentiment is stronger and deeper than the anti-League sentiment is if the Republicans win by a decisive majority. For it requires a greater effort to dig out facts and then take an active, progressive, and unselfish stand than to rest in a passive, emasculated, or negative position. Although civilized man knows that it has been only through a kind of progressive altruism that the human now differs from the animal (sometimes), he is slow and timid in applying its principles. With the exception of the partisan and prejudiced vote, or the vote of those considering other issues more important, those neither for or against the League will, for the most part, vote against it; that is, they will passively vote for

Harding (whatever that means).[x] And one of the common reasons of neutral voters for not being interested in the League or in any other important issue, for that matter, is that they don't understand it.

Whose fault is it that they don't understand it? Theirs, partly— but it is more than theirs—it is the fault of an inadequate system or rather of no-system of federal procedure for accurately presenting to the voters, in an unprejudiced way, the fundamental premises at issue in important public questions.

So what will the result of the election mean—conclusively? That the "ins" are out or in, and the "outs" are in or out. That some people will feel better or worse, and that the usual inferences will be drawn, favorable or unfavorable, vague or cock-sure, good or bad, according to the predilection, blood-pressure, size of soul or pocket-book, etc. It will mean that the little cross-currents of local, traditional, inherited, political, personal, racial, provincial, partisan prejudices have so mixed up and deformed the bigger problems that we have a substantial jumble before us instead of a conclusive answer! It will mean that another conventional process of party determination is over; that the machinery of one party is perhaps a little better greased than that of another. It will mean that in another few years or so the usual feeling of dissatisfaction toward those in office will appear: "We're tired of 'em, let's try the 'outs' "; and then the Republican, Democratic or some other party (make X here) will go in and . . . over again "dal segno."

To present more thoroughly and comprehensively the important truths underlying national questions and to find out what the people are thinking about them may not be the tremendously difficult problem which some believe. To those fine old ladies in the Senate, any plan to this end seems hopelessly impracticable. They like to call it impossible and waive discussion; for presumably they cannot so easily scold and pick up their skirts and step over this kind of a path—or put obstacles to it in the mouths of Washington and Lincoln—for the 20th century is not, not yet, a contemporary of the 19th—except to 19th century minds. To some anything apparently new is painful, and we'll have to admit that any such plan is comparatively new, for

[x] The Republican platform straddled the issue of our entry into the League of Nations. But Harding, in his inauguration speech, made it clear that he did not intend to promote our entry into the League.

only recently (about 300 B.C.) Aristotle (or was it Plato?) inferred that if one wanted to find out what the Athenians were thinking about—*specifically*, it might be a good plan to ask them—*specifically*.

An attempt to suggest a reasonable plan fairer than that of party campaign platforms for more clearly presenting the fundamental premises relating to public matters, for encouraging serious and accurate thought about them, and then of more effectively registering public opinion has been put into the form of a constitutional amendment (and accompanying it is a discussion of the plan in its fundamental aspects).

It was somewhat surprising to find that most men in political or public life (including editors) are not interested and that most everybody else is. Hence we're not worrying too much about the shock that may come at seeing our composition in print—or because there is much danger that this "transcendent-panacea" (a "label" not a "hyperbole")—will be precipitately adopted—by Congress or in a party platform—for what party is there that will take any chance of voting itself out of existence—even to win an election!

Your very truly,
Chas. E. Ives,
38 Nassau St., N. Y.

SIX

LETTER TO
FRANKLIN D. ROOSEVELT
and MEMORANDA

INTRODUCTORY NOTE

IN 1935, Rep. Louis Ludlow, of Indiana, introduced a resolution in the form of a constitutional amendment limiting the authority of Congress to declare war.[y] It was proposed that except in the case of invasion war could be declared only after a majority vote in a nationwide referendum. The resolution was not immediately accepted, and it was reintroduced several times between 1935 and 1938. After its reintroduction in 1937, a national poll indicated that 73 per cent of the people were in favor of a referendum of that type. Passage of the resolution was considered likely when it came before the second session of the 75th Congress in January, 1938.

Ives, of course, was all in favor of the Ludlow Resolution, as it was precisely the sort of procedure for finding the true feeling of the

[y] Ludlow's plan is explained in his book, *Hell or Heaven* (Boston, 1937).

people that he had advocated approximately twenty years earlier. So he assembled some of his writings from the World War I period and sent them with letters to President Roosevelt and other high government officials. On the date of Ives' letter (Jan. 6, 1938), President Roosevelt wrote to Speaker William B. Bankhead, saying, "Such an amendment to the Constitution as that proposed would cripple any President in his conduct of our foreign relations, and it would encourage other nations to believe that they could violate American rights with impunity." The House returned the resolution to committee.

The materials in the Collection relating to this document are:

1. A letter of November 15, 1935, from the Rev. Wendell J. Clark of Bethel, Conn., thanking Ives for letting him see "Memos in re Papers on Matters of Economics, Relations Between Nations, Referenda, Etc.," and informing him that he had used them in a sermon. This was the year (1935) that the Ludlow Resolution was first introduced.
2. Three complete typed versions of the "Memos," the final one together with a letter to President Roosevelt.
3. Several carbon copies of the letter and "Memos" finally sent to Roosevelt and others. This version is shortened and the language is toned down considerably, especially in the references to politicians.

The version given here is a combination of the third typing mentioned above in Item 2 (called MS. 1) and Item 3 (called MS. 2).

The letter is from MS. 2.

Section I is from MS. 1 with slight alterations based on MS. 2.

Section II is from MS. 2 with insertions from MS. 1, the most important ones being the anecdote about the Southern soldier and the ending, from "Who makes war? . . ." onwards.

Section III is from MS. 1.

The letter is reproduced as it is. The punctuation of Sections I, II, and III, since the material is expository, has been revised.

LETTER TO
FRANKLIN D. ROOSEVELT

January 6, 1938.

My dear Mr. Roosevelt:—

I am taking the liberty of writing you to say that it seems to me that the Ludlow Bill should be discussed and then passed. It will bring before the people matters not among the most difficult for them to think about and act wisely upon. The successful and eventual working out of the plan, at least as to its fundamentals, to a great extent, depends obviously upon its not being misunderstood by other nations and upon their cooperation.

This understanding and cooperation probably will take time to develop but because they probably lie more or less dormant today may not be a good reason why this bill should not be passed. The writer believes that the American people are courageous enough to be willing to make a start in this great matter. Perhaps the people, before the bill is passed, should be given a chance in prior referendum, to say whether they want to take this responsibility or not (see Section 3, Page 2 of enclosed suggested amendment). However, in the present instance, this may cause delay and so not be advisable.

Whether this War Referendum Bill is passed or not, it seems to the writer that if a way could be found (which would receive a fair and right understanding) so that the government of this country could ask the governments of all countries, if they will also put the matter of war before all the people, one of the greatest moves onward and for the good of humanity would begin.

In view of the condition in which the world finds itself today, it would seem that now is the time for all existing governments to think, or at least to start to think, of possible and practical ways which would not be readily misunderstood, (there must be ways within the realm of human possibilities) which will bring the people of the world together—in a "man-to-man" way—something greater than a "government-to-government" way—and let all the people stand up and say what they think about "WAR."

The difficulties of working out the move suggested above, for many reasons—diplomatical, economical, political, even constitutional —may seem to many overwhelming, insurmountable and hopelessly impossible—but I don't like to think a move of this kind is impossible just because it has never been tried.

The enclosed memoranda and a copy of a suggested amendment made by the writer some years ago, you may be willing to look over.

With best wishes, I am

Sincerely yours,

CHARLES E. IVES.

MEMORANDA

[x]Of all the departments of human life and its fundamental activities, the one that has been the slowest to develop and the weakest in showing progress is social evolution, especially as to the relations between nations. A fundamental reason for nationalism was fear, and it still is, not in quite the dull form it was once, say, in the days of the feudal barons, Indian tribes, etc. People grouped themselves together to protect themselves from other groups. Today, except in a very few lands (in fact, the exception is almost negligible), neighboring towns or neighboring families do not dig moats around themselves and try to settle the bargains and problems of common life by

---

[x] At the beginning of this section there is the reference, "See page 4— Chapter I—Foreword." The reference fails to connect to any available published or unpublished writing of Ives. The content suggests that it could have been taken from an early version of "The Majority," or from some of the "People's World Nation" writings.

the axe. A few soft-headed, thick-skinned political parties may try to get "theirs" this way, but nowadays most people in most countries live without chronic fear of their neighbors and are now strong enough to settle their differences with their brains, instead of the coward's way of beating around the bush with a gun.[a] But generally speaking, governments have not grown out of the baby age of social evolution.[b] They, that is the politicians in control of them, can get more limelight, publicity, vainglory, so-called fame and like appeals to the vanities—and probably more money—by singing the same old platitudes ("bunk" is a better translation); and the defenseless, inarticulate millions are so used to it that they (too many of them, at least) accept it. And so, outside of the personal work and problems of their own lives and activities, they give more of their spare thought and time than is necessary to the easy unessentials, which include, among others, the radio sap, the movie mush, the tabloid lolly pop, etc., because these wares are easier to eat, easier to sell, and easier to make money out of than the products of a stronger manhood. But give these millions a fair chance to get their teeth into stronger food, and then, in the opinion of the writer, it will not be many generations before all these various political groups throughout the world—with their medieval stuff well organized, fancy labels, and strutting leaders—will be recognized as being as useless to humanity as a policeman in Heaven. And what will do this, and where is its foundation? The respect for, and the use more and more, of the innate something that the Creator has put into the minds and hearts of men. And thus men, and so mankind, will soon begin to feed on their own food, and they will handle it well and grow strong on it, and the emasculated commercialized "candy" will gradually become a nausea to the majority. There are signs of this transition.

Eventually, the working out of the great and serious fundamental problems of life between men and between nations will be put in their natural battlefields: the minds, hearts, and souls of all men in

[a] A note on the back of the page reads: If cowards fly over & drop bombs on your children,—get up & kill the cowards—that's not declaring war,—you just enter the war to kill a skunk for the good of humanity—that's a very different thing than starting war to get more money or land, as a "hog" tries to get "his" in the pigsty.

[b] The following passage, "They, that is the . . ." to "Eventually, the working out . . ." was omitted in the material sent to President Roosevelt.

this world—Humanity. "But," Rollo[c] says, "how can this be done?"
And somebody may say to Rollo, "By trying every fair and open way
the human mind can try, and not by saying it cannot be done—and
not by lolling back and letting this group and that group, and this
leader and that leader, or this party and that party, or some political
manoeuverer or some other self-seeking partialist, have the whole say
—not by the conventional ineffective ways, platitudes, dogmas, headlines, and half-truths which confuse all issues and all ideals. Millions
of people can be interested sincerely and seriously in their own great
problems—but this will not be done by saying it can't be done, and
then leaning on the hitchin' post through Eternity."

Most Americans, at least the majority of them, still have enough
independence of thought and action to work out their own way of
progress to better things. And it won't be by imitating or by swal-
lowing down whole any pet formula of Europe, Asia, or Africa. That
the processes will have some things in common with those of men
in other parts of the world is quite probable. But they will not be
taken "hook, line, and sinker" from any "ism" of any other country.
They will grow from the soil and the mind of the people making
them.

II

Suppose the governments of all nations in the world should ask
today the following questions of all citizens: what do you think the
people's answers would be? In the final analysis, the writer believes
the answer would be: "No more war in the world."

Citizens: Ask your governments to ask you these questions:

Do you, citizens of all countries and lands in this world, want to
have the say, directly and forever, as to whether there shall be war*

* The word "war" in the above intends to refer to a premeditated and official
declaration of war against any other nation or nations that have made no official
declaration of war, and does not refer to matters of invasions or attacks upon
a country's citizens or territories made deliberately by another government—
in general, offenses which require immediate action. Though it may lead to
war, and in some cases it is quite right that defensive action should lead to
war, if a coward flies over and drops a bomb on a sleeping child's head, the
only thing for a man to do is to rise up and get that dehumanized pigeon
whether it brings us to war, hell, or Heaven.

[c] A character appearing frequently in the margins of Ives' manuscripts, who
was the personification of the conservative. After a particularly unconventional passage, Ives would jot a note to the effect that "Rollo" would never
like it. (See entries under "Rollo" in the index of Kirkpatrick's *Catalogue*.)

or no war when for any reason, or at any time, your government—
that is, those in control of the government—would desire or believe it
necessary for your country to declare war on any other country or
other nation?

Do you demand that before war is declared you be given completely, truthfully, the reasons and premises which have to do with
the situation, [in order] that you may know all that there is to know
about the causes[d] of this contention—not the evidence rigged up by
some political party, nor by the politicians in control of the government, nor by half-truths in newspaper headlines or other lines—but
the truth, as far as it is within human power to present it—the truth
that can be obtained from every source and from every side, in all
countries affected in any particular controversy, situation or dispute.
In a word, do you want to sit in judgment and have the say?

Do you believe that the cause of war has much, if anything, to do
with the will of the people?

Do you think that any nation declaring war first in any dispute
has done so because the people, after knowing all the truth underlying the presumed reasons for war, have demanded that war be
declared?

Of the millions of men (mostly young men), how many of all that
were killed in any war knew all the premises of the contention between the nations involved, and then gave their direct consent to
war and their readiness to be killed?

Of the millions that have been in active service of nations declaring war first, how many had any say as to whether there should be
war or not?

The perennial answer of not all but of too many of those in charge
of the governments and armies is: "It can't be done. People must
trust us to know the best there is to do. How could the people decide?
It takes political experience, technical knowledge of diplomatic mat-

[d] The following note is written in pencil on the back of the first page of
Section II, MS. 2: I mean, by cause, the real beginning—not after babies have
been bombed to death by cowards starting the war. If war must be made—the
people shall start—after knowing all all all there is to [know]. They will rise
like men—as though to say—"People rise & be men" do it yourself—will you
run around & [illegible]—don't let the political liliputions do it—it's for you
to say & do—not Hitler, Roosevelt, Stalin—Hitler etc. etc.—Rise & tell them
to "Shut up"—or they will soon [last three words illegible].

ters. The average man is incapable of handling these difficult problems, etc., etc., etc."

These old ladies may be wrong.

There has been no war (at least for a good many years) when the main, underlying reasons could not, if presented, have been understood by all the people, except possibly the nice village idiots. However, in past ages the process of getting all the premises before all the people, if it had ever been attempted, would have been a slow, difficult, if not impossible, job. But today the means of communication which science has helped us out with would make the job less difficult.

And some of the "male old ladies" ask: "Do you think that no nation, or group of states or of nations, ever entered a war with a just reason?" "Yes, [we answer] but only as a defense after another nation had declared war. For instance, France and England, after Belgium had been dishonored. Yet the German people had practically nothing to do with starting the war. A few politicians, as usual, maneuvered the whole thing, and incidentally took a good many years to do it. The German people had for years been fed half truths, as usual, and were trained to fall for them, and for that matter, so were the people of all countries. The same can be said about the row in the Balkan States that gave Wilhelm a kind of an excuse for starting his war. A few princes, parties, etc.—not the people."

Then the Rollos ask: "How about the war against slavery in the United States in 1860? Did not the North have just cause for entering the war?" "Yes, [we answer] but what started the war? The people of the South? No. A few politicians and slave owners in power in the South, helped by the newspapers. The people were not consulted."

The following is an incident in this connection which is of interest.

In July, 1913, Mrs. Ives, her father, and I went to Gettysburg for the 50th Anniversary of the Battle of Gettysburg. One evening while walking down a road, on each side of which the Southern and Northern soldiers were camped and holding forth reminiscences, there was one old Southern soldier sitting in a group of veterans, talking somewhat as follows:

"Now I have had plenty of time to think about this war during the last fifty years. I have lived back in the mountains, and have had plenty of time to think, and I have come to the conclusion that it was a rich man's war. Down where I came from, and in other towns in the South, only a comparatively few owned slaves—the more money a man had, the more slaves he had—and those of this minority group did not want to have their property taken from them, so they practically started the war by secession. The rest of us people did not own slaves and had nothing to say about it. We were just handed out bunk by the newspapers, and by the politicians—that the Northerners were coming down to kill us and our families, and we had better join in to protect ourselves—a lot of hot-air speeches, parades, brass bands, etc.—and thus we got it in the neck. IT WAS A RICH MAN'S WAR."

All the other old Southern soldiers around him seemed to rather agree with him as far as we could hear.

In reviewing the national and political history of most countries, a distinction has to be made—a distinction difficult to make, but there is a distinction—between "war" in a broad sense (a somewhat premeditated movement organized officially to some extent, and between groups in a country or between countries) and an uprising of a local character, relatively sudden and unpremeditated, of the people in a community against some injustice, indignities, which brought hardship, suffering, and unbearable living conditions. But today most people are realizing more and more that there are stronger and more effective ways of righting wrongs than the old-fashioned Wat Tyler way.[e] And in most of the world those days of wholesale intolerance are over. War between nations is the *one* perfectly stupid thing that still hangs over the world. The great majority of all people realize that. They look upon it as a weak symptom of suspicion, fear, and so, too much of physical cowardice. It is but the way of the medieval half-wit. It settles nothing and never will settle anything except the bottom of the graveyard. And when the day comes when those men now doing the bossing in all governments will see what the people

[e] Leader in the English peasant revolt of 1381, who gained concessions from Richard II by violence. The concessions were revoked by Parliament a year later.

see, and feel what the people feel—war between nations will stop. Who makes war? The People?
NO, THE POLITICIANS.

III

†If you want to find the best way to make things worse in the above matters (Foreign Relations), take the advice of any well-known authority on international law; or if you want to be reasonably sure what the right ways may be, ask any old experienced authority on international relations, any old master on treaty-making, put down exactly the opposite to what the expert's advice is, and you may be somewhere near right.

Some of the things that cause bad feeling and suspicion between nations are the result of the old, and today unnecessary, habits—tariffs, custom duties, etc., and treaties between a few nations and not between all the nations. Some day there will be a universal treaty for all, and then no treaties will be necessary.

Who gets it in the neck? The Politicians?
NO, THE PEOPLE.
Who has the whole say in all countries? The People?
NO, THE POLITICIANS.
In what country in the world do the people rule?
NO COUNTRY.
What country in the world is bossed by a few politicians?
ALL COUNTRIES.

But some "MORNING GLORIOUS" (not tomorrow) these answers will be "right-about-facing" and the Tread up the Mountain, resounding around the World, will bring a New Horizon to All.

[Section IV is an excerpt from *Essays Before A Sonata*—the paragraph beginning on page 62 and ending on page 63. A copy of the brochure, "A Suggestion for a 20th Amendment," was also attached to the papers.]

† This section has a reference "From Section C—Chapter IV," which fails to connect it to any available work of Ives. But the second paragraph ties it to the end of the first paragraph of the "People's World Nation" material, which also has an enigmatic reference. See p. 228, fn. h.

SEVEN

A PEOPLE'S
WORLD NATION

INTRODUCTORY NOTE

Oᴺᴇ of Ives' most persistent
ideas, from the beginning of World War I in 1914 onwards, was that
the people of the world (not the politicians) should unite to form a
"People's World Nation." A large folder in the Collection contains
manuscript material ranging from approximately 1914 up into the
period of World War II. Newspaper and magazine clippings saved
by Ives (often with notes written in the margins) show that he followed eagerly any development that supported his general idea. He
was, of course, passionately in favor of the League of Nations, and
he had the good fortune to live long enough to see the formation of
the United Nations.

Here is a list of manuscript materials in the Collection which are
relevant to Ives' "People's World Nation" scheme:

1. A four-page, double-spaced typescript which, according to a
   pencilled note, was read before a manager's meeting (Mutual
   Life Insurance Co. of New York) on June 11, 1916. The note
   must have been added much later, as the date cannot be cor-

rect. On the second page a reference is made to President
Wilson's "fourteen articles (as outlined in his speech of January 11th)." Wilson's speech outlining his Fourteen Points took
place on January 8, 1918. The paper tells of Ives' attempt to find
out whether people really ponder the great issues of the day.
After talking to about a hundred men in all walks of life, Ives
reports that only two were unwilling to express an opinion. The
document draws up a list of war aims and peace terms, support-
ing Wilson's "fourteen articles" and the formation of a League
of Nations. It insists that "there be no secret alliances between
Count So-and-So and Lord So-and-So," and that every detail
of the peace discussions be placed before the public. Parts of
the document, according to a pencilled note at the end, were
sent to the papers after 1918.

2. One typed page proposing a "People's World Union" on which
pencilled notes begin in the margins and continue on through
five added pages. The typed page corresponds closely to pages
1 and 2 of Item 3 (below), while the pencilled notes are the
draft for the material beginning on page 4 of Item 3. The typed
page appears to be of the World War I period, while the
pencilled notes seem to be in the handwriting of the World
War II period.

3. A set of carbon copies (eight pages, renumbered in pencil)
which outline a proposal for a "People's World Union or
World Nation." The first three pages are from World War I
material, as a pencilled note indicates, the next two are possibly from the World War II period, and the last three are
clearly from the latter period. The assembly of the renumbered
and new pages took place in connection with an occasion
which is explained under Item 4.

4. Two separate typings of the first two pages of Item 3, with
some revisions and deletions. A note at the end reads: "The
above are two pages from a rather long article—memoranda,
papers, etc., written after the 1914 World War started—going
into the plan in some detail. The old pages are being revised
and brought more up to date. A complete copy will be sent
later." There is no evidence in the Collection to indicate that
this intention was ever carried out. It is the second typing of

the two pages on the "People's World Nation" that provides the explanation for Ives' reworking of the old material during World War II. To these pages is clipped a description of a piece called "The War Song March." The composition is a reworking of a World War I song, "He is there" (May 30, 1917), and it includes a new verse which reads, in part: "Then it's build a People's World Nation/Every honest country free to live its own Native Life." A note at the bottom of the page which describes the piece reads: "Sent by the League of Composers, New York, to the New York Philharmonic as its program notes,[g] and to the Columbia Broadcasting Co. radio announcer."

5. Assorted manuscript pages from the World War II period, all dealing with the idea of a "People's World Nation," the "One Hope of the World." These pages contain repetitions of ideas that are expressed with greater clarity in the earlier writings.

The version of the "People's World Nation" given here is based upon the most complete document, Item 3, to be referred to as MS. 1. In several cases, revised readings have been taken from Item 4, to be called MS. 2, but the deletions made in that version have not been observed. Some marginal additions to MS. 1 have been noted. The punctuation in the text has been revised slightly, but the marginal notes are given as they are.

The pages 3–8 of Item 3, which Ives did not have retyped to go with his program notes for the "War Song March," bear the note, "for small printing on back," implying that Ives may originally have had a circular in mind, such as he produced for his "Twentieth Amendment" scheme. From these pages, four paragraphs have been omitted here, as they deal with the problems of placing issues before the people—problems which are discussed fully in "The Majority." The final paragraph, written at the time of World War II, but containing significant reminiscences of 1914, is given.

[g] The conductor, according to correspondence in the Collection (drafts of letters in Mrs. Ives' hand) was to have been Artur Rodzinski. However, the performance never took place.

A PEOPLE'S WORLD NATION

THE first great move for the people of this world to make now is to build a People's World Union or World Nation[h] (or call it the United States of the World), under whose constitution each country will be free to live its own native life, and the people free to work out for themselves their own problems in a fair, open-minded "will-of-the-people way"—not a way bossed by the pet slant of some old boss. No country shall try by force to capture another country—no more sneak-thieving by medieval-minded dictators. No country shall join another country unless it shall be by the open, fair, and direct will of the people of all countries concerned. No country shall force or try to force on another country any economic [or] political plan, system or "ism." Each country will work out its own natural ways from the soil up to better things, and after careful thought, [to] the will of the people—processes that will come in a gradual growth, perhaps several generations, and not by any sudden, underhanded, dark-age bossy gouge of any one group. All the people shall be given

[h] This opening for the first sentence is pencilled into MS 1. In all other versions, the sentence begins, "In this connection (see 3rd Section, Chapter I B, page 138), a People's World Union . . ." The page reference is enigmatic. Ives' largest prose work is the *Essays Before A Sonata,* but the MS is numbered by chapters, and the numbers are never as high as 138. The next largest MS is "The Majority," which in its final form has only 84 pages. But some of these pages are renumbered, the numbers reading as high as 208 in one instance. This suggests that the above reference might be to the MS of an early, much longer form of "The Majority." This speculation does not seem unreasonable on the basis of content.

228

openly the facts, premises, and truths having to do with the fundamental problems of life in a direct will-of-the-people way; and "where
there's a will, there's a way."[1] Also, other kinds of unnatural barriers
which have caused some bad feeling and suspicion between nations
will be removed or lowered, [such] as the old unnecessary habits:
tariffs, custom duties, etc., treaties between a few nations and not
between all nations. Under the People's World Nation there will be
a universal treaty for all, and private treaties, as such, will have
no part.

Under the People's World Nation there shall be in place of national armies throughout the world, A People's World Nation Army
Police Force. Its principal duty will be to stop all criminal acts of
any country, especially that [act] of sneak-thieving its way into another country. Fundamentally, its work will be analogous to that of
the usual town and city police in most countries today—who get the
horse thieves—and the People's World Nation Police will just as
efficiently get worse thieves than that, such as these cowardly bombing baby killers, and of course the lesser criminals who break the
"People's Law."[j] But there is one thing in their work which the
People's World Nation Army Police shall not do[k] under any conditions—forever and ever—in any way whatsoever—and that is to use
aeroplane bombs. Anyone who does shall be stoned to death—not
buried in graves but in swill piles—and any man who ever says that
bombing is right will be beaten on the jaw until the doorbell to Hell
rings them in!

Now there is one thing for Americans in these United States to get
up and do if we are MEN with the strength and courage of most
of our forefathers, and that is to do a bigger job than one which just
has to do with our own national defense; to help defend Humanity
from having to live or die in a world too much disgraced by medieval

[1] The following note is added in the margin of MS. 1: In other words,
let the people think for themselves and not just imitate their neighbors
or some conceited Jabberer, who crawls up in the limelight & looks down on
the people, & tries to tell others what to do.

[j] The remainder of this paragraph was not included in MS. 2 (program
notes for "The War Song March").

[k] The following insert is found on the back of p. 2, MS. 1: unless it be
found that there is absolutely no other way in which the PXXA Police can
stop a criminal slaveland country from bombing—a cowardly way of fighting—
the most cowardly way in the history of the world.

slavery, dark-age bossing by "half-wit" slave-making bosses, a world of animal-like suspicion, also disgraced by too much pragmatism, greed, and thievery—thievery between countries enslaving the minds and souls as well as the bodies of mankind.[1] A People's World Nation in which every honest country will be free to live its own native life with the help of its World Army Police will bring the greatest hope of the world today to its realization; a world where men can stand up as men and friends, and "do unto others as they would be done by," not just exist as cowardly suspicious enemies, slaves of dictators —a world in which the people will have more to say and the boss politicians less, and the dictators nothing to say, except perhaps to some of their slaves in hell. And some morning glorious (but not quite tomorrow) the trend up the mountain resounding around the world will bring a new and radiant horizon to all.

•   •   •   •   •   •

One summer morning nearly thirty years ago, there probably came to millions of people a thought, as it came to one man who remembers the clear, but sudden, picture of [in] humanity forced on the world, as when the first news of the Kaiser's hog-march through Belgium was read on that early morning train. The same thought must have come to all Americans in one form or another. Before this there had been a general feeling that the world was now stronger and above these little medieval fusses—that the world now had grown to strong manhood and that sneak-thieving through Belgium was hardly more possible than if Connecticut had hog-marched through Rhode Island to get more fish.[m] So now the one big thing for the

[1] A pencilled note on p. 8 of MS. 1 with a reference to this place in the preceding text reads: This was written before the present war of Dec. '41, in fact quite some of it is from some memos, papers, letters, etc. written, some of it, a few months after the war of 1914 started. Many, it is remembered, were convinced that something described above as a People's World Union could & should be worked out. Now let this war stand as the first big movement to build the People's W. U. and then everybody who has done his part in the war in any real way will go down in the history of the world as builders of the greatest movement ever in history.

[m] The following insert is written on the back of p. 7, MS. 1: And at this time, the thought was in many minds, at least in a general way, that if the people of all the countries in the world could stand up together, know each other in some kind of natural man to man way—these old aged national ways of greed, any hogging suspicion and nation conceit—the ways of the slave making tyrants—a world union of real men could be born—the hope of all people of this world.

people in the world today is to make a man's world and not a sneak-thieving, sissy, molly-coddle, suspicious world to live in and die in. And the writer is morally certain that millions and millions of people —yes, the great majority of people in our universal planet—feel and believe that the one hope of the world today is for all people to stand up as strong and honest men, "to do unto others as they would be done by" and get together as friends and not as suspicious cowards, and then work and build a People's World Union (Nation), where every honest man and every honest country has a fair chance to work out their own problems in their own way and live their own natural life—a life that God Almighty will be proud of.

EIGHT

THE AMOUNT TO CARRY
and CORRESPONDENCE
WITH DARBY A. DAY

INTRODUCTORY NOTE

I N 1910, the firm of Ives and Myrick established a training school for agents. Charles Ives supplied the agents with concrete help in the form of a pamphlet called "Life Insurance. The Amount to Carry, and How to Carry It." The school and the material Ives prepared for the agents had far-reaching, and still continuing, effects in the insurance business.

In 1920, Ives wrote an article for *The Eastern Underwriter* (September) called, "The Amount to Carry—Measuring the Prospect," which was reprinted in pamphlet form for the use of agents in the same year, and again in 1922. This pamphlet bears only a slight resemblance to the earlier one. While the earlier pamphlet was purely technical, the 1920 one was unavoidably affected by all the deeper questions Ives had on his mind at the time. There is no better illustration of the interrelation of Ives' business activities and his philosophical brooding than the opening sections of the 1920 version of "The Amount to Carry," in which he draws an analogy between the broad general principles on which progress is based in the business world and those on which it must be based in the political world. Progress has lagged in the political world, he says, but hope can be gained from the better conditions in the business world, where "fundamental truths and laws . . . come more readily and nearer home to the individual, and can be more readily and widely distributed and known." Just as the development of life insurance came in response to a long-felt human need, so, he feels, will come political institutions which respond to long-felt human needs. The argument followed in the introductory sections of the pamphlet is closely related to that pursued in "The Majority."

With all his visionary tendencies, Ives seldom lost sight of how minds more prosaic than his would react (to his music as well as to his writing), and he inserts a considerate warning to his insurance agent readers before he starts his discourse, telling them that "the subject matter relating to practical agency work begins in Section IV, part 4." But for the reader who does not skip his opening paragraphs, he inserts at an appropriate time a note offering to mail a copy of his "Twentieth Amendment" proposal "to anyone interested enough to write for it."[n]

The materials in the Collection relating to "The Amount to Carry" are:

1. Two copies of a pamphlet, "Life Insurance. The Amount to Carry, and How to Carry It," Second Edition, n. d.
2. A page from the above pamphlet marked for insertion in the manuscript of 1920 (Item 3, below).
3. The MS of an article for The Eastern Underwriter, Salesmanship Edition, September, 1920, called, "The Amount to Carry —Measuring the Prospect."
4. A copy of the above article reprinted in pamphlet form by Ives and Myrick, 1920.
5. Several copies of the 1922 printing of the above pamphlet (Item 4).

[n] In the Collection there is a letter from one Irving P. Wilt (Oct. 11, 1920) who requested a copy of the article. Since Ives was inclined to save such letters, this was probably the only request he received.

The three opening sections and the closing section (which is just as applicable to composing music as it is to selling insurance) of the 1920 version of "The Amount to Carry" are given here, reproduced literally with the exception of a few minor changes in punctuation.

Also given in this chapter is an exchange of letters between Ives and Darby A. Day, manager of the Chicago office of The Mutual Life Insurance Company of New York. It is another illustration of the permeation of Ives' ideals into his business activities.

THE AMOUNT TO CARRY—
—MEASURING THE PROSPECT

SUGGESTED PRESENTATIONS, SELLING PLANS AND FORMULAS
WHICH WILL GUIDE AND ASSIST THE AGENT IN
MAKING PROPER ADJUSTMENTS OF INSURANCE
PROTECTION TO CARRYING ABILITY AND NEEDS

The subject matter relating to practical agency work begins
in Section IV, Part 4

THERE is an innate quality in human nature which gives man the power to sense the deeper causes, or at least to be conscious that there are organic and primal laws (or whatever you care to call the fundamental values of existence) underlying all progress. Especially is this so in the social, economic, and other essential relations between men.

This intuitive and vague appreciation has apparently been more in evidence than the ability and quickness of men to analyze, or the interest to make sustained effort to discover and then in practical ways to benefit by, the lessons that can be learned from this intuition. From evidence in all civilizations, the instinctive reasoning of the masses has been the impelling influence in social progress; the intellect has been subordinate, has not kept up as far as it might with the lessons which this mass intuition threw off. Perhaps for some good reason the mind has to learn by the "dramatic." But the "fundamental," and the search for it, is seldom dramatic—it seldom makes a noise theatrical enough to stir the unthinking. Perhaps for some good reason, nature or a higher power has made it easier for man, when considering life from the standpoint of utility, to find an immediate appeal in the superficial, to show more ostentatious enthusiasm for the effect than for the cause. But for our part, we would rather believe that this has been so because, for physical reasons, the premises of, or the lessons from the deeper impulses have not been universally distributed, hence only the few have been able to observe them, and the many have not.

But a change in this relation is fast taking place. In a word, as the truer premises are becoming more widely distributed, the intellect —the majority intellect—grows in power to appreciate them; superstition is giving way to science, and in spite of an apparent or temporary lowering of ideals in some directions, which may be due to the sudden and over-intensive material development witnessed during the last hundred years, the influence of science will continue to help mankind realize more fully, the greater moral and spiritual values. As Voltaire suggests, "a little science takes us away from religion, and a great deal brings us back to it."

Progress Has Lagged

Some may say that the evidence of this change or progress in some of the present day relations between men is not as visible as they would wish; they cite, perhaps, the "political." Unfortunately, progress in this relation has "lagged," to say the least. There are still too many men who would rather read the gossip about a political candidate than the "platform" (assuming that platforms are worth reading.) There are still too many who will walk a mile to hear a self-advertised spellbinder say nothing in a spectacular way who won't lift a finger to read even a digest of—say, the covenant of the League of Nations, or any other important measure before the public. The cause of so much interest in the superficial which still remains in our political life is probably due, in great part, to this same insufficient "premise distribution." The Minority Mind has been too timid to trust the Majority Mind, and hence reluctant to pass around the "facts." Perhaps we can expect little progress politically until some practical plan can be worked out to encourage people to think, and then to act, in terms of principles and convictions rather than of persons and parties. Perhaps we will have to get rid of all parties, or at least the prejudices which they thrive on, before political progress will be more secure.

(Note—A suggestion to this end, if we may be forgiven a digression here, in the form of a constitutional amendment, together with an article discussing the plan in some detail and from various aspects, will be gladly sent by the writer to anyone who is interested enough to write for it.)

But this wholesome progress of learning the many lessons, of fundamental truths and laws, is making better headway in the economic and business relation. Naturally, here, the premises at issue come more readily and nearer home to the individual, and can be more readily and widely distributed and known, for one reason, because the personal interest in both the "causes and effects" is common to all. The improvement in service and increase in efficiency nowadays in most lines of business, is but an evidence of this gradual progress in learning how to discard the superficial for the fundamental—that is, a greater number of premises, essential truths, natural laws, or whatever they may be called, are being observed by a greater number of minds.

II

Life Insurance Doing Its Part

The foregoing, which will probably bore more readers than it will interest, is offered because to the writer there seems to be in the development of life insurance as an institution an interesting analogy —in theory, at least. The need for life insurance was felt by man long before the actuary discovered the mortality table. Before sufficient premises were gathered to build the institution, the family paid the claim; now the company pays it. Gradually enough premises came before enough minds, and an insurance organism was recognized; the companies were organized. Then came the period of bringing more minds to recognize the service of the institution as something supplying a need which had been long intuitively sensed. Here, an emotional appeal to the moral and altruistic side of human nature had to start men in overcoming prejudice and in accepting the service as a social duty.

This period is fast closing. Men are finding one of their instinctive wants acceptably satisfied, as soon as they understand what life insurance is for. As its functions become more and more a matter of common knowledge, the need for emotional processes becomes less and less. They will have their uses to some extent, probably for a good many years, and it is to be hoped they will—if for no other reason than for the sake of the color and variety they [emotional processes] may give the other processes, and to keep the technical points from becoming over-prosaic.

It can be said, at least of this country (perhaps it is even truer of some other countries), that the development of life insurance, particularly in the manner of presenting its services to the public and in increasing the benefits, has become more and more scientific in its work—that is, the fundamental in each essential premise has become clearer and clearer to more minds. Life insurance is doing its part in the progress of the greater life values.

III

GROWTH OF INSURANCE INTELLIGENCE

As a result of this progress of wider acceptance, fewer agents are jumping around in a casual way looking for the one extraordinary chance and missing the many ordinary ones. There is less speculative and more professional thought going on. There is less guesswork and more science. Fewer agents are interested in the "gossip" around the "sensational case," and more agents are interested in ways of working out legitimate methods than in ways of "working a bluff." And somewhere here, as the process of increasing the benefits becomes more definite and perhaps more wholesome, a kind of paradox may be observed: the larger the proportion of agents writing the small policies, and the smaller the proportion of agents writing large policies, the larger the small policy.

We believe one of the reasons for this is that the premises having to do with insurance fundamentals are being more widely distributed; that is, there is more intelligence on the part of both buyer and seller. The manner of selling is becoming more and more scientific. Agency work is becoming more a question of how the individual need can be accurately determined, rather than of why it should be considered at all or as such. The great majority of men today, in this country at least, know, perhaps only subconsciously, that a life insurance policy is one of the definite ways of society for toughening its moral muscles, for equalizing its misfortunes, and hence—the old problem—of supplying a fundamental instinctive want. Because this is now appreciated, no matter in what degree, the normal mind today knows that to carry life insurance is a duty—though it may consciously think of it purely as a duty to the family, and only that. Thanks to the pioneer agents of the last two or three generations, who pounded out the "gospel," perhaps only crudely, and with methods more emotional and personal than we have to use today—thanks to these persistent distributors of premises, the business man, the professional man, the wage earner of 1920, *admits* this duty. And what interests him now is to know how he can do his duty as it ought to be done. In answering this "How" more accurately, the agent has many chances of effectively pressing home the perennial "Now!"

•   •   •   •   •   •

IX

Not Complicated

To one who has had the patience to read all of the foregoing there will possibly come a thought, that the plan is involved, that it is too full of technical complexities. The justice of this criticism is more apparent than real. For what are technical complexities, anyway? [From] whence do they come if not from the natural evolution of the business? Why make believe they don't exist? Why not see if they have their lessons for us—and, if so, learn to use them or not use them, so that, in any event, our work may be made more valuable and comprehensive.

The method outlined in this paper, or any similar one, becomes less and less complicated the more thoroughly it is learned and the longer it is practiced. Whoever takes the trouble to know whatever

240   *Other Writings*

he has to know, whether it be a problem of "transmitting the molecular force," or of "selling a book," in as perfect a way as he is capable [of], and then keeps *at it and at it* until all sides of his problem may become as clear to him as the sun was to Galileo, *will* find a way of making his message clear to the dullest listener. Truth always finds a natural way of telling her story, and a natural way is an effective way, simple or not.

All fundamental aspects of anything—moral values or an organized business activity—have their complex side; all are part of the natural laws coming up from the roots. Any man, in any valuable work—no matter how limited his capabilities and power of expression seem to him at the start—who sincerely seeks to find the truths and essentials so often confused with or covered up by the immediate and superficial, and who constantly tries, as well as he knows how, to present them in preference to the easier, the more expedient, or the less substantial, will find a way to the *kind* of success he wants. And the way will be simple enough to be understood by the many, and complex enough to be of some value to all!

CORRESPONDENCE WITH DARBY A. DAY

THE MUTUAL LIFE INSURANCE COMPANY OF NEW YORK

Chicago, Ill.
February 7, 1920.

Darby A. Day,
Manager,
The Temple,
108 S. La Salle Street.

Messrs. Ives & Myrick,
Managers,
New York.

My dear Boys:—

You will note that I am addressing you jointly, because I believe that the accomplishment of January is too "goldarned big" to give credit to either one of you, solely or individually. It was a glorious month, a wonderful achievement, and we are proud of you, as proud can be! Sorry the country is so darn dry, or we would drink to your health.

In the language of Bill Smith, of Seattle, "more power to

you," and may it be but a fore-runner of twelve Three-and-a-Half-Million-Dollar months, is the wish of

Yours very sincerely,

Darby A. Day

February 11, 1920

Mr. Darby A. Day,
108 So. La Salle Street,
Chicago, Illinois.

Dear Darby:—

Thank you for your letter of the 9th.

As it so happens that Mike° has had more opportunity of seeing you than I have, I want to take this chance, if only in a line, to tell you personally that the interest and encouragement you have always shown us is appreciated.

We will see you, I presume, at the Managers' Meeting next month. It strikes me, as it does Mike, that something might be done or at least considered at that time—from the standpoint of just common ordinary business progress, to say nothing of that of the policy-holders,—towards bringing the Company nearer to what (we think) an Insurance Company ought to be. And one thing that might help would be to have a few insurance-intellects hashed in between some of those great-legal-financial-souls that have been our guides in various directions for some years past. A few capable insurance men who are vitally interested in the progress of the Company from a bigger standpoint than that of traditional finance, or of merely keeping the assets safe for the ladies, on the Board of Trustees might be a help to some members of the present Board, who are vitally interested—in what, we won't try to find out. Isn't it reasonable to suppose that some of our guardians ought to have a little more knowledge of life insurance fundamentals than they have? And if they did, would more interest be generated in the solution of the problems that we are up against?

One of the handicaps to better service is the fact that the majority

° Ives' partner, Julian S. Myrick.

of clerks are inadequately paid. This is a situation the Trustees ought to know about without being told. They ought, at least, to have imagination enough to sense situations like this. Mr. Dexter, as far as I can judge, is the only officer who has "creative-impulse"—(is that the right word?); and he can't do much in working out any constructive ideas if the Trustees, including the President, show no interest. The sub-normal interest, lack of incentive and enthusiasm of the clerical body is just one of the many things that show the results of loose-jointed, unrelated processes which all—from the noblest Director (whatever that means) down to the lowest mortality-killer—have been satisfied with.

Having got this off my chest,—which I didn't intend to do when starting,—I presume you now think it is time for me to close, and so do I.

Sincerely yours,

Charles E. Ives

NOTES

1. This theory is expressed by the following passage in *Facts and Comments* (New York, 1902), pp. 47-48: The antagonism between intellectual appreciation and emotional satisfaction, is essentially the same as one which lies at the root of our mental structure—the antagonism between sensation and perception; . . . the primary purpose of music is neither instruction nor culture but pleasure; and this is an all-sufficient purpose.

2. *What is art?* . . . , trans. Aylmer Maude . . . (New York and Boston, 1899), p. 47: . . . it is necessary, first of all, to cease to consider it a means to pleasure, and to consider it as one of the conditions of human life. Viewing it in this way, . . . art is one of the means of intercourse between man and man.

3. *Essays*, 2, III, 236: How sincere and confidential we can be, saying all that lies in the mind, and yet go away feeling that all is yet unsaid, from the incapacity of the parties to know each other, although they use the same words! My companion assumes to know my mood and habit of thought, and we go on from explanation to explanation until all is said which words can, and we leave matters just as they were at first, because of that vicious assumption.

4. "The Method of Nature," I, 208: Yet when Genius arrives, its speech is like a river; . . . Has anything grand and lasting been done? Who did it? Plainly not any man, but all men: it was the prevalence and inundation of an idea.

5. *Nature*, I, 9: Our age is retrospective. "The American Scholar," I, 89: The next great influence into the spirit of the scholar is the mind of the Past, — . . .

6. Channing, "Christianity is a Rational Religion," *Works*, pp. 233-234: I propose, first, to show that Christianity is founded on and supposes the authority of reason, and cannot therefore oppose it without subverting itself. . . . I trust I have conveyed to you my views in regard to the first characteristic of this highest power of the soul. Its office is to discern universal truths, great and eternal principles.

7. "Success," *Society and Solitude*, VII, 284: We are not strong by our power to penetrate, but by our relatedness. The world is enlarged for us, not by new objects, but by finding more affinities and potencies in those we have.

8. Bernard of Morval, monk of Cluny (fl. 1150), *De contemptu mundi* (critical edition, H. C. Hoskier, London, 1929). Probably known to Ives in a translation by J. M. Neale called "The rhythm of Bernard de Morlaix, monk of Cluny, on the celestial country" (New York, 1864). Several well-known hymn texts have been extracted from Neale's translation, among them, "Jerusalem the golden," on which Ives wrote pieces for band and for organ. Ives' teacher at Yale, Horatio Parker (1863-1919) made his international reputation with an oratorio on this text called "Hora novissima" (1893). Ives wrote a cantata called "The Celestial Country" on a hymn-text by Henry Alford, also dealing with the theme of the Heavenly City, which was performed at the Central Presbyterian Church, New York, 1902. The "Celestial City" is mentioned constantly in Hawthorne's story "The Celestial Railroad" in *Mosses from an Old Manse*. This story formed part of the subject matter of the Concord Sonata.

9. "Beauty," *Nature*, I, 29: For although the works of nature are innumerable and all different, the result or the expression of them all is similar and single. Nature is a sea of forms radically alike and even unique. A leaf, a sunbeam, a landscape, the ocean, make an analogous impression on the mind.

10. Henry A. Beers, *A History of English Romanticism in the Eighteenth Century* (New York, 1898), pp. 1-2: . . . the reader will be invited to examine a good many literary documents, . . . Even then he will hardly find himself prepared to give a dictionary definition of romanticism. . . . Romanticism, then, in the sense in which I shall commonly employ the word, means the reproduction in modern art or literature of the life and thought of the Middle Ages. . . . It is the definition Heine gives. . . .

11. "Poetry and Imagination," VIII, 70: And when life is true to the poles of nature, the streams of truth will roll through us in song:
"Woodnotes, II," *Poems*, 53: For Nature beats in perfect tune, / And rounds with rhyme her every rune, / Whether she work in land or sea, / Or hide underground her alchemy.

12. Ives actually attempted to effect such a change from representative to direct government through referendum by means of a twentieth amendment to the Constitution. He had a circular describing his proposal distributed at the Republican Convention in Chicago in 1920, and he mailed it to the editors of major newspapers and to important public office-holders. The only important figure who gave him a serious (although negative) response was William Howard Taft (letter of June 19, 1920).

13. "Modern Painters, IV," *Works*, VI, 66: I have also been more and more convinced, the more I think of it, that in general *pride is at the bottom of all great mistakes*. All other passions do occasional good, but whenever pride puts in *its* word, everything goes wrong, . . .

14. "Montaigne; or, The Skeptic," *Representative Men*, IV, 151-152: Remember the open question between the present order of "competition" and the friends of "attractive and associated labor." The generous minds embrace the proposition of labor shared by all; it is the only honesty; nothing else is safe.

15. David Willis Reeves, "Second Connecticut National Guard March," published in New Haven by C. M. Loomis, and copyrighted in 1877. Ives' copy is in the Collection at Yale. The margins contain some jottings toward a work called "Decoration Day." The march is referred to again by Ives on the margin of a sketch for "Yale-Princeton Football Game": Reeves 2nd Reg. Quickstep—always played by Brass Band at Games & reunions etc. (see Kirkpatrick, *Catalogue*, pp. 10, 30).

16. Carlyle, *Sartor Resartus; the Life and Opinions of Herr Teufelsdröckh*, *Works*, I, 210: Was it not the still higher Orpheus, or Orpheuses, who, in past centuries, by the divine Music of Wisdom, succeeded in civilising Man? Our highest Orpheus walked in Judea, eighteen-hundred years ago: his sphere-melody, flowing in wild native tones, took captive the ravished souls of men; and being of a true sphere-melody still flows and sounds, though now with thousandfold accompaniments, and rich symphonies, through all our hearts; and modulates, and divinely leads them.

17. "Plato; or, The Philosopher," *Representative Men*, IV, 77: These things we are forced to say if we must consider the effort of Plato or of any philosopher to dispose of nature,—which will not be disposed of. No power of genius has ever yet had the smallest success in explaining existence. The perfect enigma remains.

18. "Spiritual Laws," *Essays* 1, II, 156-157: Let a man believe in God, and not in names and places and persons. Let the great soul incarnated in some woman's form, poor and sad and single, in some Dolly or Joan, go out to service and sweep chambers and scour floors, and its effulgent daybeams cannot be muffled or hid, but to sweep and scour will instantly appear supreme and beautiful actions, the top and radiance of human life, and all people will get mops and brooms; until, lo! suddenly the

great soul has enshrined itself in some other form and done some other deed, and that is now the flower and head of all living nature.

19. "Milton," XII, 163: For who is there, almost, that measures wisdom by simplicity, strength by suffering, dignity by lowliness? Obeying this sentiment, Milton deserves the apostrophe of Wordsworth:

> "Pure as the naked heavens, majestic, free,
> So didst thou travel on life's common way
> In cheerful godliness; and yet thy heart
> The lowliest of duties on itself did lay."

20. In autobiographical material quoted by Cowell (p. 131), Ives states that he first heard the music of Stravinsky in 1919 or 1920. The work was *The Firebird*, ". . . and I thought it was morbid and monotonous; the idea of a phrase, usually a small one, was good enough, and interesting in itself, but he kept it going over and over and it got tiresome. It reminded me of something I had heard of Ravel, whose music is of a kind I cannot stand: weak, morbid and monotonous; pleasing enough, if you want to be pleased."

21. "The Old Manse," *Mosses from an Old Manse, Works*, II: Happy the man who in a rainy day can betake himself to a huge garret, . . . the secrets of which I never learned, being too reverent of their dust and cobwebs (p. 26). . . . The occupants, at various epochs, had left brief records and ejaculations inscribed upon the walls. There, too, hung a tattered and shrivelled roll of canvas, which on inspection proved to be the forcibly wrought picture of a clergyman, in wig, band, and gown, holding a Bible in his hand. . . . The original had been a pastor of the parish more than a century ago, a friend of Whitefield, and almost his equal in fervid eloquence [perhaps the Rev. William Emerson, first owner of the house, 1765, ancestor of Ralph Waldo Emerson]. I bowed before the effigy of the dignified divine (pp. 22-27), . . . and I could not but muse deeply and wonderingly upon the humiliating fact that the works of man's intellect decay like those of his hands. Thoughts grow mouldy (p. 29).

22. This story is related by Professor H. A. Beers in "A Pilgrim in Concord," *The Yale Review*, III (1914), 683. He describes his visit to the first session of the Concord School of Philosophy in 1879. Speaking to his host at the ancient tavern about Concord's literary inhabitants, he mentioned Alcott. The innkeepers reply was, "Oh, Alcott! The best thing he ever did was his daughters." It seems probable that this was the source of the story, Ives supplying the name of Staples, who had once been the keeper of the inn, long before 1879. The anecdote does not appear along with other well-known Staples anecdotes which are in various sources on Thoreau.

23. "Conclusion," *Walden*, 354:
> "Erret, et extremos alter scrutetur Iberos.
> Plus habet hic vitae, plus habet ille viae."
> Let them wander and scrutinize the outlandish Australians.
> I have more of God, they more of the road.

24. "Where I lived," *Walden*, 99: Little is to be expected of that day, if it can be called a day, to which we are not awakened by our Genius, but by the mechanical nudgings of some servitor, are not awakened by our newly acquired force and aspirations from within, accompanied by the undulations of celestial music, instead of factory bells, and a fragrance filling the air—to a higher life than we fell asleep from; . . . All memorable events, I should say, transpire in morning time and in a morning atmosphere.

25. "Economy," *Walden*, 78-79: I would not have any one adopt *my* mode of living on any account; for, beside that before he has fairly learned it I may have found out another for myself, I desire that there may be as many different persons in the world as possible. . . .

26. "Conclusion," *Walden*, 356: I learned this, at least, by my experiment; that if one advances confidently in the direction of his dreams, and endeavors to live the life which he has imagined, he will meet with a success unexpected in common hours. He will put some things behind, will pass an invisible boundary; new, universal, and more liberal laws will begin to establish themselves around and within him; or the old laws be expanded, and interpreted in his favor in a more liberal sense, and he will live with the license of a higher order of beings.

27. In *Dial*, but quoted from Van Doren, p. 93, which reads: The silent influence of example . . . is the true reformer. . . . Society are more benefited by one sincere life, by seeing how one man has helped himself, than by all the projects that human policy has devised for their salvation. . . .

28. "The Village," *Walden*, 191: I am convinced, that if all men were to live as simply as I then did, thieving and robbery would be unknown. These take place only in communities where some have got more than is sufficient while others have not enough. The Pope's Homers would soon get properly distributed.
> "Nec bella fuerunt,
> Faginus astabat dum scyphus ante dapes."
> "Nor wars did men molest,
> When only beechen bowls were in request."

"You who govern public affairs, what need have you to employ punishments? Love virtue, and the people will be virtuous."

29. This idea, developed in Ives' essay, "The Majority," was carried out by Ives in his personal life. Although he was the senior partner in the insurance firm of Ives & Myrick, which issued over $49,000,000 of insurance in 1929, the year before he retired, Ives refused to take a propor-

tionate share of the business, drawing only enough to meet the needs of his family, and a certain fund to be used for expenses connected with copying, publishing, and performing his music. From the latter fund, he made numerous contributions to needy organizations devoted to the publication of new music by other composers (see Cowell, pp. 119-120).

30. During World War I, Ives wrote a great many notes formulating what is described in portions of the manuscripts that still exist as a "People's World Union (or call it the United States of the World), under whose constitution each country will be free to live its own life, no country shall try by force to capture another country—no more sneak-thieving by medieval dictators."

31. In E. W. Emerson's *Thoreau* see pp. 14-16, and 124-125 (Notes) for boyhood stories; pp. 131-134 (Notes) for the letter to Ellen Emerson (July 31, 1849); pp. 68-70, for ministrations to the runaway slave, as related by Moncure D. Conway, a preacher from Virginia who lived for a time in Concord near the Thoreaus. Sam Staples was a Concord "character" who rose from hostler and bar-keeper to constable, and later Representative in the General Court. He was Thoreau's jailer in 1846 when Thoreau refused to pay his poll-tax in protest against the war with Mexico, and later, his friend and rodsman on surveying expeditions. E. W. E. gives a long note about him (pp. 136-138).

32. Van Doren, p. 43, quotes Stevenson as follows: "Thoreau is dry, priggish, and selfish," and has "none of that large, unconscious geniality of the world's heroes." Robert Louis Stevenson, *Familiar Studies of Men and Books* (London, 1882) reads: With his almost acid sharpness of insight, with his almost animal dexterity in act, there went none of that large, unconscious geniality of the world's heroes (p. 129). Thoreau is dry, priggish, and selfish (p. 160).

33. "Walking," *Excursions*, V, 247: We walked in so pure and bright a light, gilding the withered grass and leaves, so softly and serenely bright, I thought I had never bathed in such a golden flood, without a ripple or a murmur to it. . . . So we saunter toward the Holy Land, till one day the sun shall shine more brightly than ever he has done, shall perchance shine into our minds and hearts, and light up our whole lives with a great awakening light, as warm and serene and golden as on a bankside in autumn.

34. Apparently a mixed recollection of "Woodnotes" and the passage from Emerson's essay "Nature" (cited above) with the following lines from "Ponds," *Walden*, 207: Standing on the smooth sandy beach at the east end of the pond, in a calm September afternoon, when a slight haze makes the opposite shore-line indistinct. . . .

35. "Tuesday," *Week*, I, 201:
> Low-anchored cloud,
> Newfoundland air,

Fountain-head and source of rivers,
Dew-cloth, dream drapery,
And napkin spread by fays;
Drifting meadow of the air,

. . . .

36. "Sounds," *Walden,* 126: My house was on the side of a hill, immediately on the edge of the larger wood, in the midst of a young forest of pitch pines and hickories, and a half a dozen rods from the pond, to which a narrow footpath led down the hill.

"The Ponds," 207: Standing on the smooth sandy beach at the east end of the pond. . . .

"The Ponds," 206: I have in my mind's eye the western, indented with deep bays, the bolder northern. . . .

37. "Monday," *Week,* p. 185: Travelling on foot . . . when I reached the railroad in Plaistow, I heard at some distance a faint music in the air like an Aeolian harp, which I immediately suspected to proceed from the cord of the telegraph vibrating in the just awakening morning wind, and applying my ear to one of the posts I was convinced that it was so. It was the telegraph harp singing its message through the country, its message sent not by men, but by Gods. [For a discussion of the many references to the Aeolian sounds of a telegraph wire in Thoreau's *Journal,* and its deep spiritual significance to Thoreau, see Van Doren, p. 113.]

38. "Sounds," *Walden,* 123-124: I love a broad margin to my life. Sometimes, in a summer morning, having taken my accustomed bath, I sat in my sunny doorway from sunrise till noon, rapt in a revery, amidst the pines and hickories and sumachs, in undisturbed solitude and stillness. . . . I grew in those seasons like corn in the night, and they were far better than any work of the hands would have been. They were not time subtracted from my life, but so much over and above my usual allowance. I realized what the Orientals meant by contemplation and forsaking of works. For the most part, I minded not how the hours went. The day advanced as if to light some work of mine; it was morning, and lo, now it is evening, and nothing memorable is accomplished.

39. "Sounds," 136: Now that the cars are gone by and all the restless world with them, and the fishes in the pond no longer feel their rumbling, I am more alone than ever. . . . Sometimes, on Sundays, I heard the bells, the Lincoln, Acton, Bedford, or Concord bell, when the wind was favorable, a faint, sweet, and, as it were, natural melody, worth importing into the wilderness. At a sufficient distance over the woods this sound acquires a certain vibratory hum, as if the pine needles in the horizon were the strings of a harp which it swept. All sound heard at the greatest possible distance produces one and the same effect, a vibration of the universal lyre, just as the intervening atmosphere makes a distant ridge of earth interesting to our eyes by the azure tint it imparts to it. . . . The

echo is, to some extent, an original sound, and therein is the magic and charm of it. It is not merely a repetition of what was worth repeating in the bell, but partly the voice of the wood; the same trivial words and notes sung by a wood-nymph.

40. The first line of William Cullen Bryant's "Death of the Flowers" reads: "The melancholy days are come, the saddest of the year." The last sentence of Emerson's essay "Nature" (*Essays 2*, III, 188) contains the following phrase: ". . . it [wisdom] enveloped us in dull, melancholy days, for in days of cheerful labor. . . ."

41.
Dear Father,　　　　　　　　　　　　　New Haven Apr. 1 '94

Rec'vd your letter last evening after I had returned from New York. I left here at 10:35 and reached the city at a little before one o'clock, and went immediately to the Theatre in time to get a good seat in the family circle (top gallery). I could see quite well and could hear very plainly. I bought a libretto with both German & English words. I read the plot over thouroughly two or three times so I could understand and follow the German words better. I could easily see what Wagner tried to [do]. You wouldn't notice the music or the orchestra, as it all seems to be a part of and go along with the action and story, I don't mean that you wouldn't notice it, because one is interested in the play, but, that it feels as if it was only made to help one pay attention to the action. I don't remember of any particular piece or song that you would notice simply for the music itself unless it was the "Song of the Rhinedaughter" at the beginning of the 2nd Act. There are some things that don't seem exactly natural. For instance in one place, Siegfried is supposed to be greatly furiated at Brünhilde and she has a long song in which she is greatly excited and upbraids him, but he, instead of interrupting her waits until the orchestra plays a long intermezzo, and then begins, and there were several other places like that struck me as being rather unnatural, although there was probably some reason for it. They bring a horse on the stage, and it is supposed to be on the shore of the river but you can hear his hoofs striking the timbers of the stage, which spoils the effect. And then the using of so much horn and kettledrums, grows awful tiresome towards the end. And about all I can remember of the orchestra now, is that it was all diminished chords, wholes [whole-notes], and trombone. Of course I don't mean to criticize but [crossed out: there are just things] this is just as it seemed to me, but probably if I had studied it more before, I would think differently. But anyway the horse ought to have had some dirt to walk. I wish I had time to study and hear all of his operas. Everything all together is great and you can see just what his idea was, and it seems funny that nobody thought of it before. Although it does seem that if he had had more rhymn [rhythm] or connected melody (you know what I mean) in his music, and if the action was more natural, and if the plot had more sense to it, as it was just a common fairy story, and when you think·of it, it looks like a great deal of work over nothing, or if it was a fact in real history, or taken from some noted book, so that some educational benefit could be gotten from it. Will send the program and libretto, when I send wash, as I want you to read it over and tell what you think. . . .

42. "Spiritual Laws," *Essays 1*, II, 148: You think because you have spoken nothing when others spoke, . . . that your verdict is still expected with curiosity as a reserved wisdom. Far otherwise; your silence answers very loud.

43. Boston, 1837. A public meeting concerning the murder of Elijah P. Lovejoy (Alton, Ill.) by a proslavery mob. James T. Austin, attorney general of Mass., said Lovejoy died as a fool. Wendell Phillips spoke in Lovejoy's favor, carrying the sentiment of the meeting with him. See *The freedom speech of Wendell Phillips, . . . With letters from eye witnesses* (Boston, 1891).

44. If Ives were directing his remarks at any one person among the composers of the time who were using Indian and negro material, it would appear to be Henry Gilbert (1868-1928), whose ballet, *The Dance in Place Congo* was performed at the Metropolitan Opera House in 1918, approximately the time Ives was writing the "Epilogue." Gilbert's piano pieces include "Indian Scenes" and "Negro Dances." The leading composer using Indian material was Arthur Farwell (1872-1952).

45. *The introduction to Hegel's Philosophy of fine art*, tr. from the German with notes and prefatory essay by Bernard Bosanquet (London, 1886), p. 60: The universal need for expression in art lies, therefore, in man's rational impulse to exalt the inner and outer world into a spiritual consciousness for himself, as an object in which he recognizes his own self.

46. Autobiographical notes quoted by Cowell refer (p. 73) to Mrs. Ives and "Ralph D. Griggs" as the only persons who liked Ives' more problematical music in the earlier days. Although Ives was never one to get names or titles exactly right, it is very strange that he should have given the wrong Christian names to one of his oldest friends—the man who, according to a draft of a letter in the Yale Collection, came nearest to taking his father's place.

Cowell must have been misled also by material from Ives other than that quoted in his book, as he states (p. 31) that Dr. Griggs was pastor of the Center Church, New Haven. The *Historical Catalogue . . . (Center Church)*, compiled by F. D. Dexter (New Haven, 1914) lists no one by the name of Griggs, either as member or pastor. The pastor in the period 1882-1902 was the Rev. Dr. Newman Smyth. That Dr. Griggs was active in the music at Center Church, however, cannot be doubted, as a number of marginal notes on Ives manuscripts (listed in Kirkpatrick's *Catalogue*) mention that he sang pieces by Ives there during the years Ives was at Yale (1894-1898).

A note in the issue of *The Yale Review* containing Griggs' article on Debussy (1912) states that he was "instructor in singing, and lecturer upon developments in modern music" in Vassar College. A letter in the Collection from Canton, China (Aug. 27, 1921), connects him without question to one "John Cornelius Griggs, B.A. Yale, 1889, Ph.D. Leipsic, 1893, Assoc. prof. Engl., Canton Christian College, 1919," described in Yale alumni records. His dissertation, *Studien ueber die Musik in Amerika*, was published in Leipzig in 1894.

47. David Stanley Smith's years of study at Yale with Horatio Parker overlapped those of Ives. Having followed a successful and conventional career as a composer, succeeding Parker as head of the Yale School of Music, he was more than once the target of Ives' caustic comments, although the two were good friends, if music was not concerned (see Cowell, p. 66).

48. The above passage in the text may help to explain what has been to many of Ives' admirers an enigma: that he never seemed to resent or resist the pressures which drove him into full-time activity as a business man in the period when his creative urge as a composer was at its peak. He said in a letter to Henry Bellaman, quoted by Cowell, p. 97: "I have experienced a great fulness of life in business. The fabric of existence weaves itself whole. You cannot set an art off in the corner and hope for it to have vitality, reality and substance. . . . My work in music helped my business and work in business helped my music."

49. H. K. Moderwell, as quoted by Mason from *The New Republic*, October 16, 1915 (Mason, pp. 247-248): I like to think that ragtime is the perfect expression of the American city, with its restless bustle and motion . . . As you walk up and down the streets of an American city you feel in its jerk and rattle a personality different from that of any European capital . . . This is American. Ragtime, I believe, expresses it. It is today the one true American music.

50. Mason, pp. 278-279: He must love his cause so singly that he will cleave to it, and forsake all else. Now what is this cause for the American composer but the utmost musical beauty that he, as an individual man with his own qualities and defects, is capable of understanding and striving towards? And what is the 'all else' that he must forsake, save those types of musical beauty which, whatever may be their intrinsic worth, do not come home to him, do not arouse a sympathetic vibration in him, leave him cold? He must take sides. He must be, not a philosopher, but a partisan. He must have good hearty enthusiasms, and good hearty prejudices. Only so can he be an individual.
    It matters not one jot. . . .

51. Brander Matthews, *The American of the Future, and Other Essays* (New York, 1909). Ives may have had this statement in mind, p. 18: The New Englanders long ago relapst from orthodoxy into unitarianism, and

then their wavering faith faded into a chilly agnosticism, until now their piety often takes the mild form of ancestor-worship, revealed in not a few of them by a high opinion of themselves as descendants of their sainted forefathers.

52. Insert for 2nd Edition of "Essays before Sonata" (if there happen to be one). (Probably in Epilogue.)

What are the usual fundamental qualities of genius—? A general estimate would probably include "capacity for taking infinite pains," power of imagination & intellect, emotional & creative-instincts desires & impulses; but underlying *this*—there must run—and the more I observe, the surer I am that this less commonly accepted element, is of great underlying importance—is *"self-restraint."* This, if more carefully analyzed, is found to rest on something that has to do with "moral character," a power of balance or poise. All great men have that & are given little credit for it. All near geniuses or self-appointed geniuses, loudly talk about "their need of freedom," to do any & live any way they want— Listen to one talk, and you'd soon find that [what] he is wildly enthusiastic [about] is selfishness not freedom. He thinks he must be free from the ordinary sacrifices of everyday life. His comforts first—that of others, his children, wife, friend second—or nowhere. He must be free to express his great soul but forgets, that unfair & impatient, or even indecent treatment of his wife—means that he hasn't a great soul to start with—but forgets that if he is [isn't] willing to earn or try to earn an honest living— he isn't a man——big enough to have aspirations worth expressing. In a word—genius is indicated by that self-restraint, that "great poise of soul"—which can control the emotional & intellectual impulses, as a "man" not a degenerate. (Illus) A man who said he was fond of music from & in his cradle, & who wanted everybody to know it—who was passionately fond of Bach & Beethoven so didn't have to study them hard —who was passionately fond of Schubert's songs—but always sings Massenet to the ladies, who said he was passionately fond of counterpoint, but alway sidestepped his classroom work,

> A great Ceasar Frank who worked hard in life—teaching etc.
> composed evenings and vacations, instead of looking for a
> rich patron, to let him lie in bed—and pocket hers.

who said he was passionately fond of beautiful women—married (one) an affinity and soul-mate at 18, raised a large family—and left them (overnight) all (trusting) for providence to look out for them both,— for he must be free to express his great soul. Look into this man's or any similar character's (art) music—live with it long enough—& you will gradually feel the decadent part of the man's soul—making a strenuous perhaps beautiful sound,—but you can't live with it long—any more than he could live with his family—freedom to express the great was not what he was after—it was hog-hearted impulse to be recognized as a genius—not to be one. His mind (& heart) was too little to know that great self-restraint of genius. He was a coward—was afraid that his great soul would keep him from thinking too much. Quote Hadley Economics, p. 50.

[Arthur Twining Hadley, *Economics: An Account of the Relations Between Private Property and Public Welfare* (New York and London, 1896). Hadley, later president of Yale (1899–1920), was Professor of Political Economy at the time. The book was used as a text when Ives was an undergraduate. The passage referred to is probably, "The evils of thinking too much, and trusting Providence too little, seem small in comparison with those which arise from trusting Providence for everything and not thinking at all."]

53. Helmholtz, p. 358, reads: At every step we encounter historical and national differences of taste. Whether one combination is rougher or smoother than another, depends solely on the anatomical structure of the ear, and has nothing to do with psychological motives. But what degree of roughness a hearer is inclined to endure as a means of musical expression depends on taste and habit; hence the boundary between consonances and dissonances has been frequently changed. Similarly Scales, Modes, and their Modulations have undergone multifarious alterations, not merely among uncultivated or savage people, but even in those periods of the world's history and among those nations where the noblest flowers of human culture have expanded.

Hence it follows,—and the proposition cannot be too vividly present to the minds of our musical theoreticians and historians—*that the system of Scales, Modes, and Harmonic Tissues does not rest solely upon inalterable natural laws, but is at least partly also the result of esthetical principles, which have already changed, and will still further change, with the progressive development of humanity.*

54. Pole, p. 15, reads: On the other hand, the notion most generally prevalent among *musicians* is, that the rules of their art are founded on imperative natural laws, which will not admit of violation and scarcely of alteration. Musicians are aware that great changes take place from time to time as the art advances, but they account for this by the assumption of a gradual progress in science, every change involving, as they think, either the discovery of some new natural law, or the extension of some old one.

55. At the end of Ives' song, "In the Alley, after a session at Poli's" (*114 Songs*, p. 121) there are two chords over which occurs the note, "change 'swipe' ad lib." These chords are long, arpeggiated triads on B flat and D flat, placed between two D major chords, D major being the key of the piece. If the term "swipe" refers to their function in the harmony, it may be a colloquial way of saying that the chords are borrowed from another key. If it refers to the manner of playing, it may be

a way of describing the motion of the hands "swiping" across the keys in executing a long, arpeggiated chord.

56. Ives' reaction to the harpsichord was not a common one among musicians at the time this article was written (1924–25). Wanda Landowska had made her first American tour in 1923, but most musicians (especially pianists) were not convinced that the harpsichord was more than an antiquarian curiosity. Ives seems to have been able to disregard the instrument's relatively slight volume and to appreciate its superior richness produced through couplings and varied registrations.

57. The fundamental chord is:

58. The second possible fundamental chord is:

59. The third possible fundamental chord is:

60. In the illustration below, No. 1 is the chord in its first form, consisting of five tones at intervals of five quarter-tones (being expressed in

notation either as major seconds a quarter-tone sharp or minor thirds a quarter-tone flat).

No. 2 is the chord which results when the second note (D) is "thrown up an octave."

1. 2.

61. The following paragraph was crossed out in the typescript (MS. 3). The version given here is the first and longer one from MS. 2. It reads: Another way of treating the general subject is as Mr. [Hans] Barth [b. 1897, gave his first major performance on his quarter-tone piano in Carnegie Hall in 1930] has done. He uses practically the same number of notes as in the diatonic system dividing them between two pianos— each using six or seven notes a whole-tone apart—a plan of substitution rather than of extension but the more I hear his music the more I like it—it has many beautiful periods & effects, it produces a composite result that is fascinating. It is a practical way of accustoming the ear to 1/4 tone combinations & intervals. It attempts no pure 1/4 [tone] harmonic basis and the usual rules of the diatonic system may apply. It has the advantage that any piano music may be readily transcribed. But the plan obviously can include no perfect fifths & a good part of the twenty-four quarters are not used—or if so only as passing notes.

62. Perhaps because there was some confusion about the reference, the following passage was not included in the printed article: "A quotation from Hauptmann [Hauptmann's name appeared just above the sentence, in reference to a previous passage, but these words are Pole, p. 127] is interesting in this connection—
It is by no means impossible that composers [Ives omits "of genius"] might someday open for themselves a considerable field for novelty and origi- nality by shaking off the trammels of our restricted modern tonality.
And Dr. Pole said over fifty years ago—
It is doubtful whether the imperative adoption of modern tonality is an unmixed good, for it cages us in a somewhat narrow circle [p. 126]."

63. In his *Dante*, Sedgwick quotes Plotinus from Maeterlinck, *Ruys- broeck l'admirable:* "The first thing is to render the organ of vision analogous and similar to the object which it is to contemplate. The eye could never have perceived the sun, if it had not first taken the form of

the sun; in the same way, the soul could never see beauty, if she were not first beautiful herself, and every man must begin by making himself beautiful and divine in order to obtain sight of what is beautiful and divine (Sedgwick, p. 137)." The reference to Plotinus in the "Postface" as well as the one in *Essays Before A Sonata*, p. 97, may have come from Sedgwick's *Dante*.

64. To the friends of *The News*, who may take up this work, the question may come,—Why did he write a book? It is a natural inquiry. It has assailed hundreds before our day; it will afflict hundreds in the years to come. And probably there is no form of interrogation so loaded with subtle torture as this very one, unless it is to be asked for a light in a strange depot by a man you have just selected out of seventeen thousand as the man most likely to have a match. Various authors have various reasons for bringing out a book, and this may or may not be the reason they give to the world; I know not, and care not. It is not for me to judge the world, unless I am elected.

It is a matter which lies between the author and his own conscience, and I know of no place where it would be less likely to be crowded. But my reason for writing a book is so novel, so different from all others, that the public may be pardoned for feeling an intense desire to know it. Some have written a book for money; I have not. Some for fame; I have not. Some for love; I have not. Some for kindlings; I have not. I have not written a book for any of these reasons, or all of them combined. In fact, gentle borrower, I have not written a book at all—I have merely clipped it.

65. Richard Melancthon Hurd was not a politician, but was a classmate (Yale, 1888) and frequent correspondent of Henry L. Stimson, who had been Secretary of War under Taft. Ives would have known him because he was a Yale man and because he was active in New York as president of the Lawyers Mortgage Company. If he had anything to say about the "people's government," it was entirely unofficial, as he did not hold public office. The other possible Hurd is Edward Payson (1841–1927), a corporation officer with extensive business interests in Mexico and South America. He likewise held no public office, and he seems to have had no connection at all with Ives.

66. As Secretary of the Interior under Harding in 1921 (a year after Ives wrote this essay), Albert B. Fall was placed in charge of the administration of oil reserves at Teapot Dome, Wyoming, and Elk Hills, California. He secretly leased the reserves to Harry F. Sinclair and Edward L. Doheny. A Senate investigating committee in 1924 revealed that he had accepted "loans" from these two men totalling $125,000. In 1927, Fall was convicted, fined $100,000, and sentenced to a year in jail.

67. Francisco Ferrer y Guardia (1859–1909) was a Spanish Socialist and educator who advocated secular education. Matteo Morral, an em-

ployee in his school, attempted to assassinate Alphonso XIII in 1906. Ferrer was charged with complicity, but was released. In 1909, after violence in Barcelona, he was arrested again, and was hanged after a trial so questionable in its methods that it aroused international protest. In 1912, his innocence was affirmed, and his property was restored to his heirs.

68. If article #4? (or preamble) does not suitably supply a starting point for recording majority expression, an amendment could be adopted, with a design of the process and providing that all future amendments be drafted from majority-suggestion & ratified by majority approval. An amendment covering the whole procedure, would, it strikes us, be a more effective way of starting the plan than a *series* of majority-amendments or separate laws.